Unfolding the Past

Unfolding the Past

Elizabeth Wilson

BLOOMSBURY VISUAL ARTS
LONDON • NEW YORK • OXFORD • NEW DELHI • SYDNEY

BLOOMSBURY VISUAL ARTS
Bloomsbury Publishing Plc
50 Bedford Square, London, WC1B 3DP, UK
1385 Broadway, New York, NY 10018, USA
29 Earlsfort Terrace, Dublin 2, Ireland

BLOOMSBURY, BLOOMSBURY VISUAL ARTS and the Diana logo are
trademarks of Bloomsbury Publishing Plc

First published in Great Britain 2022

For legal purposes the Acknowledgements on p. 285 constitute an
extension of this copyright page.

Cover design: Adriana Brioso
Cover image © Cornell Capa/The LIFE Picture Collection/Shutterstock

A catalogue record for this book is available from the British Library.

A catalogue record for this book is available from the Library of Congress.

ISBN: HB: 978-1-3502-3259-4
ePDF: 978-1-3502-3260-0
eBook: 978-1-3502-3261-7

Typeset by Deanta Global Publishing Services, Chennai, India
Printed and bound in India

To find out more about our authors and books visit www.bloomsbury.com and
sign up for our newsletters.

For Ellie,
my best critic

'*The eternal is in any case far more the ruffle on a dress than some idea.*'

WALTER BENJAMIN

Contents

1

Outside looking in

On a fine morning in the first weeks of the Covid-19 pandemic, I ran into my former publisher, Ursula Owen, co-founder of Virago Press, by a local bus stop. It wasn't clear if we were self-isolating yet or not, so we spoke to each other from a safe distance on the pavement – two militant feminists, now surprised to find ourselves in our eighties. In this disorienting new world of imminent confinement, our encounter felt like one between ghosts wandering around Limbo.

To my amazement, Ursula said: 'I've been rereading *Mirror Writing*. It's so good – I think it was before its time. It really should be republished.'

I was too touched to think of a generous reply – for example, I could have thanked her for publishing the book in the first place, but I was too startled to be polite. Instead, we exchanged anxieties about our health, the state of the world and the incompetence of the government.

Mirror Writing was published in 1982. It was a kind of auto-biography, an account of that period of my life when I was preoccupied with the creation of a gay persona. I later came to have reservations about the book's very camp approach, not because I repudiated camp, but because camp comes with its own problems. It operates as a defence against hostility and hurt, twisting trauma into a joke. My defiant lesbian identity was also protective; like a camp pose, it warded off pain, doubt and ambivalence.

Mirror Writing was a hybrid, because, in a further defensive move, I used my own experience to propel me beyond the personal into an analysis of autobiography as a genre of writing – since, after all, intellectual analysis, like jokes and defiance, is yet another form of defence, keeping emotion safely at arm's length. So – like many autobiographies, I suspect – *Mirror Writing* was a fiction as well as a hybrid. It was a work of disavowal, neutralizing traumatic aspects of my childhood and its legacy of self-doubt and rejection.

Camp, then, is defensive, yet, in spite of my reservations, *Unfolding My Past* does, like *Mirror Writing*, recall the past in a spirit of camp humour. Camp is a satirical posture, tinged with black. As an attitude that originally arose as a defence against oppression, it has the power to demystify pomposity and self-importance, while at the same time being quite forgiving. Camp positions itself as an artificial attitude to life, or rather it exposes and celebrates culture as inherently artificial. Artificiality is often posed as being morally inferior to 'the natural', but I shall be defending the artifice of fashion and the other cultural forms that I researched.

I return to life writing to explore what might be called the autobiography of my research. I see this as an unfolding, in the way that the arrival of a new garment in its outer casement is a moment of anticipation before you open the box, turn back the tissue paper that wraps the dress, lift it out and unfold it. That unfolding is only the start of a relationship, which begins as the dress or jacket adjusts itself to the wearer's body and develops, as the garment becomes familiar, is worn and at length becomes well worn, by which time experiences and memories are captured in its folds and it has become part of your life and part of your personality.

The unfolding of a dress also provides a metaphor for my relationship with my work, my writing, the cloth of which is woven out of my life. By this I mean to suggest that the subjects I wrote about over several decades were as much a reflection of my inner life and personal history as a search for objective knowledge. My work was also underwritten by a politics, the embers of which persist today.

In the decades between the 1980s and now, literature has expanded into forms that *Mirror Writing* did, perhaps in a small way, anticipate. There were other outliers, among them Elizabeth Hardwick's *Sleepless Nights*, a short work somewhere between fiction and autobiography. In it she wrote of her life at one remove, as I later did of mine, approaching the pain of her separation from her husband, the poet, Robert Lowell, obliquely, through stories of women and men she had known. She wrote of their emotional trauma rather than directly of her own. That, at any rate, is how I understood *Sleepless Nights*.

Since the last decade of the twentieth century and into the twenty-first, distinctions between fiction and autobiography and even the boundary between academic and personal writing have begun to break down. Such distinctions were never entirely rigid, but genres have become more porous as the author has evolved into an ambiguous figure and writing into an act of self-creation more ambitious – and yet also perhaps more limited – than the recreation of an objective world. Novelists and historians continue to describe large events, but it is impossible for a writer today to present the panorama of a whole society in quite the magisterial way that nineteenth-century novelists were able to do. The omnipotent narrator may still exist but has become a less familiar figure. Individualism has swelled. Readers and writers yearn to interrogate their own feelings and vicariously experience the inner lives of others. The subjectivity of a single consciousness is a more feasible subject than a social panorama, when a global world in turmoil seems too vast to be reduced to one coherent narrative, no matter how all-embracing. Ideas and politics are more swayed than ever by the power of the personal – although readers and writers still do seek, of course, to understand the world objectively.

My first published writings were political forays into the 'underground' press in the effervescent years of the Miss World demonstration, Gay Liberation and left-wing militancy, yet within a surprisingly short time I published my first – academic – book, a critique of the institutional sexism of the welfare state. I considered myself to be a polemicist and almost at once began to feel uneasy about the label of academic writer. I struggled to escape from it, because I felt it cordoned me off in a non-literary writing zone, restricted to abstract thought. I was always trying to establish a foothold on more expansive and promising territory. I searched for some non-existent genre, for some literary peninsula, or at least an atoll, from which I could launch ideas in the context of personal experience rather than, or as well as, disembodied theory, or at least could anchor in daily life ideas that might otherwise have seemed remote. They would be more accessible, I believed, in the context of lived reality.

I had started out as a political writer, but in this search for 'everyday life' – or rather, some different way of writing about it – I found myself abandoning more conventionally political subjects such as social policy. I moved instead into the research of consumption and the surfaces of life, fashion, spectacle and entertainment, urban social life, countercultures, art, film and, more unexpectedly, sport. All these were theatres of performance and had their passions, their fans and their costumes. As my research into dress developed, the very fact that colleagues and comrades often reacted with surprise or disapproval to subject matter they considered trivial alerted me both to its inherent importance and to my own emotional engagement with it. As well as being a researcher, I was a fan.

Researchers often talk about being in love with and passionately devoted to their subject. Research involves emotional commitment; researchers are drawn to subjects that have meaning to them in terms of sensibility, childhood memory or obsession. Research is more than an intellectual pursuit, more than the detached gathering of data. A research project is, in the end, a kind of love affair – and sometimes a love–hate relationship.

Individual human histories reside in many research works, not least when oral history becomes part of collective memory. Material culture concerns itself with objects that also have their own autobiographies and research can also tell their stories. Memories cling to the folds of a dress or to the pattern on a plate. Objects represent past experience in a congealed form. When brought into conversation with history, they illuminate social and cultural practices and deepen our understanding of our own lives and the lives of others, past and present.

My research into fashion led me to counter-cultural or alternative dress, sometimes referred to as anti-fashion. I branched out further from that, to explore 'bohemian' lifestyles, anti-establishment cultures and the mad personalities that thrived in those eccentric circles. This research in turn directed me towards the great cities in which it was possible for them to exist. As I moved into these new areas of mass culture, I found a world consciously dedicated to the promotion of pleasure and excitement. The urban scene provided a stage for the display of 'appearances' and the costumed variety of social life. Dress was a key that unlocked this spectacle of modern life and the problematic consumer world in which we live.

Fashion was traditionally suspect, and still is, because it prioritized pleasure and was often associated with sexual display – although it is just as often concerned with rules and conformity. In fact, consumer society as a whole is devoted to the search for pleasure, yet always disavows mere gratification or 'entertainment', seeking to clothe its enjoyment in moralism. If it is ambivalent about fashion, that is because fashion betrays this unacknowledged truth.

Through the study of fashion, or rather, dress, I came to understand that love of fashion was in part a search for personal identity through aesthetic experience. Fashion was more than frivolity – was, in fact, the very opposite. The search for the right style of dress could devour an individual's existence or a fashion faux pas cause, in extreme cases, murder. Less luridly, it was a search for authenticity.

The intensity it revealed went far beyond dress. It was found in the obsessive involvement of audiences and fans with sport, film, music and fiction. This was also a search for meaning, not through ordered reflection, but rather through kinetic cultural experience. When the Liverpool football manager, Bill Shankly, allegedly said: 'you think football's a matter of life and death? I can tell you it's a lot more important than that', he wasn't joking. We know that sport is more than mere amusement and, for better or worse, it plays a much more significant role in the lives of many of its supporters than the politics that actually influences their existence. It may be less universally recognized that popular drama, films and stories play a similar role in fans' lives. They can be props to self-esteem, sources of self-confidence, anti-depressants, obsessions, even sources of enlightenment.

As my work developed, I noticed that my investigation into pleasure linked what seemed to others to be diverse fields of research. I wanted to understand why spectacle, narrative and sport aroused such intense emotions in readers, viewers and participants. My research was about their search for meaning, expressed through aesthetic experience and was an attempt to understand this. But this attempt – which I never thought fully to explain – to find connections between diverse cultural experiences brought me up against another restricting aspect of academic writing, for, as publishing has expanded, marketing distinctions have been established and enforced. It is not only that academic writing has too often been separated off from literature, as if facts and truths could be divorced from the style in which they are expressed. Divisions into subjects have been established, and this frustrated me. My work appeared to extend into fields not thought of as being connected with one another in any way as I wandered off from social policy into dress history, urban studies and the analysis of film. For this promiscuity, academics from those 'disciplines' attacked me as an invader into their territory, and I myself worried that perhaps I was nothing more than an intellectual butterfly, flitting from subject to subject with no clear commitment to any particular one. I feared I was a dilettante who flouted lane discipline, a kind of intellectual drunk, weaving about while in charge (or not) of my vehicle. The annoying result in practical terms was that my books, on fashion, on urban life and on tennis, for example, were promoted and reviewed in different journals or different sections of magazines by different specialists, were to be found in different areas of bookshops and consequently had different readerships. Fashionistas were amazed to discover my fiction, sports writers derisive that I'd written about clothes.

In 2017, a Swedish industrialist I met in Stockholm suggested a different way of looking at it. My problem, he said, was that I suffered from 'brand diffusion'. This was a flattering excuse, implying that it was only due to the extensive range of my interests that I wasn't better known as a writer, but it was a fact that, to me, my work formed a coherent whole, and frustrating if no one would recognize that: for there is an organizing theme that unites my work and an underlying rationale in my eclecticism. Over and above that, I strove to be a 'writer' rather than an 'academic', though I was always haunted by the fear that I was simply a failed popularizer.

In considering my research work as a personal journey, I was inspired by a misremembered quote from George Devereux: 'All research is a form of autobiography.' I may have invented this, as I haven't been able to trace it, but when I came to prepare these chapters, it seemed strikingly relevant. Devereux, an ethnologist, psychoanalyst and trained social scientist, challenged what he saw as the false objectivity of science. This was a daring position to take because the idea that research might be subjective challenged entrenched assumptions. As a rational quest for knowledge, research seeks solutions to problems and promotes the Enlightenment purpose of mastery over our conditions of life. In the current era of 'fake news', rational evidence is often scorned and paranoid rumours gain credibility, but I am not suggesting that all facts are relative or that there is no such thing as verifiable reality or truth. In exploring the personal element in research, I am not endorsing a slide into subjectivism. I am simply suggesting the stunningly obvious: that meaning is emotional as well as rational.

Devereux deployed psychoanalytic ideas in his anthropological work. He believed that there is 'countertransference' in research, just as in therapy. The patient projects onto his therapist feelings related to past experiences and conflicts; this is known as transference. Countertransference refers to the response of the therapist, whose own emotions are equally at play as s/he reacts to the patient. In a similar way, the feelings of the researcher for their subject necessarily colour the relationship. There is no one-way encounter: the active researcher investigating the passive object of research. A researcher's personality and experience colour the perspective they bring to bear on their subject – and that subject may in turn alter the researcher's views. The enterprise therefore includes elements of hidden autobiography and self-reflection.

Autobiography in a specific sense is an exploration of the way in which work and personal experience are imbricated – or perhaps entwined is a better word, or even entangled. In tracing the relationship between my personal experience and my choice of subjects to research, I have seen aspects of my life in a different light, have understood my parents differently (and unexpectedly) and have had to continually reassess what exactly I was doing. I see now how I was drawn to certain subjects because I felt I was and would always be an outsider. My mother's sense of shame in being divorced cast a shadow over my lonely childhood as I inevitably absorbed her guilt and shame. Deeply affected by her sense of social failure and of being discarded and marginalized, I felt that I too was destined to be an exile from exciting worlds that were forever closed to me.

Mine may be an ambiguous form of life writing because it is not the simple exposure of a life. It approaches a life at one remove, through a different kind of lens. I wanted an audience to see life and what I wrote about through my eyes, rather than simply seeing me. Writing was my form of communication precisely because it was a screen as well as a lens. It was almost as if writing was more than the simple act of recording. It was the formaldehyde in which my thoughts and feelings were preserved, and the preservation process changed them so that they were no longer painful, especially when filtered through more abstract or objective topics. They were no longer raw fruit, but crystallized, more artificial and more exotic.

Writing was a form of escape, and I wrote from a young age, but before writing came reading. Reading was my first (virtual) escape route. Books gave me imaginative entry into many worlds, historical or fictional. I was described as a 'withdrawn' child, because I withdrew into reading, which was a place of safety. Yet books could give one

Figure 1.1 *Photograph of me with photograph of grandmother behind me. Author's photograph.*

sufficient courage to encounter everyday life again. Reading might be 'escapist'. It was also restorative. In any case, whether it was good for me or not, I spent hours and years reading and sitting in libraries. How perfectly suited I was to the silence of the library and the out-of-body world of the book.

2

First came reading

Every Thursday, a Harrods van drew up outside our front door and the driver, uniformed in green, delivered a cardboard box tied round with pink tape. It contained the weekly volume from Harrods' lending library, chosen by my mother after she had read the book reviews in the *Daily Telegraph* and the *Sunday Times*. Usually it was a novel, but books on history, popular psychiatry and the Cold War turned up from time to time.

The delivery to our terraced house was out of place in the marginal social world of my childhood. At the lower end of the street, tall, stuccoed mansions had fallen into decay, and flats and rooms were rented out to Jamaicans. At the cross-street intersection, four 'prefabs', rushed up after the war, stood on a bomb site, already looking oddly temporary and out of place. Beyond this, at our end of the road, the atmosphere subtly changed. Most of the Edwardian houses in this section of the street were divided into flats rented out to office workers, all of whom were safely white.

The whole district – from Queen's Tennis Club, a couple of streets away in slightly smarter Baron's Court, to West Kensington's North End Road with its market stalls, its council flats, hardware and electrical shops – formed an indeterminate social no man's land. This made the area appropriate for my family, which had lost

Figure 2.1 *Photograph of my mother aged twenty-one. Author's photograph.*

any clear place in society. My grandparents had spent years in West Africa and belonged to a class of colonials that was beginning to drop out of circulation. My father was absent, chief administrator in Sierra Leone. The British Empire had its own hierarchy of importance and snobbery. On this social scale, Sierra Leone was a small and unimportant colony at the bottom of the ladder. One of my grandmother's ancestors had been a Nabob with the East India Company, and her grandfather had been an officer in the Indian Army, a staple of the Raj, the empire's grandest jewel. My mother clung to these not especially distinguished forebears as tokens of status, whereas, to my grandmother, the African afterthought at the bottom of the imperial pile represented a demeaning decline.

We were still officer class – just about – but something had gone wrong, and our circumstances did not match the family self-image. My mother hated our shabby street and wished we lived in gracious Kensington, a mile or so to the east. We went to church and to the dentist there, and for walks through its elegant little side roads lined with early Victorian villas. We ventured past Notting Hill Gate as far as the Portobello Road market, but never further than that, for at the end of the streets that slipped down towards Notting Dale lay the wild wastes of Ladbroke Grove and Paddington: the Slums. My grandmother expressed pity and compassion for individuals in trouble, but slum dwellers in the mass frightened my mother. Those who lived there were uncivilized, violent, a threat.

In fact, our relative poverty, our 'reduced circumstances', could not for a moment be compared to the real, rock-bottom poverty of Notting Dale and Kensal Rise, so vividly described by the politician, Alan Johnson, in his autobiography, *This Boy*. My grandparents owned a four-storey house with electric light and hot and cold running water. The Johnson family – Alan, his sister and his ailing mother – lived in two rooms with a shared outside lavatory, damp and cockroaches. They didn't even have electricity, only gaslight.

Nevertheless, our downward mobility created an atmosphere of deprivation. We were somehow shut out from our rightful place in society, and a sense of disillusion and disappointment pervaded our existence. Unanchored sorrow and unstated regrets weighed down home life. This mood was not improved by the wider gloom of the post-war austerity years, when it was fashionable for the middle classes to indulge in self-pity and to refer to themselves as the *nouveaux pauvres*, resentful of the efforts of Clement Attlee's government to create a more equal society. Perhaps the use of French was to show off their cultural capital or to make their condition sound more exotic. It certainly expressed my mother's resentment of the new welfare state, set in place by the hated Labour Party. Like every other child, I qualified for free orange juice and cod liver oil, but my mother refused to claim these for me, since they were tainted products of state socialism.

The arrival of the Harrods van drew attention to our peculiar status. My mother and grandmother often told me we had no money, yet we shopped at Harrods, then the most opulent department store in London. Our ugly, uncomfortable house was full of inherited antique furniture, but the bathroom was located on the top floor, and this was rented out to 'paying guests', so we used a makeshift bath in the chilly basement scullery and washed at the sink. At odds with the Georgian cabinets and desks, relics of my grandparents' years in West Africa also littered the house. Leopard skins, a crocodile's skull and an elephant's foot – the latter bizarrely converted into a sewing box lined with pink satin: a truly Surrealist object – were souvenirs of my grandfather's big-game hunting expeditions. A keen amateur photographer, he recorded these as well as many other aspects of African life. In one, presumably taken with a delayed shutter action, he is seated, clad in pith helmet and khaki shorts and surrounded by his bearers dressed in white uniforms. The empire was nothing if not a fancy dress party.

We had moved to London in 1945 from Exeter in the West Country. In Exeter, my grandfather had visited his friends from the Home Guard and fellow retired doctors from the Medical Board on which he sat. (This board determined recruits' fitness for call-up to the armed forces and, in this society at war, with strict food rationing, my grandfather told us how he was regularly offered meat, eggs, bacon or Christmas turkeys from local farmers, desperate to keep their sons at home on the farm, in the vain hope he would declare them unfit to be recruited. He always refused, of course. I felt sorry for the farmers, anxious to keep the farm going and not to have their sons slaughtered.) My mother accompanied him on social visits, and I often went too, but my grandmother hardly ever left the house. My mother also had a few friends of her own, fellow volunteers at the WVS (the Women's Voluntary Service) or the mothers who met at my private kindergarten.

In London, her social circle was non-existent. My grandfather died soon after the move and in our new house my grandmother lived entirely in the basement, moving only from her bedroom along a dark corridor lined with tin trunks (not wanted on the voyage) to the kitchen, where she sat by the coke boiler in an ancient deck chair and read the *Daily Telegraph*. She left the house once a year, accompanied by my mother, to visit my grandfather's grave in Highgate Cemetery.

The cold, dark house was painted throughout in chocolate brown and sallow cream. The ground floor dining room, with its Jacobean sideboard and glass-fronted bookcases, was never used, and a fire was lit in the sitting room only at weekends or on winter evenings so that I could do my homework there. Homework, the focus of my mother's anxious attention, represented the education she'd missed

Figure 2.2 *My mother and I facing the future in September 1939.*
Author's photograph.

Figure 2.3 *With my mother in austerity London. Author's photograph.*

out on and was determined I should have. We had even moved to London so that I could attend a better school. Education was a mark of social status as well as a passport to financial security, but books weren't there just to prop up our shaky hold on middle-class lifestyle. My mother loved reading. The historical novels of Walter Scott and Harrison Ainsworth, and biographies of the Tudors were her favourites. She'd taken me around all the ancient buildings in Exeter that had survived the Blitz, and in London there were many more visits to churches, palaces and museums, where I learned not only about history but also about architecture, costume and furniture.

I don't remember learning to read. I read and was read to every day, and by the time I was eight or nine years old was deep into everything I could lay my hands on: Enid Blyton; *The Family at One End Street* (this, about working-class kids, seemed very exotic to me, who was never allowed to play in the street); Kenneth Grahame's *Golden Age, Winnie-the-Pooh, Alice in Wonderland* and *Through the Looking Glass, The Children of the New Forest* (about plucky Cavalier children and how they survived the wicked Cromwellian Puritans); and *My Friend Mr Leaky*, a children's tale written by the eminent scientist, JBS Haldane. All I remember from this last book is the description of how best to eat a mango (in the bath, because the juice gets everywhere), which fascinated me, although – or because – I had never seen a mango. My mother was unaware that Haldane was a committed Communist, which was just as well, because the news would have appalled her.

When, in 2019, I read Lucy Mangan's *Bookworm*, a chronicle of her childhood reading, I recaptured through her vivid descriptions my enjoyment of the books I'd read so long ago. I experienced again the joy and purity of that pleasure of childhood reading. Lucy describes herself as a bookworm in a wholly positive way, reminding her own readers that love of books can instil ideas of solidarity, kindness, generosity, grit and many other qualities needed to lead a good and useful life, yet 'bookworm' seems a strangely negative way to describe a book lover. The worm eats its way into and eventually destroys the book it feeds on, but surely no reader, however avid, would want to destroy a book. 'Bookworm' is a hostile metaphor, positioning the reader as a desiccated destroyer, burrowing away in archives and dust, a Mr Casaubon devoid of human feeling. For me, reading was the opposite and opened a gate to worlds of passion, excitement and romance. I completely endorse Lucy's view of reading and books as forms of expansion and enlightenment. They are a broad highway to a better world that I feel everyone should tread and I'm baffled and saddened by those who don't care for books or reading. Yet there was a dark side.

My mother was thrilled when my English teacher told her I was a 'voracious reader' and I imagine Miss Harrison intended it as a compliment, yet the adjective strikes a sinister note. The Shorter Oxford Dictionary defines 'voracious' as: '1: greed in eating, greedy, ravenous, insatiable; 2: extreme eagerness in the pursuit of some desire or interest' – and I was a greedy reader. Like a greedy eater, I swallowed my intellectual food whole, gulping it down without proper chewing, so that I suffered from chronic mental indigestion. I was a binge reader and would devour anything in print just as some people binge on junk food as readily as on wholesome fare. (So perhaps in that sense I *was* a book worm.) My mother forbade children's comics, because she considered them vulgar, but I was allowed to read anything else, and I did.

I was often 'lost in a book'. I was solitary and withdrawn. At children's parties, I refused to join in, escaped to an empty room and found a book to read. I was even known to snatch a book from another child because I'd decided I had to read it now, right this minute. Where reading was concerned, I was a stranger to deferred gratification and my mother, who indulged her only child in many ways she couldn't afford (clothes, later on), never refused to buy me a book. Only in my teens, when I began to read books she disapproved of and formed opinions that frightened her, did she realize that reading is a dangerous activity.

By a sad paradox, the love of books my mother so eagerly encouraged became my escape from her over-anxious and eventually stifling attention, as I silently shut myself off in an imagined world of my own. She rested her thwarted hopes for happiness in me and the intensely close relationship we'd had when I was a small child was meant to continue forever, but, even before I reached my teens, I was beginning to resent her and barricaded myself away from her over-protective anxiety behind an invisible wall into the alternative universe of reading. She longed for companionship, but I was never lonely and no longer needed her, since I lived in the world of whatever book I was reading at the moment.

Walter Mehring, in flight from Nazi Germany in the 1930s, recognized that reading could be an addiction and, in his autobiography, *The Lost Library*, he describes how you can

> Become as addicted to reading as to any other intoxicant... especially ... Europeans, who from long heritage are as dangerously given to books as they are to alcohol. You reach for a book as you reach for a drink, to escape the depressing banality of newspaper headlines, to wash away the disgusting aftertaste of the medicines served up in the hospital known as Contemporary Civilisation. And there's nothing so good as a potent brew of well aged pathos, preferably distilled in verse. At once you feel cleansed and ennobled. The trouble is that you don't stick to the select vintages very long. And in reading, as in drinking, you incline to mix the cocktail stiffer and stiffer.

At the age of thirteen, I could hardly have matched the bitter cynicism of this Jewish exile, but I certainly clutched the bottle, dependent on my daily fix. I read in bed when I woke up, I read the cornflakes packet and the newspaper at breakfast, I read at school during 'break', I read on through the school day, escaping to the library whenever possible, and I ended the evening by reading in bed again before I turned the light out and fell asleep.

Mehring was right about something else too: 'you are looking for self reassurance and for a general absolution'. I didn't recognize it at the time, but I too was looking for 'absolution'. I was looking for an escape from the guilt that haunted me at home, as if I were responsible for my mother's restricted existence – as, actually, I partly was. To an outsider, I must have appeared 'spoilt', since everything was devoted to me and my privileged education, and I was guilty of seeming ungrateful, by taking it all for granted and simply retreating into my books instead of being a companion for my mother. A 'spoilt' child, however, usually means an indulged child and, although I was given everything to stimulate and encourage me, the emphasis on achievement was unrelenting and when one year my work went downhill, my mother was distraught and accused me of not trying, when in fact I was upset by the death of my grandfather.

Mehring's word, absolution, implies forgiveness for sin and perhaps my sin was to reject my mother rather ruthlessly, although I didn't recognize that yet. I just knew I hated it when she questioned me about my homework, wanted to know what I'd done at school and who my friends were (naturally, as a solitary child, I didn't have many and those I did have were other, not very popular girls), what I thought about what I was reading and – when I returned from my fortnightly Sunday visit to my father and stepmother – what we'd had for lunch and what we'd talked about. I had little to report on that front, since as soon as I arrived at the Roehampton flat, I seized my stepmother's pile of women's magazines and installed myself on the window seat, where I disappeared behind the moss-green velvet curtains. Reading was my cloak of invisibility.

It had developed other magical properties. By reading, I escaped into an imaginary world where I did not live in an embarrassingly shabby and eccentric house and my mother wasn't so awkwardly different from all the other parents. When I was reading, I no longer felt self-conscious about my background – and myself. The abjection of my downtrodden mother ceased to be a burden and source of guilt, but, as I grew up, her self-sacrifice became my guilt and our ugly home an aesthetic prison.

Literacy, the ability to read – and also to write – was perceived as an unmixed good in mid-twentieth-century Britain. It was an essential part of modern life; no citizen could function fully or negotiate the welfare state without it, and it was a cause of dismay that a worrying minority of recruits to National Service turned out to be functionally illiterate, in spite of having endured years of compulsory schooling. Reading was also a marker of social standing; to refer to a person as 'uneducated' was a euphemism for the 'working class' and implied a certain contempt.

For centuries, authorities had feared the influence of books. Indeed, the idea that knowledge is dangerous went right back to the story of Adam and Eve. Powerful interests such as the Roman Catholic Church had tried and usually succeeded in restricting and policing access to books considered too dangerous for the general population – and especially women – to read. When the French revolutionaries stormed the Bastille, they found few prisoners, but thousands of forbidden books.

Until the industrial period, the only book to be found in most ordinary Western households was the Bible, but control of what the common people might read was undermined by the arrival in the eighteenth century of the market in books and publishing and by the democratic belief in free speech. There still lingered a feeling that books were not to be trusted. Novel reading, in particular, like an obsession with clothes, was associated with weak-minded women and is still seen as (and is) a predominantly female activity. It was a form of escapism, a form of doing nothing when you could be doing something useful and practical around the house. Reading could be dangerously close to daydreaming. It could also be a self-important claim to superiority.

By the mid-twentieth century, the idea of reading as dangerous had been consigned to the past, yet conflicts still sprang up sporadically in the law courts, British ones, anyway, when judges tried to decide whether innocent women might take to lesbianism if they read Radclyffe Hall's *The Well of Loneliness* (more likely to have put them off, I should have thought) or whether 'your wives or your servants', as a barrister during the *Lady Chatterley's Lover* trial expressed it, should be permitted to read DH Lawrence's creakingly explicit novel.

In truth, the politicians, prelates and aristocrats were right. Reading is dangerous. It can give you ideas. After we moved to London when I was eight years old, I became more and more aware that my family was different from the others. This led to social embarrassment and a feeling that I myself was somehow different and didn't belong to any secure social world. Books provided unlimited ammunition for escape into an imaginary world and supported my growing distance from my depleted family; this distance was increased by my education. My situation was a version, with a twist, of the story that became well known after the Second World War: of the working-class child who goes to grammar school and as a result is alienated from their background. In my case, school simply acquainted me with a different section of the middle class, the liberal intelligentsia.

Had I gone to a different girls' school, I should have found plenty of fellow students with a colonial, imperial background, but at St Paul's I encountered girls, many Jewish, whose parents were musicians, psychiatrists, journalists, dance band leaders and Labour politicians, as well as businessmen and lawyers. That and its London constituency meant it was not quite like other famous 'public' schools such as Roedean School or Cheltenham Ladies' College. It wasn't remotely 'jolly hockey sticks'. It had an air of the urban, the worldly, the glamorous. Perhaps as schools went, it was even slightly 'fast', its social mixture more hedonistic and even raffish than that of other schools. It introduced me to new, liberal ideas and set me on a road that led away from my background, now a source of embarrassment, towards an imagined world of sophistication and success.

It was not only that I was exposed to more progressive political views. It may have been a reaction to my mother's divorce that caused me to fall so heavily for the world of romance, and this led in directions beyond my conscious choice. I didn't read *Madame Bovary* until years later, but in my teens I was as much a romance-mad Madame Bovary as Emma herself and I have never quite managed to cast off the heightened romantic sensibility that developed partly through my promiscuous adolescent gulping down of all those romances about fatal love and thwarted passion.

My first love was Richard Coeur de Lion. He was the most romantic hero in the world to my nine-year-old self, not because he fought in the Crusades – and I didn't understand what they were anyway – but because he inspired passionate love; from his wife, Berengaria, who, when he was bitten by a snake, sucked the poison from the wound, and from his page boy, the minstrel, Blondel, who serenaded him from outside his prison and thereby somehow rescued him. The word 'metrosexual' hadn't yet been coined, but the legend of Richard the Lionheart transcended the banality of fairy story happy endings to reach for something different and intangible.

As soon as I arrived at my secondary school, I made straight for the junior library. There, I found popular classics by E. Nesbit and Mazo de la Roche, and a shelf of Baroness Orczy romances about the Scarlet Pimpernel. I was completely ignorant about sex as my mother could not bring herself to discuss it. The Baroness conveyed a sentimentally blurred idea of erotic love with her use of cloud-wreathed euphemisms, and this vagueness fitted my ignorance. Her writing was incoherent and her plots far-fetched, but I didn't notice that, as she'd created an ideal of impossible passionate love that I found irresistible.

In the lax, late-eighteenth-century world of the English aristocracy, Sir Percy Blakeney had, unusually, married for love, only then to discover that his French wife Marguerite had sent royalists to the guillotine during the ongoing Revolutionary Terror, or so he believed. He still secretly adored her but banked down his passion beneath a façade of exquisite, but frigid courtesy. The violent intensity ('intensity' being the Baroness's favourite word for sexual feeling) of his desire occasionally threatened to break through, but he never lost control. Ironically, once his wife believed he no longer cared for her, she fell more in love with him. The thrills of rejected love and wilful misunderstanding heightened erotic yearning. This had the irresistibly masochistic appeal of having it both ways. It was the ideal erotic romance: the love that is inevitable, yet impossible. It was the exquisite agony of a passion that is not fulfilment, but longing.

Equally romantic was Sir Percy's double role as the idle, effete aristocrat who lived a secret life as the heroic Scarlet Pimpernel, saving aristocrats from the Jacobin terror. In the 1934 film version, re-released in the late 1940s, Leslie Howard was perfectly cast as Sir Percy, combining camp languor with smouldering romantic 'intensity'. This was apparently genuine, as off set, he was having a torrid affair with his leading lady, Merle Oberon. By the time I saw the film, Howard had himself become a tragic war hero, shot down by the Germans when on a civilian flight from Lisbon. This gave rise to theories that he was involved in espionage, and he certainly was involved in anti-German propaganda. So he was a modern version of the perfect tragic, heroic and unattainable lover, a role he also played in *Gone with the Wind*, another of my favourite teenage films.

I soon left Baroness Orczy behind and read every novel I could lay my hands on: Agatha Christie and Ernest Raymond, LP Hartley's *The*

Go-Between, another tragedy of thwarted love, Alberto Moravia's post-war bestseller, *The Woman of Rome*, about a prostitute, and Colette's novels about lesbian and heterosexual love. One minor novel, Edith Templeton's *The Island of Desire*, made a deep impression. In its final pages, the heroine, travelling on the Orient Express away from her failed marriage, succumbs in her sleeping car to the ticket collector, a complete stranger. Afterwards, she claims that he had provided her first encounter with what erotic love really is, 'although he was not a gentleman . . . was brutal . . . and had not even pretended to have any feelings for her'. Yet of all her subsequent lovers, he alone appeared in her dreams. As I now realize, but didn't at the time, this effectively eroticized rape – she tries to refuse, but he takes no notice. The linking of sex and violence was actually quite a theme of the period, seen in the popularity of DH Lawrence novels and acted out in real life by Ted Hughes and Sylvia Plath, with jealousy, cruelty, infidelity and violence mistaken for the truest proofs of passionate love.

Even more thrillingly, I discovered Lord Byron, the perfect embodiment of impossible love. Fame followed by outlawry and exile; his love of boys, his incestuous relationship with his half-sister, his death while in pursuit of Greek liberation – he was the perfect romantic anti-hero. Peter Quennell, a mid-twentieth-century bohemian and man of literature, who seems to have been a romantic himself and was married several times, wrote two volumes about the notorious poet. These presented him so alluringly that I immediately and completely fell for the dark glamour of the aristocrat who was, 'mad, bad and dangerous to know', an epithet never to be surpassed. I don't know whether I was in love with Byron or actually wanted to *be* Byron – or both. Either way, there was an ambiguous narcissism in the blurring of incoherent desires without a real-life object.

Reading, then, could be dangerous. In my teens it provided a substitute for the 'real life' I thought would never happen, but eventually 'real life' did turn up and provided at least some kind of antidote to the melodramas of my imagined world. Meanwhile, my harried mother was saddened by the way reading had antagonized me, and she became distraught when books even more shocking than Colette's *Chéri* came along. She was particularly appalled by Simone de Beauvoir's *The Second Sex.*

It was only after my mother's death that I understood her life better through fiction, but by then, of course, it was rather too late. Even as a small child, I knew my mother was sad. One of my first favourite children's stories was the tale of a donkey, driven to market by his master. Looking round at the profusion of produce on the market stalls and especially the flowers, the donkey was entranced. 'What pretty flowers', he murmured wistfully. And there was something of that donkey about my mother: a grey, submissive beast of burden with myopic eyes and a wistful longing for the beauty and happiness symbolized by the flowers, a glimpse of escape from the drudgery of daily life in wartime, at the beck and call of my invalid grandparents and preoccupied with anxieties about my withdrawn behaviour, all on top of the bombing, ration books and queues. Worse than any of that was the shame of the divorce.

At first, there was nothing odd about my father's absence. He was legitimately abroad in Africa, defending an obscure corner of the British Empire against the enemy. Many families were fragmented during the war, men fighting in distant theatres of combat, women working, children evacuated. In any case, non-standard households had been more common before the war than they became afterwards: 'families' often included lodgers, children informally fostered by aunts or grandparents, unmarried sons and especially daughters still living with parents into middle age.

In 1940, my mother was one of those dutiful daughters. Unfortunately for her, she took on the role just as it had been abolished

forever by the war and she took it on permanently, because my parents'
marriage broke down. In those days, a middle-class woman involved
in a divorce brought disgrace and stigma upon herself. One member
of any failing marriage had to be the 'guilty party'. The gentlemanly
norm was for the husband to take the blame, whatever the actual
situation, so that his wife could divorce him and be recognized as
'innocent', but my grandparents so strongly disapproved of divorce
that they prevailed on my mother to seek a judicial separation instead.
This would mean that neither party could remarry. Why they did this
was a mystery, since they never went to church and had no religious
beliefs, but, as a result, my father, who did wish to remarry, divorced
my mother. For this, my grandparents denounced him as an epic cad,
while my mother became the 'guilty' one in the eyes of the world. At
my school, only one other girl had a divorced mother, and she was a
member of the Labour Party, which associated divorce with socialism
and made it seem even more dreadful to my mother. It was as if she
felt she was being punished for some real wrongdoing; she seemed
almost to identify with the smear of guilt, and, under the influence
of my grandmother, she became ever more locked into attitudes that
had vanished, swallowed up in the war. My father was demonized
as selfish and heartless. I was successfully alienated from this man
whom in any case I barely knew.

My immersion in 1970s feminism enabled me to understand my
mother's predicament in a wider social context. I read Alison Light's
exploration of popular fiction from the interwar period, *Forever
England*, and understood that my mother's restricted life had been
the fate of many single as well as abandoned women. If a wife was
lucky enough to have a considerate husband earning enough to keep
her in comfort, she could lead a life of leisure, with a nanny and maids
to do the domestic work, leaving her free for tennis, bridge parties or
whatever else took her fancy. My aunt Erica, my father's sister, was one

such married woman. Unusually for the time, she had a university degree, but once married, devoted her days to playing golf.

A spinster's life was very different. Women novelists of the period explored the fate of these unmarried women, indignant at the limited lives they led. One such novel was Radclyffe Hall's *The Unlit Lamp*. It was a better book than *The Well of Loneliness*, for when Hall was writing about lesbianism, she overplayed what was intended as tragic so that it became self-pitying, even maudlin – or so I felt, but *The Unlit Lamp* was an eloquent plea for single women to be allowed to fulfil themselves. In *Dutiful Daughters*, Nicola Beauman rediscovered – and having founded Persephone Press, eventually republished – that and many other fictional accounts of thwarted women, prevented through lack of an independent income from fulfilling their potential, or doing so only at great cost. The financially dependent unmarried daughter of the house was confined to a life of trivial pastimes, flower arrangement and paying social calls. Lacking the status of the married woman, she remained a marginal figure, at the beck and call of her parents, never fully adult. My mother was in an even worse situation, abandoned by her husband and responsible for a child. There was to be no independence from her parents now.

She could have stepped from the pages of one of those novels and it became a further source of tension between us that she never seemed quite grown-up socially. Actually, she was rather tough and made as good a life for me as she could. She found work, looked after my grandmother and me and eventually became a secretary. Yet her timid naivety and exaggerated fears of many aspects of modern life made her appear in middle and old age to be embarrassingly 'girlish'. She never cast off the authority of the father she adored and the mother who did so much to interfere with her marriage.

As a child, I loved my grandparents. They always seemed selfless and concerned only for our well-being, but in adult life I recalled incidents which made me suspect that, probably without conscious intent, they'd undermined their daughter's marriage from the beginning and kept her tied to them for reasons arising from some psychological need of their own. My grandmother never raised her voice. She was an unchanging, reassuring presence, but her chronic headaches required continual quiet at home. At the age of twenty-six she'd been diagnosed with an incurable brain tumour and given six months to live, but my grandfather somehow persuaded the top neurologist of the day, Sir Victor Horsley, to operate. I was training to become a social worker when I came across an account of one of Horsley's famous operations, described by Ernest Jones, Freud's disciple and amanuensis, in his autobiography. Jones described how he could 'still hear the gruesome sound of Horsley's bone-secateur scattering chunks of skull all over the floor'. Yet my grandmother survived the ordeal and lived to the age of eighty-nine, still plagued by her headaches. As my father remarked acidly, 'Your grandmother's been dying for the last forty years', but she outlived everyone, including him.

The dramatic story of her operation was one of the few she would tell and retell about her adult life. She seldom mentioned Africa and refrained from asking me about my life at school or my work. What she liked to talk about was her distant early childhood, a theme she returned to again and again. It was a story that haunted us all. It was like the first chapter of a fairy story, but one with no happy ending. It was as if she'd been cast out of paradise at the age of six when my great grandfather, a wealthy rentier, 'lost all his money'. There was the move from the big mansion on the outskirts of London to a pokey house in some meaner, suburban location. Instead of eight servants, they had one.

This long-ago event was still vivid to my grandmother and overshadowed my own childhood, making everything in the present

Figure 2.4 *My grandmother. Author's photograph.*

shabby and a further shame to add to the disgrace of my mother's divorce. We were 'poor relations' and destined to be so forever and ever, it seemed. My grandmother's brothers had revived the family fortunes and were now rich and successful again, one a QC, another a rear-admiral, but my grandfather never made much money and I think he must have been essentially a wanderer.

A Scottish highlander born in New Zealand, he returned to London and wanted to join the navy as an officer, but he couldn't afford to. He trained as a doctor instead and became a GP on Exmoor, but my grandparents didn't stay in the West Country long. My grandfather treated patients for free if they couldn't afford to pay and he presumably simply couldn't make a living. He probably didn't cultivate the better-off families assiduously enough to gain their patronage. Perhaps the move to Lynmouth had represented a hope and idealism in the young couple that didn't survive. Certainly, when Lynmouth was flooded in 1953, the disaster really upset my grandmother.

I don't know where they went next, but, when the First World War broke out, my grandfather became a naval medical officer, later a ship's doctor and then a doctor in West Africa. This was 'the white man's grave', and a strange choice for a semi-invalid, who'd survived tuberculosis with only one lung and suffered from chronic asthma, but he loved to talk about life in 'the Tropics' and interested himself in African medicine.

In the house in Exeter, my grandparents slept in separate bedrooms, while my mother and I shared the third bedroom, as if we were sisters. Shortly before she unexpectedly died, my mother suddenly one day, without any preamble, blurted out the information that, when she was five years old, my grandmother gave birth to stillborn twin boys. The way she suddenly told me this made me feel that it must have been searingly meaningful to her. She never complained of being rejected by her mother, but she sometimes let drop details about her childhood that to me suggested rejection – and it was always clear that my grandmother very much preferred boys to girls. Perhaps the stillbirth was the key to my grandmother's retreat from life into the past, long ago as it was, the source of her polite distance from my grandfather, a permanent wound that had shaped her personality as I knew her, in-turned, stoical, shut up in herself, a recluse. Yet I felt closer to her than to my mother. It was from her I took my refusal to be impressed or to admire, turning a coldly critical eye on received ideas, becoming a sceptical nay-sayer. But she was also calm, when my mother was always so anxious, agitated by emotions that already upset me when I was still quite small. Each evening, my mother and I said a prayer and she read a hymn to me before I went to sleep. One summer evening, as she read the hymn, *Abide with Me*, she began to cry and, still crying, hugged me tighter and tighter, murmuring, 'I love you best in the whole wide world'. It was so painful, so frightening; not a reassuring love, but a desperate need, at least as I see it now. And it still upsets me to hear *Abide with Me*.

It's not uncommon for children, as they grow older, to find their parents embarrassing and to come into conflict with them, but what was corrosive about my home life was that I knew my mother herself was ashamed of being divorced, shabby and rejected, and was even ashamed that my father had been an administrator in Africa and not the Raj. I was encouraged not to talk about him and found it hard to explain his work to my school friends. The feeling that my family couldn't be talked about increased my shyness and withdrawal. For many years, I found it difficult to talk to people, sometimes impossible. If the doorbell rang, I didn't answer it. If the telephone rang, I ignored it. I was secretive.

When I was nineteen, I discovered that my mother had been reading the diaries I obsessively kept. What she discovered was that now I was at university I'd slept with a boy. This so horrified her that she relayed my exploits to all and sundry – our GP, former teachers, her cousin, who was a lawyer, worst of all, the boy's father and, even more dangerously, my Oxford tutors, which could have led to my being 'sent down'. Yet, when she arranged for me to meet the former teachers and other adults to whom she'd told my shocking story and dragged me round to visit them, I didn't shout at her or storm out of the house. I went along with it, sat embarrassed, drinking tea and left without anyone having said anything. I simply withdrew. I communicated only with myself in an echo box of dreams. Perhaps those visits were her only way of punishing me or of making me 'see sense'. It was quite understandable that she was worried and distraught, but the humiliation of having my private life exposed in this way caused a rift that was never mended. The drama could be said to have had its comical or even farcical side, but neither my mother nor I found it funny. It crystallized the way we were always somehow at cross-purposes and unable to understand the other's point of view, her hysteria set against my mutism.

In 1970, my mother was selling the house in West Kensington after my grandmother's death, and, by now immersed in the alternative society, I took a friend, Peter (now Bette) Bourne, to see if there were objects she wanted to get rid of that would be suitable for his Portobello Road stall. He was already selling the crocheted tank tops I made while I sat in meetings at work. My mother was very taken with Peter and gushingly pressed on him various items. There were cushions and I think some textiles, perhaps some ornaments. Then, unexpectedly, she brought out my black ribbed silk, Jacques Heim (diffusion line) A-line evening dress. Purchased for a dance at Oxford, it had been out of fashion for a long time; also, I no longer went to balls, but I still treasured it. To my horror, my mother paraded it in front of Peter: 'Why don't you have this? *She* never wears it.' I was speechless with shock as Peter accepted the gown immediately and I was somehow unable to protest or stop it happening. After Peter left, my mother said: 'What a wonderfully good-looking boy. All that curly hair! Wasted on a man, of course.'

This small event somehow typifies the way we misread each other's feelings. It didn't occur to her to ask me if I wanted to keep the dress – she just assumed I didn't value it. Also, I didn't give her much help with the house clearance or reflect on how the move must have been a difficult emotional event for her.

I took my last photograph of her in Kew Gardens. She has taken off her spectacles – all through her life she hated wearing them – and looks at me distrustfully, like a small animal, unsure if I am going to bite or stroke her. The following year, my partner had a baby daughter, but by that time my mother had unexpectedly died while

I was on holiday. I wonder if the baby might have brought about a better relationship, but it was not to be.

For a long time, I felt guilty for not loving my mother more. I think she longed for love, but no one ever loved her as she should have been loved. Her parents were quite neglectful of her when she was young. Her father, a doctor, didn't notice she was short-sighted and, when she was sent off to boarding school, they thought she was backward until her myopia was diagnosed. As a teenager, she was left alone in London when her parents were in Africa, yet in retirement they restricted her life when they needed her to look after them.

Is this a fair account? Probably not. Were they able to read it, surely they would protest that it wasn't like that at all. Perhaps it is not surprising that I was desperate to break free, but this is not a bid for sympathy. Our life as the *nouveaux pauvres* was far from destitution and I was given every opportunity. Unlike many girls of my generation, I was never held back and, as a result of my mother's insistence on my education, I have been able to lead a privileged life. When my partner (from a working-class family) told her sixth-form teacher she wanted to go to Oxford, the reply was: 'Girls like you don't go to Oxford.' They refused to put her name forward. That could not have been more different from my own experience.

In a wider sense, I belong to the lucky generation that was young at a time when things seemed to be getting better and life in the post-war world was opening out – the *trentes glorieuses* of Keynesianism and welfare capitalism. I sometimes think: Was that really as good as it was ever going to get? Couldn't we have gone so much further, done so much more? As it is, I have often felt that I have spent my life picnicking on the edge of a volcano. As war, floods and famine raged around other parts of the globe, I enjoyed the continually multiplying pleasures of 'the western way of life'.

Yet we were all unhappy in the home of my childhood and that was a reality too. The three adults felt they had failed in some way. They had disappointed themselves and one another. It was as if unhappiness was both a sin and its punishment.

So that was the house I grew up in, the house of reading. Its interior embalmed a suppressed oedipal drama, frozen, dead quiet. The actors held their positions in rigid immobility. Nothing happened. My father was a rare alien intrusion, an insect buzzing against the glass dome that preserved our life in a vacuum. I read and read.

3

Researching my life

I became a researcher by accident. It was never part of my 'life plan'. I had no plan. When adults asked: 'what do you want to be when you grow up?' my mind went blank. I had no idea; baffled because the quizzing adults always asked what I wanted to *be*, not *do,* as if a wardrobe of costumes awaited me and all I had to do was choose an identity. Perhaps boys were asked what they wanted to *do*; but I was a girl.

In one sense, it didn't matter, for so long as I was at school, life didn't stretch beyond university and my mother did have a plan. It was taken for granted that I'd go to Oxford or Cambridge. No one doubted it, although my stepmother tried to pour cold water on the idea. 'Surely you don't want to be a bluestocking, do you?' she screeched, but actually I did. I saw nothing peculiar about a girl going on to higher education. For one thing, my paternal grandfather was a professor and my aunt had gone to university. In any case, I had no idea how few girls in Britain entered higher education in the 1950s, because most of the girls at my school *did*. The whole sixth form was being prepared for the Oxford and Cambridge entrance exams, so to me it seemed normal, inevitable and unremarkable. There wasn't anything particularly clever about it. It was just what we did.

I was the most naïve brain box in the world and, for years after I left Oxford, negative or patronizing attitudes to educated women would continue to amaze me. I shouldn't have been surprised, because the principal of my college, addressing us in our final year, told us that: 'You are being educated to be the wives of diplomats.' This was a snobbish way of making a husband employed in the civil service sound glamorous and important, but what shocked me most was the idea that all the free education being lavished on us was nothing more than a preparation for marriage. Yet I faced a dilemma. As far as I was concerned, education was about amassing knowledge and finding out about things that interested me. It had nothing to do with entering the world of work and earning a living and, frankly, that was a world I was not particularly keen to join.

As soon as I got a place at Oxford, the chorus of adults was back and now they were eager to tell me about the wonderful social life I was about to experience. They raved about sherry parties in ancient buildings, about tea parties with walnut cake, about punting on the Cherwell and about summer balls that went on all night, ending with the dawn breaking over Magdalen Bridge. They seemed blithely uninterested in the course of studies I'd chosen to follow.

I think I half-knew, even as an undergraduate, that there was something overwrought about this myth of a Bright Young Things Oxford. It was hard to live up to. There was a feeling one ought to be having 'fun' all the time – at least for girls, who were theoretically in short supply, so that too many evenings without an invitation spelled social failure. The burden of being special made us all slightly hysterical – although special is not quite the right word. As young women, sometimes demeaningly referred to as 'undergraduettes', we occupied a space halfway between irruption and anomaly. This may have been behind the principal's decision to bring us down to earth and remind us to start thinking about marriage.

On one hand, we were elevated above our social status. Girls from middle-class homes dated aristocrats and foreign princelings. On the other hand, we were unlikely to go out with any of the few African or Indian students. Some of these would return to their own countries to become politicians, leaders, even heads of state, but silent racism rendered most of them socially invisible as students. In a way the racism was worse, because it was so buried. No one bothered about Cecil Rhodes in those days, but in 1996 when I returned to give a talk on coffee houses and the rise of café culture, an African postgraduate in the audience reminded me that merchants had traded slaves in seventeenth-century coffee shops and that these had not just been centres of political and philosophical discussion and enlightenment, or homes from home for bohemians.

By the end of the 1950s, about as many Oxford undergraduates, men and women, came from grammar schools as attend from the state sector today, but I seemed to meet only boys from private schools. It was they who threw sherry parties and were skilled punters. Many years later, I met an ex-grammar school student who'd been at Oxford at the same time as me. Grammar school boys like him, he said, had been too much in awe of female undergraduates to think of asking them out. It seemed to be our social, rather than our intellectual superiority, that had been off-putting, but that was just one aspect of the silently stifling straitjacket of class. We were aware we had rivals. There were nurses and French au pairs in Oxford, and we suspected that they might be more 'earthy' – our word for sexy – than we were. It was rumoured that French girls didn't shave their armpits, a deeply daring sign of 'earthiness'. No doubt some of them even 'went the whole way'. We imagined them as more attuned to the physicality of life than us high-minded bluestockings – well, certainly I did. And they probably were.

So, the romance of Oxford was tinged with uncertainty. Our female status was shaky. No one knew quite what to do with us. The few women dons at Oxford were treated as eccentric caricatures. Unlike most of my contemporaries, I had read Simone de Beauvoir's *The Second Sex* and there was no way back from that. I don't know how I discovered it; probably I read an article in the *New Statesman* or a report in *Picture Post*. These publications contained dispatches from time to time on the intellectual climate in Paris and I expect that was how I found out about existentialism, the movement with which de Beauvoir was associated.

The Second Sex created a huge stir that spread beyond France. The broadsheets would not have ignored a book that created so much controversy. It therefore seems less surprising that I'd read it than that so few of my fellow students knew about it (none, in fact), although the boyfriend I slept with had read it, which was probably his main attraction. Anyway, the result was that I was excessively attuned to the subordinate position of women at a time when no one else was. Yet, when I heard the stories of a don so eccentric that she set fire to her own hair with her cigarette, or of another who wore a French sailor's beret and was sometimes seen drunk and stumbling about in St Giles, I laughed as heartily as anyone at these absurd creatures.

My fellow students on the English literature course immersed themselves in Malory's *Le Morte d'Arthur* and *Sir Gawain and the Green Knight*. Surrounded by ancient architecture, it was easy to enter a pre-Raphaelite dream. The fantasy of being a Tennysonian maiden veiled with romance the startling inequalities confronting women at every level. The poetry of love, betrayal and chivalry glowed like stained glass against the pedestrian, welfare state world of post-war Britain, but, in spite of being a diehard romantic, I did not fancy myself as Guinevere or the Lady of Shallot. The romantic medievalism I encountered was too heavily steeped in Christianity.

Oxford was saturated with piety. Every Sunday morning, bells from all the church spires rang out in an endless carillon, one answering the next in a counterpoint of chimes. At first, they sounded beautiful, but, after a while, their insistence became domineering and oppressive in their demand that one capitulate to Faith. All branches of belief, from the Jesuits to Christian Science and beyond, had a foothold in Oxford and Christianity seemed to have a particularly strong relationship with the English School. JRR Tolkien was in the middle of publishing *The Lord of the Rings* and male undergraduates went into raptures over goblins and the heroic struggle between good and evil. Women were almost entirely absent from the novels, but no one noticed. To my dismay, I also found C. S. Lewis's unconvincing (at least to me) defence of his faith, *The Screwtape Letters*, on many of my fellow students' bookshelves, along with, astonishingly, *Winnie-the-Pooh*.

Most of the literature we studied was shot through with religion. I could respond to the poetry of the metaphysical poets, because it was beautiful, but the hollow, vatic cadences of T. S. Eliot's *Four Quartets* struck me as cold and strangely unpoetic. Too many of the writers we studied were always banging on about God. I'd expected Oxford to be full of existentialism and left-wing ideas, so the religious atmosphere lowered my mood and was all too compatible with the dank climate and the mist rolling up from the Cherwell in the mauve dusk of November afternoons.

I endured in sceptical silence my tutor's interpretation of *King Lear* as Christian parable. I failed to respond to Edmund Spenser's *The Faerie Queene*. Although my core interests were literary and artistic, I preferred to hang out with social scientists, undergraduates who'd more sensibly chosen to read PPE (Philosophy, Politics and Economics) or 'Greats' (Philosophy and Classics), and who introduced me to Émile Durkheim and Ludwig Wittgenstein (well, the name, anyway), writers with more relevant things to say, I felt, about modern life than *Beowulf*. Yet, although I may sound negative in retrospect, I didn't feel negative at the time. I loved Oxford. I loved

Figure 3.1 *Radcliffe Camera and All Souls College, Oxford. Author's photograph.*

just being there. I loved the buildings, and of course never went near the Cowley motor works, nor even knew they existed. I had all this free time and could listen for hours to Schubert's Unfinished Symphony. Doing nothing could be elevated into an art, a melancholy mood elaborated into a philosophy.

Faded memories of an Oxford distant in time are of no special interest or relevance today. In any case, nothing can surpass *Brideshead Revisited*, which still gilds the university with its glamour of backwardness. More interesting is the continuing hold of Oxbridge over the British cultural imagination. During my time as governor of an inner London comprehensive school, I was surprised to find that, for this and other local schools, to get one or two students into an Oxford or Cambridge college was the unchallenged marker of success. It did represent success, but might there not have been other good universities? And wasn't getting a student from an asylum-seeking family into *any* kind of higher education a more meaningful measurement of success? At the same time, while politicians attacked the ancient universities for having too few state-educated and too few ethnic minority students, and while there was also dismay at the disproportionate presence of Oxbridge graduates as actors, writers and directors of so many prestigious cultural institutions, the stated goal of equality could not compete with the Oxbridge glamour that continued to grip the nation's imagination. The blame lies less with the universities or their successful graduates than with a vision of Britain that is somehow still locked into a romance of dreaming spires and floating punts on glassy rivers. Oxbridge is an enduring part of the reactionary and ultimately imperialist myth of Britain.

I had never pictured my future as marriage to a diplomat and in any case no future diplomat proposed. Perhaps my mother's divorce had put me off marriage altogether, but neither did I think of myself as a 'career woman'. At the end of the fifties, marriage or career for women were less starkly posed as alternatives than they'd been before the Second World War, but the choices of work on offer were hardly inspiring to a romantic like me: schoolteacher, secretary or probation officer.

In our final year, there was a rush of engagements among my friends. For them marriage beckoned. I dimly recognized in them a certain determination in the last year, a sense of purpose to that end. No-one said: 'I'm looking for a husband', but it was the unspoken necessity. Marriage was a default installation without which you couldn't download all the other programmes for adult life. It was an imperative internalized by my friends; it turned out to be the point of it all, but I didn't seem to have had the programme installed. The small group of lawyers among my fellow women students were the only ones who seemed determined to have a career as well as a husband.

How many different kinds of marginal could there be? After the diaspora from university came a more uncertain time. I'd never considered staying on to do postgraduate research. It was primarily nineteenth- and twentieth-century culture and literature that interested me. I must have felt that, if I'd stayed on, I'd have been locked into medievalism forever. I opted for a crash course at a secretarial college, since teaching and social work sounded unbearably dreary. I think I should have preferred to be someone's muse, but I didn't know any artists or geniuses and anyway I wasn't beautiful. Later, in my first social work job, one of my colleagues, married to a painter, regularly turned up at work with a black eye, having, she said, 'walked into a door', so perhaps life as inspiration to a genius wasn't the solution either.

I'd had all that education, but at the end of it I had no idea what to do with my life and felt unfitted for any occupation. In my teens I'd thought I might want to be a journalist, but my withdrawn, shut-off personality was utterly unsuited to that. I could never have surged out into the real world, badgering people for interviews and sniffing the wind for the latest topic of the day. Such a life would have been impossible for someone as shy and silent as I was.

After a short spell as a publisher's secretary, which didn't pay a living wage, I changed course and opted for social work training after all. This meant two more years of study, now at the London School of Economics, which was perfect, since all I really wanted to do was to go on reading and sitting in a library, learning about things. At Oxford, I'd had free tuition and, because of my mother's 'straitened circumstances', a maximum grant from my local authority. They now paid for two more years at university, first a social science conversion course, then a training in mental health work. Higher education was free. I took it all for granted. I didn't appreciate how lucky I was and how generous society was to me. It was the way things were then.

In the 1990s, I was a member of the Isaac and Tamara Deutscher Memorial Prize Committee. One year, I chaperoned the prize winner back to his Bloomsbury hotel after the celebration dinner and, as we walked through the quiet streets, I boasted to him of the free higher education we British enjoyed. His awed response made me feel very proud – which shows how dangerous it is to boast. I must have been tempting fate, for only a few years later free university education was abolished.

My two years at LSE were as intellectually stimulating as the Oxford English course had failed to be and better suited to my incoherent radical ideas. Richard Titmuss, Peter Townsend and Brian Abel-Smith were spearheading the Rediscovery of Poverty. This was part of a progressive mood that would soon bring a Labour government to power. Life in 1950s Britain had remained, in moral and cultural terms, quite Victorian. Now social attitudes were shifting. Sexual scandals shattered stuffy moralism and Mary Quant dresses symbolized emancipation – mine was a khaki pinafore dress with buttons down the front and godet pleats at the hem. The stiff culture of the early post-war years was breaking up.

The 'liberation' offered women was double-edged at best. They were 'freed' by the birth control pill to have sexual relationships before marriage, but little else changed. Attitudes even worsened, because the main point of young women now seemed to be their sexual availability. When I wrote an essay on the position of women, my tutor, Peter Townsend, dismissed the subject as unimportant and irrelevant and spent the rest of the tutorial flirting with my much prettier fellow tutee. The message was clear: only plain girls are feminists. Richard Titmuss's daughter, Ann Oakley, has described how her mother seethed with frustration as she stood ironing the shirts worn by her husband, the professor. In 1965, Hannah Gavron committed suicide a year before the publication of her pioneering book, *The Captive Wife*. This was an investigation into the difficulties faced by educated mothers – difficulties that overwhelmed her own life.

The male radicals campaigning against poverty were simply blind to and uninterested in the position of women. By contrast, the Mental Health Course had definite views on the subject. 'We want to help women be better mothers', one of my supervisors told me. Freudian theory was deployed effectively to restrict women to their eternal nurturing role. Psychoanalysis became a lifelong interest, but I rebelled against its use to justify such a conservative view of women and, by the time I left, I was politicized but conflicted about the work I had embarked on. I may have excelled at exams, but I was hardly the ideal social worker.

The Rediscovery of Poverty agenda implied that decent wages, proper working conditions, education and good housing were the best way to combat social problems such as delinquency and depression. The Freudians, by contrast, saw these problems in psychological terms. If, for example, a woman was the victim of domestic violence, it might be that she unconsciously 'needed' this and was therefore the author of her own situation; or, to take another example, it wasn't bad housing that caused a mother's depression, but her inner psychological conflicts dating back to childhood. To rehouse her would therefore be pointless. This is not as much of a caricature as it may sound. The dilemma between inner and outer change was inherent in the whole social work enterprise. The psychological climate of the period, the interest in motivation and in the personal and childhood experiences of welfare clients were in many ways more humanistic than present-day managerialism, with its emphasis on drugs and conscious effort, but was too often disfigured by class and gender prejudices. Many social workers were dedicated to helping their clients out of poverty. Nevertheless, in the 1960s, social work had not caught up with the way society was evolving and often seemed conservative and punitively judgemental, more concerned with the morals and behaviour of the poor than with their material conditions.

The squalor and poverty I encountered in the East End appeared too vast for individual solutions. I wasn't even temperamentally suited to social work. I was not a practical person, not a doer or an organizer. I was a passive daydreamer and never felt comfortable in the down-to-earth social work role. I didn't even enjoy talking to people, still less did I like asking them about their private lives. It was excruciating to be tasked with trying to help a mother on benefits to 'budget' successfully, when I myself was a spendthrift who thought nothing of buying a new dress or some books every month, regardless of my overdraft. Still only in my mid-twenties, I had my political convictions, but they were of little help when I was confronted with women whose life chances were so much narrower than my own. One particular situation that condensed my sense of alienation was the case I was assigned of an Irish Catholic mother of six, living in a rundown tenement. She wept as she told me she was pregnant once more. They hadn't any money. The pregnancy was making her ill. Abortion was the only sane solution, but the Roman Catholic Church forbade it. There was nothing I could say. To me, my role was inauthentic or, rather, useless. The woman's GP told her husband that his wife would die if her pregnancy went on, so it was terminated after all. The doctor had the authority I lacked.

The post-war expansion of the welfare state had been developed in an attempt to create a fairer and more equal society, but paradoxically it was one in which morality was much slower to shift. It was assumed that women would return to the home. Their role was to remain domestic. This society was still to be a patriarchal one constructed around conservative social values, especially those concerning women and the empire. The empire itself was already disintegrating, but its values remained embedded in the nation's psyche.

And yet – perhaps accidentally – the welfare state provided a springboard from which to leap towards further innovation: new writing, avant-garde art, jazz, modernist architecture, the Beats, the Existentialists, above all, sexual emancipation. Britain at the end of the 1950s seemed to be full of young ideas and experimental thinking. The banners of radicalism fluttered under the stormy skies of a world threatened by nuclear disaster and the earliest portent of cultural crisis to come was the Campaign for Nuclear Disarmament. By 1960, the new, the hip, the cool were everywhere – in art, in literature as well as politics – and, as the decade progressed, the force for change became a battering ram against the barriers of convention. In terms of changes to the law concerning personal behaviour (abortion law reform, the partial decriminalization of same-sex relations), the 1960s became known as the 'Permissive Society', but, although the word 'permissive' contained paternalistic overtones, there was much more to it than either legislation or permission.

There was a new space of the imagination. In *Bomb Culture*, his account of those years, Jeff Nuttall, the now-forgotten doyen of what was known as the International Underground, identified the violence that roiled beneath the surface of the welfare state. The horror of the Nazi concentration camps haunted the post-war world and was reinforced by fears of nuclear annihilation, but it came with an undertow of fascination. In the aftermath of war, Nuttall felt, people were 'eaten up by repressed violence'. He pointed to all the artistic movements – Romantics, Symbolists, Dadaists, Surrealists, Existentialists, Action Painters and Beat poets – that had been fascinated by the writings on sadism of the Marquis de Sade. In the 1960s, the Royal Shakespeare Company put on a controversial play about de Sade; Nuttall found Nazi overtones in literary life and a 'rash of sado-masochism in the arts'. At the time, the 1960s, the clichés of 'Swinging London' had more to do with miniskirts, models and zany fun, but Nuttall was prescient. The complacency of the post-war settlement would be shattered.

As experimental art, new politics and the loosening up of personal lives exploded tantalizingly all around, I was marooned in work that didn't suit me. I was a social worker with unfulfilled ambitions to write at a time when 'do-gooding' was going out of fashion and seemed held back by moralism and by class and gender prejudice. I felt cut off from the cultural ferment that seemed just beyond my reach.

My first social work position was at St Bartholomew's Hospital. The trial of Stephen Ward, who was at the centre of the Profumo scandal, was taking place at the Old Bailey nearby. Every day at lunchtime, I emerged to inspect the inquisitive crowds outside the courts. I stared at them with a blasé disdain from behind my dark glasses. That was me then, defiantly lesbian, fashionably dressed and intellectually unshockable, but my *sang froid* was a sham. Really, I knew so little of life and was cut off and on the sidelines. I was a textbook case of making the worst of one's opportunities.

Dark glasses provided a convenient mask and served the second purpose of preventing me from seeing how little I saw. American modern jazz musicians referred to them as *shades*. The Tonton Macoute and the Existentialists wore shades. In communist Czechoslovakia, sunglasses were denounced as symbols of capitalist decadence; youth on the streets of Prague were forbidden to wear them and if they did were punished with fines or even imprisonment – which should destroy the illusion that style signifiers are unimportant. In the West, shades were everywhere and were everywhere cool, along with Gauloises cigarettes, at a time on the cusp of the 1960s when there was a famine of style signifiers. There was no millennial babel of piercing, tattoos, cosmetics, labels, trainers, the rifling of decades and the style diarrhoea of postmodern fashion – but at least we had dark glasses. I was still frozen behind mine.

In the nick of time, new movements – gay liberation and women's liberation – came to my rescue. Later on, Michel Foucault, one of the theory heroes of the 1970s, would tell us that no one is ever liberated, but we didn't know that then and I escaped to my own liberation, however partial, and away from the work I found unsympathetic. Still a psychiatric social worker by day, I spray-painted feminist slogans on the walls of psychiatric institutions at night, went on demonstrations and sit-ins and wrote for underground magazines in what now seems a surreal double existence. But life was like that then. Boundaries collapsed and 'normality' was challenged. In those years, work and politics became one. I joined a feminist collective, which produced a movement magazine, *Red Rag*. I wrote a *Red Rag* pamphlet: *Women and the Welfare State*. A feminist publisher read it and gave me a contract to turn it into a book. It was an authentic piece of social research, but it was also my revenge on social work, for the years when I'd felt out of place, marginal and disregarded, but now I, who never said anything, had begun to speak and I shall be forever grateful to the women's movement, which gave me my voice.

Student activism matched the rediscovery of Marxism in the universities. Trade unions were militant and equal pay for women was on the agenda. Feminists in London and in cities all over the UK moved in an alternative society, part 'underground', part hippie, part hard-left politics. The women's movement was a world unto itself, but even as the economy was tanking, society seemed to be moving our way as we forced ourselves onto the agenda. The expansion of higher education was an important part of this expansion of ideas and politics. In the early 1970s, I left social work to become a lecturer at a polytechnic, where I had time to read, write and possibly think and at the same time found subjects that inspired me.

Teaching mature students was a very different proposition from social work and freed me from the burden of guilt and false consciousness. I enjoyed my work. The academic world in the 1970s was less bureaucratic and money-driven than it is today. The marketization of higher education had not yet taken place. I did my own thing in a little-respected, but interesting part of the sector. Lecturers in the then-polytechnics were not at that time required to undertake research, so mine felt slightly illicit. It was my secret vice. I was essentially an amateur researcher, with no higher degree and sometimes with little grounding in the subjects I chose. I had become an academic almost by accident. I didn't even really regard it as a job. It seemed more like a continuation of my higher education grants, a kind of superior form of state benefit, which fed my reading habit.

Since that distant period, much has changed. It would be easy to preserve it in the formaldehyde of nostalgia, to overlook the facile 'revolutionary' rhetoric, half-baked utopianism and negative consequences of some of the ideas from that time, but, in addition to the genuine progress that was made, there was a value in the questioning of the 'taken-for-granted' and conventional 'common sense' of everyday life. It was right to challenge cultural convention. With my fellow activists, I set out to question established ideas and embarked on a life of research determined to do just that.

4

Bodies in the library

The British general election of 2010 brought public libraries into the limelight. Threatened closures symbolized the arrival of 'Austerity' – the slashing of funds to benefits, housing programmes, the NHS, the police and local councils. Starvation of the mind was surely the worst cut of all and the incoming coalition government was denounced as a hard-faced clique of philistines. The government's recipe for recovery bore down on the poor, while enforcing a template for schools that rejected the idea of 'education for education's sake' (an outmoded, sentimental idea) in favour of education as largely a technological training for future participants in 'the world of work'. Education was to become utilitarian; forget about art, the humanities and the fulfilment of human potential. Education was and ought to be an adaptation to the world as it is; it shouldn't encourage students to get het up about how it could be and ought to be better. So far as welfare was concerned, helping people in need had turned into 'service delivery' and a whole dehumanized managerialist vocabulary had spread like a rash over higher education while we weren't looking. Students had become customers and their results were 'outcomes'. At one stage, it was even suggested that we should be producing a 'graduate personality' as though students were packets of biscuits, all to be cut from the same mould. Certainly, the management was less concerned with the expansion of minds than with avoiding trouble by observing 'procedures'.

Figure 4.1 *Highgate Local Library. Author's photograph.*

The cuts came despite the protests. Some protesters argued that culture wasn't as important as welfare (would you rather have a new hospital or a ballet company? – which is the wrong question) but volunteer groups formed to keep the threatened libraries going. These were already community centres, with children's play areas and computers for those deprived of access to the internet because they had no 'device' of their own. They were more than lending libraries for the affluent with time to read for pleasure; they performed a social function. This was a continuation of the Victorian ideal. In the nineteenth century, they built libraries as an improving alternative to the pub and later the music hall. Libraries were about education and the improvement of the mind. Knowledge was the key to wisdom and responsible behaviour. In industrial society, reading – the right reading, of course – was no longer considered dangerous for the ignorant. On the contrary, it was a path to success and a worthwhile life.

In the twentieth century, the consumer society and cheap books changed the reader's relationship to the library. Flimsy paperbacks replaced heavy tomes. In the 'Age of Enlightenment', the library in an aristocrat's country mansion had denoted not just status and wealth, but the owner's claim to be a civilized man of culture. By the twentieth century, the books on an individual's shelves defined their personality and were part of their 'image'. Reading had been an aspect of entertainment since the rise of the novel in the late eighteenth century, but with the arrival of paperbacks, when reading as entertainment became easily accessible and relatively cheap, the library became a more specialized enterprise.

A library may represent different things to different people. For Walter Mehring, his father's library signified home. This is an appealing idea. I worked in a public library for a few months before starting university. There, every morning, a few huddled men shuffled into the reference section, where they sat all day, making no attempt to read a book, but were sometimes armed with a copy of the *Daily Mirror*, *Titbits* or a racing paper. They dried their handkerchiefs and sometimes their raincoats on the radiators, fell asleep or muttered to themselves, exiled by day from the local Rowton House (a hostel for

homeless men), where the mass murderer John Christie had recently
been run to earth. For them, the library was more refuge than home,
a temporary shelter rather than a permanent residence.

This suggests that a library cannot quite be a home, for a home is a
base: the place you start out from, the place where you 'recharge', the
burrow where you lick your wounds and, if necessary, hibernate. A
library by contrast is a destination, yet once you have arrived it does
become a kind of second home. It is a place in which to lose yourself,
to disappear. It is a 'home from home' and can certainly be a refuge, a
rehabilitation centre and perhaps an inn, the intellectual equivalent of
those hostelries of former times, which nourished travellers seeking
an overnight pause in their travels.

It is a public space (whether or not it is maintained by the
public purse), but an ambiguous one. In the library, the reader is
simultaneously alone and in company. The reader is 'in public', but
each researcher sits at their desk encased in an invisible membrane
of silence. One is alone in a room filled with people. The silence is
interrupted only by stifled scratchings like those of scuffling mice
and, from time to time, by the twenty-first-century ping of a text or
the chord of an opening laptop. Readers take off their shoes and pad
about in socks, cocoon themselves in shawls, pick their noses and
scratch their heads. These are gestures of the private sphere, things to
do when you're not under scrutiny. Every reader is visible yet behaves
as if they were not. Incognito is the default mode.

Research is a collaborative as well as a solitary enterprise, but the
library, rather than the laboratory or the 'field', prioritizes the individual
researcher. There they all sit, absorbed, alongside other strangers,
seething with silent intensity, sleepily yawning, daydreaming,
twisting their hair, scouring the web for a new dress, playing patience,
furiously typing, staring glassily ahead, their purposes mysterious,
embalmed in silence. Largely, the rules are observed and tolerance

reigns – although a 2020 report on disputes in the British Library reported that 'private' behaviour (smelly socks, viewing pornography online and drinking (only water, but all refreshments are forbidden)) occasionally encroached too far and caused complaints and even confrontations.

Alberto Manguel begins his magnificent *A History of Reading* with a description of Aristotle 'sitting on a cushioned chair with his feet comfortably crossed' as he engages with a book. Manguel discusses reading as a physical activity, but for me it was a disembodied one. My memories of reading books are not of a sofa on which I reclined or a garden in which I sat, but of removal to a disembodied world. I was levitated into an alternative universe that alone had material reality yet was wholly disembodied.

Libraries and their surroundings are, for all that, very real and define the reading experience in distinct ways. The Duke Humfrey's Library at Oxford was so ancient as to seem more like a cathedral than a secular place of learning. On the other hand, the Weston Library (formerly the New Bodleian) on the corner of the Broad, housing colonial documents previously kept in Cecil Rhodes house, where I read my father's documents, was smoothly modern, technologically and perfectly adapted to the needs of the twenty-first-century reader. Everything, down to the last beautifully designed door handle and the smooth carpeting, was designed to extinguish noise.

When I first undertook research, I used to work at the old British Library when it was housed in the British Museum. I could almost imagine that I was living in George Gissing's novel, *New Grub Street*, so little did things seemed to have changed since the 1880s. In the circular reading room, the catalogue consisted of hefty A2 tomes. Typed and handwritten entries were stuck onto the stiff paper. It was physically arduous to lift out a volume, place it on the shelf above the storage space and turn the pages. After an order had been written on a slip and placed in a box, the reader returned to their seat and waited for the rattling trolley that brought the books they'd ordered – although the hungry sheep often looked up and were not fed. The rows of desks, with their ancient dull duck egg blue leather chairs, radiated out from the centre. Each desk was provided with a blotter, before pens were banned. From time to time, a group of Japanese tourists was led in to be shown the desk at which, allegedly, Karl Marx had worked. I wasn't sure that anyone could actually know where he sat. At least, however, an Icelandic correspondent to *The Times Literary Supplement* revealed that an earlier writer from Iceland had regularly sat next to Lenin, who, when he was living in London and used the British Library, always sat at seat B13. In any case, the ghostly presence of the illustrious revolutionaries reinforced the hushed aura.

In those days, some of the more eccentric readers did seem to have stepped from a novel. I remember an elderly woman with an Eton crop who strode about in safari shorts, whatever the weather. There was a dishevelled tramp-like individual, similar to those in the public library of my teens, who wandered round the circular room with a plastic bag; in fact, there was a number of strange-looking readers who appeared lost in themselves and oblivious to their surroundings.

The Reading Room closed, to be replaced by a vacuous white space, like the inside of a roc's egg, containing nothing, apart from a small exhibition gallery and commercial outlets. (Absurdly, the museum later recreated a copy of the Reading Room in another part of the building.) I am told that, on the final day, as the books were packed onto the trolleys for the last time, there were tears and champagne. Readers made a painful transition to the new British Library, a raw red brick ziggurat at St Pancras – yet they soon forgot about the old Reading Room as they settled into the luxury of their new home. This resembled an upmarket hotel, with carpets, cafés, shops and sofas. You could almost believe that there was sleeping accommodation in the hinterland somewhere and contemplate going back to your room to have a shower. (At an American university I visited, the library was open twenty-four hours a day and did indeed have showers, so it really could have been your home.)

Opened in 1997, the new British Library represented the new millennium. Catalogues were digitized. Access to books was streamlined. Its atmosphere was in tune with the way in which research was transformed. At first, I read and took notes for my own interest and pleasure. Later, research was bureaucratized, managers took over and my amateur efforts became part of a 'Research Assessment Exercise'. It was even rumoured at one point that the university that employed me was to insist on owning the copyright to the publications of all the lecturers on its payroll.

The public, obvious core purpose of the library remained, yet a national library also represents the power both of knowledge and of the state. Entrance to the reading rooms could be restricted. Once within them, access to certain books and papers could still be denied. For example, in a previous era, British Library readers were only in certain circumstances permitted to read the pornography and sexually explicit books traditionally housed under lock and key in a place of safety known as 'Cupboard'. I was surprised to find Valerie Steele's *Fashion and Eroticism* consigned to 'Cupboard', presumably because of its title. There was nothing pornographic about its contents, but while reading it I had to sit at a desk within sight of the librarian, in case, I suppose, I became over-excited.

The library is a kind of heterotopia, that is a space that contains within itself many different and possibly incompatible purposes. It has its own ambiguities, though is no more ambiguous, possibly, than the nature of research itself. In bringing together strangers, the library could also be said to resemble other public buildings that draw people together while safeguarding their separation. The German writer Siegfried

Kracauer riffed on the hotel lobby as an anonymous space in which strangers mingled, while continuing to exist as ciphers. An individual entering the hotel lobby could be anyone; they might not be who they said they were, their reason for being there opaque. In *At Bertram's Hotel*, Agatha Christie elaborated on this anonymity, its inmates and its own existence ultimately exposed as a fake. In fact, the hotel lobby was a potentially rather sinister place and those who came there remained atomized and unknown, yet Kracauer also compared it to a cathedral. This was another public space that brought strangers together, but with the crucial difference that they had a common and transparent purpose: worship. The hotel lobby had no such moral basis and Kracauer, like Agatha Christie, wrote about it in the context of crime. The library sits between these two, somehow both secular and profane.

Yet it is much more than a hotel lobby. It can transcend the immediate purposes of its users and represent the collective aspiration of a whole society. The British Library was built with no expense spared, although Margaret Thatcher insisted that its original size be scaled down. Its architecture has been criticized, but it fits well with neighbouring St Pancras (itself a 'cathedral' of the railway age) and the purple, rust and ochre brick of that extraordinary building. It complements the station successfully, its angular rawness is unapologetic, and, with its spacious forecourt and massive filigree iron gates, it does suggest pride in its purpose, even if Eduardo Paolozzi's statue at the centre of the forecourt sends an ambiguous message. This is based on William Blake's 1795 print of Sir Isaac Newton. Blake felt that Newton represented an overly intellectual, scientific approach to knowledge and its lack of a spiritual dimension and a reverence for nature, and he intended the image to be a critique of this, yet, as Paolozzi's sculpture dominates the library forecourt, it can be interpreted as a coming together of science and the imagination, representing both science and the arts by referencing Blake and Newton simultaneously.

The library as a public institution has evolved. So has the publishing industry. Their victim has been the private subscription library, still flourishing in 1950 when my mother belonged to Boots's circulating library as well as to Harrods' but disappearing in the 1960s. Even a private library as prestigious as the London Library has had trouble in adjusting to the twenty-first century. I first heard of the London Library when I was a student and a hanger-on to a group whose parents were involved in the literary world of the period. On an expedition to the south of France, one of them brought with him an 1845 copy of Murray's travel guide, borrowed from the London Library, and read out extracts from the high Victorian commentary, which at the time we found hilarious.

The London Library then seemed to me a privileged and almost aristocratic place. I never thought of joining it until the 1980s, when it suddenly seemed quite possible. I didn't leave, even when the subscription doubled, but quite a few did at a time when membership was already in decline. An American equivalent, the New York Society Library, seems not to have faced similar problems, despite the existence of the New York Public Library, but perhaps Americans find it less difficult to pay for access and don't necessarily see a subscription as a triumph of commerce.

I liked the London Library less for its unique and priceless collections (such as the T S Eliot archive) than for its atmosphere. To pass through the door was to re-enter something like Oxford at the end of the 1950s. Its Reading Room had just the right degree of shabby elegance. The air was almost tangibly the slow air of the mid-century, everything I'd longed to get away from at the time, but which now projected its own nostalgia. One of the library's benefits was that all the books were on open stacks, so you could forage for hours in dusty, forgotten corners. One member likened searching the stacks to going into a Piranesi print, and certainly as you climbed up the stairways that grew narrower and narrower towards the top of the building, there was a vague feeling that you might be about to find yourself in a horror movie. Woodwork was blackened with a century of dust, the shelves were in darkness until you switched on a flickering light and the sense of being alone among hundreds of silent books was uncanny.

When I was creeping around alone up there, I remembered my visit to the Goethe-Institut Library in South Kensington after it was modernized. There, many books had been removed; when I commented on the bare shelves, the librarian replied that, yes, they had got rid of many of the *Buch Leiche* (book corpses). In the depths of the backstacks at St James' Square, I shuddered in momentary horror, a body snatcher among all these corpses – yet it was also part of the romance of the place.

The London Library was caught between two stools. To some of those involved in it, the unique qualities and special status it enjoyed were sacrosanct. The very anomaly of its being like a club, yet not quite a club, appeared to enhance its appeal to those who felt most passionately about it. For a few years, the then-development officer was my next door neighbour and she described how she'd tried to set up a London Library café integral to the institution. For all sorts of reasons, this wasn't feasible. The members' room, even enhanced with a coffee machine, didn't work in the same way. It didn't have the atmosphere of a café. When the British Library had been housed in the British Museum, the café had had the reputation of being a genteel pick-up location. The London Library members room seemed more like a waiting room, and waiting rooms seldom encourage conviviality, still less romance. By the millennium, the London Library was also having to compete with a literary scene in which every cultural institution – bookshops, concert halls, museums – had a café and ran promotional events, such as public lectures and discussions. Literary festivals flourished. The internet provided information on every subject under the sun.

I briefly became a library trustee, but then felt paralysed by ambivalence, because in my heart of hearts I felt it ought to be part of something to which all had access. The possibility was raised and explored of its connecting to a university, but it came to nothing. I silently wondered if there were some way of assimilating it into the British Library. I came to realize, however, that to its ardent supporters what seemed most precious about it was that it was a kind of secret, to whom membership was a marker of being in the know, of being an educated, refined person acquainted with civility and distinction. Indeed, the library was often described as a 'hidden gem' or a 'well-concealed secret'.

Phrases such as those reminded me of a visit to Oxford with my daughter. After we'd spent a day looking into hidden quads and college gardens and the back alleys behind 'the High' (i.e. the High Street), she observed that it was a place 'full of secrets'. The whole point of the London Library too, certainly to many of its members, was its existence as a place known only to the cognoscenti. Its ambience would be destroyed if it became part of the public realm. Perhaps I got it wrong – and soon after my stint as trustee ended, a new team began to solidify membership as it entered a new era, schemes for young authors being set up and literary lectures organized – but my mixed feelings were too difficult to articulate. In the end, the atmosphere that transported me back to my student years also reduced me again to the silent mutinous self I had been then.

The London Library was an example of how a library is much more than its instrumental purpose and how there are many other ways of thinking about libraries. A 'library' is the sum total of books housed in the 'library', that is a building, as well as being the building itself.

There is also the question of what distinguishes a 'library' from simply an accumulation of books. The London Library is partly defined by the way it was founded by a group of Victorian intellectuals, to promote learning, and the British Library by its aim to own a copy of every book printed in Britain, to record. I have never thought of the books I've accumulated over a lifetime as 'my library' or myself as a collector, whereas Walter Benjamin discussed unpacking his library, simply for their material existence as beautiful or interesting objects as much as for their content. His books also solidified into a distinct entity, expressive of his personality.

First and foremost, for me, a library has always been a location and a space, although its contents are, of course, crucial. As a home for bookworms, it has some of the qualities of the opium den, or whatever secret place, known only to those with a habit, where you access your drug of choice (and perhaps all drugs both enhance and destroy). It is a liminal space, like C. S. Lewis's wardrobe or Lewis Carroll's looking glass, a door to a parallel universe, where the barrier between the real and the imagined is, at least for a time, dissolved. Unlike those worlds, it is not wintry and bleak, far from it, nor is it eccentric and baffling. It is like a great city, a world to wander through to find new and unexpected places, the secret quads and gardens of the space that is dedicated to the location of a better self.

5

Dressing the post-war young woman

'The streets belong to everybody', observed Marcel Proust as he watched the Duchesse de Guermantes pass along the boulevard, incognito in her dark costume embellished only with a bunch of violets pinned to her lapel. He might have added that the city streets had begun to belong to women as well as men by the turn of the twentieth century.

I started reading Proust when I was eighteen and never stopped. The experience of reading him was unlike any other kind of reading. It was immersive, like stepping into a great sea. Some disenchanted readers complain about the length of his novel, *In Search of Lost Time*, and of the complexity of his sentences and endless paragraphs. His motifs, in the shape of characters, coming and going like *Leitmotifs* in Wagner, baffle them. They have not understood that you actually have to drown in order to experience the book fully. And that includes encounters with sea monsters, that is, with unacceptable ideas and attitudes foreign to a modern sensibility.

It was exactly what others found exhausting that I loved. The novel was so incredibly long: twelve volumes in the Scott Moncrieff translation. I lost myself for weeks and months in the *fin de siècle* world of upper-class Paris, where I met artists, writers, duchesses, courtesans and lesbians. This was my perfect alternative universe, for Proust clothed his subtle analysis of human behaviour, social custom, politics and art in extravagantly aesthetic terms. His housekeeper looked like a character from a Giotto fresco, a prostitute resembled a Botticelli, a single musical phrase reprised a whole love affair.

Later, I was to explore the historical world on which Proust based his novel – when researching my book on 'bohemia' – and rediscovered it in a different way, but already in my twenties Proust had interested me in the cultural history behind the novel. I'd been once to France, but never to Paris. This city now became the place in the world I most wanted to visit, becoming in my imagination a mash-up of the *fin de siècle* and post-war existentialism. I accessed this imaginary city through the poetry of Charles Baudelaire, through nineteenth-century novels and cultural histories of shopping and consumer culture, and also through films of the late 1930s, 1940s and 1950s, so that the city had become a virtual realm of my imagination before I ever actually got there.

When I did first visit, there were still romantic districts to explore. Belleville and the Marais were not yet gentrified. The Buttes-Chaumont Park was surreal and sinister. It is still possible to visit this Paris in films that preserve its atmosphere of post-Occupation suspicion. In Jean-Pierre Melville's *Le Doulos*, for example, released in 1963, the endless opening tracking shot follows a man as he walks alongside a canal, through tunnels, past crumbling walls and dilapidated houses in a whole panorama of decaying urban melancholy. By the time I read François Maspero's *Roissy Express: A Journey Through the Paris Suburbs*, that world had gone. Maspero, a radical publisher, described his journey through the unglamorous suburbs beyond *le boulevard périphérique*, the motorway surrounding central Paris, for it was there, Maspero claimed, that the real life of Paris in the 1990s was to be found. The traditional Paris had become a tourist centre and home for the rich. That pastiche was created and recreated in films such as Jean Renoir's *French CanCan* (1955), which celebrated an enduring myth of the Moulin Rouge and of Paris as the glamorous centre of consumption, known as the city of lights, the city of the floating world and the capital of the nineteenth century.

This had been in one sense a city of women, in that women represented a sexualized Paris as a city of pleasure: the eroticism of prostitutes and courtesans falsely romanticized. For, although in the nineteenth century, women were all too visible on the streets, impossible to banish from the public sphere, their presence was suspect, even if many, of course, were not selling their bodies. City life offered opportunities for some women, at least, to escape rural patriarchy and find a new freedom. Women as artists, entrepreneurs and artisans found opportunities in Paris and some achieved an independent life they could never have dreamt of in the provinces. By the beginning of the twentieth century, women were as familiar as their male companions in the cafés of the Left Bank, and in the cinemas, theatres and sports grounds of the city and its suburbs.

The trauma of the Great War intensified the thirst for pleasure and excitement. Spectator sport, in particular, attracted new audiences. One prominent sports entrepreneur commented that men might have stopped killing each other, but they would persist in their love of combat. Therefore sport, which was really war by proxy, would replace more refined pleasures. Sport – especially tennis – was also closely linked with fashion, spectacle and celebrity, so it is therefore no surprise that the greatest sporting star of the 1920s was a woman, Suzanne Lenglen, the French tennis player, whose balletic style was unhindered by corsets and complemented by the daringly short skirts that revealed her bare legs, untrammelled by stockings. The outfits Jean Patou designed for Lenglen hardly differed on or off court.

They were boyish and minimalist. Women had become active. They bobbed their hair. They wore makeup. They discarded the hampering corsets and bustles of a bygone age.

Then came the Second World War. The Nazi occupation ended in 1944 and victory came the following year, but the Parisians' joy was shot through with doubt. In the French capital, there were victory celebrations, but it was 'a strange celebration; close and appalling', wrote Simone de Beauvoir in her autobiography, *Force of Circumstance*; 'the past was haunting us; looking ahead, we were torn between hope and doubt; no serenity was possible.' They had to forget, and even then 'forget we were forgetting'.

The Cold War soon cooled the ambivalent mood of the immediate post-war period, and the late 1940s in France was a period of political instability, but throughout three centuries Paris never ceased to be the epicentre of fashion. After the war, this was symbolized by Christian Dior's 'New Look'. Dior introduced the new fashion in 1947 with his vision of the *Belle Epoque,* which he hoped would return women to corsets, ankle-length skirts and crippling elegance, yet his backward glance was partial, for Paris fizzed with a sense of youth and freedom. Student existentialists crowded the Left Bank boulevards. The singers of the day – Mouloudji, Yves Montand, Juliette Gréco – sang odes of hope and laments to lost love; and Gréco's informal style, her narrow tartan trousers and black polo neck sweaters announced a new spirit.

After I left university and became a publisher's secretary, I spent many weekends wandering around London, sometimes sitting in coffee bars, but never letting the men who sometimes talked to me pick me up, wondering where I could find a more deviant social circle, but not knowing how to. Someone told me of a lesbian club, The Gateways Club, in Chelsea, but I didn't know its address and would have been terrified had I found it. I wasn't unusual – many ex-students feel lonely and adrift for a while, post university, but I don't know why I was so passive. The publisher I worked for thought I was an ace secretary. It would have been difficult to work my way up in publishing, when female secretaries were expected to go off and get married, but, had I been ambitious and determined, perhaps I could have become a woman publisher. It didn't even occur to me.

I took refuge in fashion. That was another reason for the importance of Paris in my imagination. Fashion was as important to me as reading. Dress provided an anchor of normality, and I achieved some kind of confidence when I wore my Jaeger Chanel knock-off suit of knobbly apricot tweed. Its knee-length A-line skirt and short jacket, edged with braid, disguised me as the secretary I never felt I truly was. If the books I read provided an alternative inner world without any limits at all, the ensembles I'd created in my teens had acted as a mask or armour to protect me against the social everyday. Then I'd tried to bend and break the rules of fashion to craft an 'arty' appearance. These carefully planned, not always successful 'looks', concealed, I hoped, my inner faults, my social incapacity. Clothes can enhance self-confidence, and can also be used, as I used them, to hide what I felt was unacceptable about myself and my background. I presented a fashionable figure to the world to conceal my insecurities. Dress was a suit of armour, as much disguise as display, and fashion was my weapon against self-hatred. *Vogue* was my Bible as I desperately toured the department stores, Barkers, Derry and Toms and Pettits, along Kensington High Street, later Harrods and Harvey Nichols, for the magic remedy that would transform me into a glamorous being. By the time I was a student, fashion had become my obsession. In my twenties, to be well-dressed made life possible.

Since the 1990s, fashion exhibitions have become popular. They recreate past periods and atmospheres as no other kinds of exhibition can. A garment display recreating the history of a past period seems uniquely evocative. To look at models wearing the clothes the viewers themselves once wore projects a strange feeling of distance and closeness combined. A display of period interiors can achieve some of the same effect, but only garments can fully realize the sense of intimacy with which the spectator recalls the fall of those folds and the impact of that look. I felt that sense of 'oh, yes, that's how it was' strongly in 2012, when Paris hosted a major retrospective of the fashion house Chloë.

Karl Lagerfeld had been its designer since 1966, but it was founded in 1952 by a young woman, Gaby Aghion. Aghion arrived in Paris from Egypt in 1945. Cairo in wartime had been an amalgam of cosmopolitan Weimar Berlin and the interwar Riviera fused together, with officers and men from every combatant country. Now, Aghion in Paris encountered the beginnings of another new era in a hectic metropolis. She found a Paris infused with a breath of fresh air from beyond the Atlantic: America, wrote de Beauvoir, meant so many things! To the French, so recently liberated from the occupation, it meant first of all everything inaccessible, especially in the popular arts; its jazz, cinema and literature but for de Beauvoir it had always been 'a great myth' as well. And soon enough, the Quartier Latin was welcoming refugees from McCarthyism: Afro-American jazz musicians and writers, Beats and pure adventurers. William Burroughs, James Baldwin and Richard Wright all took up residence on the Left Bank during this period.

Paris became the Mecca for free spirits, not simply those seeking to escape political oppression. In the early nineteenth century, Honoré de Balzac's novel, *Le Père Goriot* concluded with his anti-hero, Rastignac, surveying the French capital as a world to be conquered, when, from the vantage point of the Père-Lachaise cemetery, he looks down on Paris spread out below. There lay the splendid world he was determined to conquer. A century later, a cluster of young French women and cosmopolitan wanderers made use of a similar metaphor to describe the thrill of coming to Paris in order to conquer it. De Beauvoir wrote that what was intoxicating about her return to Paris was the freedom it gave her, when, from her fifth-floor balcony, she looked out over the panorama of roofs and plane trees. In the early 1950s, Shusha Guppy, a young Persian student, sought, as a woman, to escape from the restrictions of her native country and she too retrospectively expressed this in *A Girl in Paris*, like de Beauvoir using the view from her attic window as a metaphor of freedom. From there, she described how the view stretched over the green canopies of trees alongside the Seine to the shimmering roofscape of the Right Bank, her view taking in famous landmarks so that on a clear day she could even see the white cupola of the Sacré-Cœur. Then, at dusk, the multi-coloured lights of the pier by the Pont de l'Alma were lit up and the embankment became a pleasure ground. And yet another young woman student in the 1950s, Gillian Tindall, also went to her window to look out at the September evening. The view sent shivers of excitement up and down her spine, she wrote, and to feel the warmth of the summer air at dusk held the promise of future loves and the adventures she would have and those she would not.

The freedom of Paris was erotic – and creative, as the novels these young women wrote proved. Their novels were some of the most popular of the period. They were autobiographical accounts by young women of their experiences, even if the ending was an abortion or disillusionment, as in Gillian Tindall's *No Name in the Street*, or, in the most famous, Françoise Sagan's *Bonjour Tristesse*, a cynicism – or irony – that was more shocking than the loss of virginity. Freedom, female eroticism and writing, united in a thrilling exploration of the future these women now felt opened before them. Yet the new freedom seemed doomed to be costumed in fashions that were astonishingly backward-looking (although an exception should be made for Balenciaga). Many women embraced the New Look (originally christened the Corolle line by Dior and intended, he said, for 'flower women') in a reaction against the deprivations of wartime. Others protested against its extravagance and exaggerated femininity. Working-class French women were reported to have attacked a luckless fashion model who appeared for a location shoot in a signature Dior outfit. It seems this was a set-up, a photographer's deliberately staged publicity event, but there were genuine protests in New York, and in London a female Labour MP denounced the backward outfits as promoting a 'caged bird' attitude and undermining women's equality.

The New Look spoke of luxury and the bliss of self-adornment and seems to have been inspired by Dior's nostalgic love of the *Belle Époque*, rather than some conspiracy to cage women in clothes that restricted movement. The dresses, haute couture of the highest quality designed for the most rarefied echelons of society, were both exquisite and sexy. Nancy Mitford's novel, *The Blessing*, idealized the post-war Parisian aristocracy, whose women devoted themselves exclusively to these fashions. A countess spread out the ten yards of her Dior gown at a ball and all the women guests wore similarly huge crinolines, their vast skirts contrasting with their naked shoulders and almost naked breasts, which perfectly displayed their heirloom jewellery. A flirtatious newlywed confessed that she couldn't think of any occasion without visualizing how she would be dressed at it, how she would appear. Indeed, she couldn't understand how there could be any pleasure in social life for people who were not interested in clothes. And what would be the point of getting out of bed in the morning if she didn't have some new and pretty garment to put on? I heartily agreed with this sentiment. (Only when I reread the book years later did I notice its anti-Semitism.)

And yes – fashion is intoxication. Yet so exclusive an obsession with appearance was certainly open to the criticisms made by Simone de Beauvoir. She loved nice clothes herself and was at pains to dress attractively, but she attacked the way in which women's fashions were part of a construction of femininity that damaged them. Elegance was just like housework, a hopeless task of trying to eternalize perfection. The woman identifies with 'something unreal, fixed': 'She has chosen to make of herself a thing.'

The Story of O, published in 1948, took to its logical conclusion feminine masochism as self-destruction. The author's name, Pauline Réage, hid the identity of the journalist Anne Declos, who had written the novel as a love letter to her lover, Jean Paulhan, who, she feared, was tiring of her. Until she removes them to be flagellated, raped and branded, its heroine is clothed in sumptuous New Look ensembles, immense gowns of heavy silk and brocade with tight waist and skirts falling almost to the floor. It was against this constricting – indeed deathly – 'New Look' conception of femininity, more influential when promoted in the mass media than in an underground pornographic classic, that the young women of the Quartier Latin rebelled. But how was freedom to be costumed? This was where Gaby Aghion found inspiration and showed her genius.

The Left Bank students and existentialist fashions of around 1950 were insufficient in themselves to provide a completely new aesthetic for the post-war young woman, so full of hope and energy. Gaby Aghion perceived a space between the stiff upper-class haute couture created for the establishment and the beatnik fashions of the street; a space in which a cosmopolitan, youthful style could develop. And she had the wit, the taste and the vision to bring it about. She created well-made clothes for a young clientele that could not afford the price of full-blown couture. These were women who led active lives and did not spend all day thinking about fashion. In many ways, this was a better solution than the 'fast fashion' of the twenty-first century, even if her designs were not available to the poorest groups in society.

Aghion aimed for a fashion that she designated as worthwhile. Her designs drew on and recreated the carefree style of the interwar 'café society'. This had flourished above all on the Riviera, where artists, writers, sports stars, aristocrats and tycoons had mingled, until it was all brought to an end by the Second World War, but was partially recreated in cities at war, where the military on leave, refugees, adventuresses, spies, civil servants and tricksters mingled. Cairo and Alexandria were two such cities, in which military personnel, both men and women, sought moments of release and refuge in the intervals of leave from the terrible theatres of combat. No wonder that they wanted to live to the full on these islands of pleasure, to experience love and to cast off restraint.

In the 1950s, the war was still entrenched in people's memories, but there was a new attitude. It had arrived with the alternative American culture that the Afro-American (and white) musicians and writers brought with them. This was *Cool*. Cool was an attitude. Cool was knowing; it was ironic. It rejected sentimentality and ideological passion. To be cool was to reject conventional attitudes and to embrace experience, but without illusions. It was, on the one hand, a philosophy in opposition to convention, but, on the other hand, it had its own standards of authenticity. Its most famous French expression was perhaps Françoise Sagan's *Bonjour Tristesse*, published in 1954, when the author had just turned eighteen and had recently dropped out of the Sorbonne. A sensation when it was published, it was the story of an adolescent girl's cool and ruthless plan to sabotage her father's remarriage. Sagan herself became identified with the (anti-) heroine and famous for her love of fast cars, which she drove bare foot (or so she claimed), and of love outside marriage.

Aghion's style, however, projected a less doomy and nihilistic form of cool, infused with the hope of youth rather than its disillusionment. She thought up simple shirt dresses, easy, slip-on coats, shifts and casual jackets: a cool, uncluttered look that spoke of freedom – the bodily freedom of comfort and the mental freedom of the casual and sporty. Soon, there were smart shorts and neat 'drainpipe' trousers. These were clothes for movement, for joyous self-affirmation, clothes for young women's busy daily lives, as students, workers, wives, free spirits. There were shorter skirts and looser tops. These were garments that encouraged movement instead of restricting it. Aghion fashions prefigured Mary Quant and were loved by young working women like me.

They were ideally suited to the heroines of the new cinema. The young women who appeared in the films of *La Nouvelle Vague* – Jean Seberg selling newspapers on the Boulevard Saint-Germain in *À Bout de Souffle* , or the heroine of *Cléo de 5 à 7*, whose director, Agnès Varda, was the only woman of the New Wave – these were young women who were seeking their path in life and searching for a direction outside the established limits of conventional society, yet retaining their femininity.

Chloé reminds us of a time when those films could be made; of a time when progressive ideals were in the ascendancy and when there was a lot of hope for the rising generation. Chloé fashion styles emerged from that heady post-war moment when culture cast off sentimentality and gazed with clear and unafraid eyes at the enormity of the future – on the one hand, the devastation of Hiroshima and the dark years of the Occupation, but, on the other, the promise of modernity and of the bright life that was to come. As the sixties progressed, fashion began to challenge its own conventions. Countercultures appeared. Now dress could be used to shock. It was becoming political.

6

Dressing the Bohemian Sixties

Bohemia was 'less a geographical location than a state of mind', observed an obscure German anarchist, Erich Mühsam, around 1900. Mühsam was murdered by the Nazis in 1934 in one of the first concentration camps. Bohemia was never risk free, and more than a few of its more outspoken dissidents paid the ultimate price for their defiance.

Bohemianism was certainly my state of mind in my twenties, when it was less dangerous than in the 1930s to be a rebel. The word itself had fallen out of fashion, but there were Beatniks, existentialists and artists and I longed to join them. I'd read all the right books and had all the right (i.e. left) views, but I didn't have the right contacts and feared I'd always be on the outside looking in, a thwarted, lonely rebel nobody noticed – because a bohemian needed an audience. It was always tempting to dismiss bohemians as attention-seeking poseurs, which was often the case, but, although bohemians were theatrical, their dissidence was seriously meant: they converted their own personalities into a critique of society.

Then 'The Sixties' came along and gave youth its chance. The tabloid press and the mass market created 'The Sixties' as a fest of free love, nudity, drugs and bad behaviour – as well as, indeed, 'fun'. At a superficial level, its radical, transformative impulse was lost or at best diluted into mere informality. Stiff 1950s manners disappeared, but capitalism rolled on. Nevertheless, the image of 'The Sixties' was more than a myth. Those who lived it believed it and its powerful radical impulse opened up new avenues of thought and activism. It began in art and then brought art and politics together. New painting, new music and new styles prefigured a new way of life. The aesthetic was key because it directly expressed ideas of social and political liberation and the defeat of the Victorianism that still gripped British customs. In *Notes Towards the Definition of Culture*, T. S. Eliot celebrated English culture as a collage of sporting events – Derby Day, cup finals, the dog races – mixed with awful food such as boiled cabbage cut into sections and beetroot in vinegar, and set against nineteenth-century gothic churches with everything orchestrated to a soundtrack of Elgar. This caricature of largely working-class culture, although he also included grouse shooting, summed up everything 'The Sixties' was determined to get away from.

The 1960s propelled 'bohemianism' into the mainstream as it was transformed into the counterculture, the Underground, the May Day Manifesto. All received ideas were to be challenged. A new world was in the making. In fact, the 1970s was the more radical decade, particularly in terms of improvements for women, but then came the twist of the 1980s, ironically with a woman, Margaret Thatcher, in charge, when it turned out you could have bohemianism without revolution. To everyone's surprise, unconventional behaviour was perfectly compatible with capitalism.

When I emerged at the other end of those years and found myself in the feckless nineties, I wrote a book about bohemians. My research exposed to me the deep-rooted contradiction that haunts – or taunts – rebellion in a consumer age. In the nineteenth century and the first half of the twentieth century, the bohemian was a well-known figure, locked in a love–hate relationship with the philistine bourgeoisie. The bohemian was the artist against society, his art too far in advance of middle-class taste to achieve commercial success. As a result, these self-chosen outcasts faced a lifetime of penury, yet transformed their poverty into a costume of defiance, literally, flaunting their rags and cast-offs. They were out to shock. The outrage of straight society was their lifeblood. When their art failed was when it most succeeded, since that was the proof of the avant-garde's superior insight into the world. Some bohemians dedicated their lives to new experiments in art, but others developed themselves as outrageous or eccentric characters: their own personalities and appearance as art, an unconventional way of life their sole artistic creation. They were the awkward squad of the cultural world, who defied conventional morality, who chose to walk in the gutter and refused to follow the rules, preferring to live on their wits or on other people.

Dedicated to failure, the bohemians were soon devastated to discover that their way of life, unlike their art, was a huge success and a lucky few made a fortune out of it. It didn't fail for long but was speedily taken up and turned into a 'lifestyle' by the industrial capitalism most of them despised. By the 1890s, the bohemian districts of Paris had become tourist attractions and the artists who had lived in Montmartre were forced to flee an area now transformed into a cheery parody of their outlaw dissidence.

Commercial imitations, from George du Maurier's bestseller, *Trilby*, to Puccini's *La Bohème* (itself based on the first popular account, Henri Murger's *Scènes de la Vie Bohème*, published in 1851), undercut the genuine bohemian way of life. Bestsellers of the 1920s, Michael Arlen's *The Green Hat* and Margaret Kennedy's *The Constant Nymph* popularized a stereotype of the beautiful girl who refuses to follow the rules and conventions by getting married and therefore dies tragically – although Nancy Cunard, the inspiration for these figures, did not. The greedy mill of consumer capitalism devoured every new trend that came its way and sold it to the very 'bourgeois philistines' from whom the bohemians tried so furiously to set themselves apart.

Originally, to be a bohemian had meant the rejection of all conventional ways of looking at things and the exploration of the forbidden. The idea was to turn the world upside down, politically as well as artistically. Tragically, the very combination of art, style and politics that made bohemianism radical, also made it commercial. Suburban consumers could steal the bohemian style. The mainstream stole the bohemians' clothes. The end point was reached when David Brooks neatly skewered the 'bourgeois bohemians' in *Bobos in Paradise*, describing with relish the hippie capitalists of Silicon Valley, with their grey ponytails, making millions while clad in track suits and trainers. The forms of shocking behaviour the early bohemians went in for, starting with untidiness, unpunctuality and neglect of housework, but progressing to free love, homosexuality, illegitimate children, drugs and alcoholism, were all seized upon and copied by the mainstream. We are all bohemians now – or at least 'bourgeois bohemians' or 'bobos' (embraced with special enthusiasm by the French). The scruffy look adopted by Dominic Cummings – briefly famous as the chief enabler of Brexit and then as a Parliamentary aide who planned to revolutionize the BBC, the civil service and parliament in short order – was widely interpreted as two fingers up to the establishment but was actually just a tired cliché that shocked no one. (For one thing we all know about semiotics now, so everyone could 'read' his style knowingly and mock its intended message.)

Attitudes towards art also changed. Well into the early twentieth century, avant-garde art attracted suspicion and hostility, sometimes verging on hysteria. Canvasses by the Impressionists and many later painters were denounced as degenerate daubs. Works by Schoenberg and Diaghilev were booed off stage and even caused riots. Today, by contrast, we live in a world so highly embellished, so resounding with artistic shock and awe, that it is almost impossible for any art to truly upset anyone. New artists and writers more easily find acceptance – and often cash. In a promiscuous democracy of taste, anything goes.

The fate of revolutionary politics has been otherwise. Its successive failures and sometimes betrayals have led to disillusionment. 'Bohemia' was an umbrella term that brought art and politics together: feminists, sexual radicals, socialists and anarchists sheltered with cultural innovators under its shade. In the 1960s, bohemian ways of life spread into youth culture via the Beats and then into rock music as the youth movement itself evolved out of a less differentiated Bohemia. This then morphed into an Andy Warhol world. Celebrities shoved aside the flaunting personalities of Bohemia and created a culture about instant fame and rapid extinction, largely uncoupled from art. The bohemians produced art; the art of celebrity is consumption.

Bohemianism was about ego. So is celebrity culture, yet some great bohemians had the steely tunnel vision that, under the right circumstances, achieves genius; they were not to be deflected. Celebrity is indiscriminate, embracing the inauthentic, kitsch and trivial as well as – sometimes – genuine originality. Celebrity culture's purpose, however, is not to create or be original, but simply to show off. It is part of a global web of mass distraction, designed to smash the diamond of an individual's will into a thousand smithereens of tweets, posts and trivialities. Consumer culture, which took up bohemian style with such enthusiasm, solicits conformity to its every latest whim; seeds of a change that were already summed up in the title of George Melly's 1960s book, *Revolt Into Style*.

From the beginning, bohemians dressed the part, sometimes to bear witness to their principled poverty, sometimes to underline their dedication to art and beauty, while untidiness and outlandishness were adopted to shock the 'squares'. With the arrival of pop music came new alternative fashions designed to identify the 'tribes' of late-twentieth-century youth culture. An exhibition to celebrate these varieties of 'Street Style' at the Victoria and Albert Museum in 1996 paradoxically signalled their decline, for, with their elevation to the museum, fixed in time, they became self-conscious and lost their spontaneity.

In 2015, the Thea Porter exhibition offered a momentary return to that period – the 1960s – that now seems more distant than ancient Rome (a time and place we so much more resemble). It was held at the Fashion and Textile Museum in Southwark. The museum, garish or bold, according to taste, stands out, painted in shocking pink and orange, in a warren of crooked little streets that are overwhelmed by the Shard and other gigantic building projects, transforming the whole district. This was formerly a Thames dock area, verging on a slum, but today, former dockers' pubs have become chic bistros, forbidding Edwardian tenements are transformed into desirable Airbnbs and the people hurrying along the pavements aspire to the tense, sporting body of the twenty-first century.

There could be no greater contrast between these streets and pedestrians and the world of Thea Porter, the colourful, exotic 1960s. Thea Porter was the epitome of that hippie era, when Western dress was infused and enlivened with Middle Eastern influences and orientalist languor. The opening section of the exhibition on the ground floor brought to life the designer's cosmopolitan upbringing, of which her work speaks so eloquently, with displays of her early paintings and photographs. There was a recreation of her London dining room with its mirror table, where she entertained the glitterati of the period; there was also a mock-up of her Soho shop.

She was born in Jerusalem, her father an Irish Presbyterian minister, but unexpectedly of Russian-Jewish origins, while her mother was a Tunisian nurse. Her childhood was spent in Damascus and, after a spell at an English boarding school, in Beirut. There she met and married a British economist working at the British Embassy. The sophisticated social life of the Lebanese capital provided an opportunity for experiments in glamorous fashion and her own wardrobe contained copies by local seamstresses of designs by the French couturiers, reproduced in beautiful local silks. Yet this life, glittering though it was, did not satisfy her latent creativity. She began to study painting, exhibited her works successfully, left her husband and, in 1964, moved to London just as the British capital was about to 'swing'. She at first decided to establish herself as an interior designer and won a commission to decorate the Syrian Embassy, but the crucial move was to open her own shop in Soho. This sold not only accessories for the home, such as rugs and cushions, but also the kaftans she at first imported from Syria and for which she was to become famous.

Thea Porter described how, from the moment it opened, her shop attracted rich hippies, actors, musicians and their women. They were entranced by the fabrics she was then selling and begged or demanded that she transform the silks into garments fit for their lifestyle and their performances. In fact, some of her earliest successes were designs for famous male pop stars of the day. Thus, as with some other women designers, it seemed that her fashion career began almost by accident and that, as is also so often the case, textiles were at the heart of her success.

After her first couture show in 1968, she was taken up and showcased by British *Vogue*, but the true secret of her success was that – apart from the exquisite workmanship and style – Porter's work perfectly matched the zeitgeist. Her own creations were made from rare brocades, silks and embroidery, often imported from the Middle East. Her styles were lavish and feminine – or, for men, androgynous – with long, floaty skirts or harem trousers and Eastern-style jackets. She drew inspiration also from the past, referencing the work of Mariano Fortuny and Paul Poiret and that Proustian period just before the First World War, when, as occurred later in the 1960s, non-Western influences enriched fashionable styles. These were her key motifs, before her style gradually mutated when, in the 1970s, she branched out into Paris, New York and especially California. From this later period, her creations for Hollywood stars such as Elizabeth Taylor and Lauren Bacall, and for Hollywood wives, among them Veronique Peck and Shirlee Fonda, revealed how she was as much in tune with California in the seventies as she had been with 1960s London.

An important aspect of the exhibition was its demonstration of the relationship between couture and the exquisite textiles she used. One Directoire-style dress was made from silk covered with Japanese figures holding parasols; its neighbour had a design reminiscent of Turkish carpeting or kelims. Her signature shapes – the abaya, gypsy dress, wrap-over dress, occasionally harem trousers – were consistent throughout, yet there was a change both in her Paris collections and in the designs she produced for her Hollywood clients. The Paris collection made more use of black and of lace and displayed a strictness of line slightly reminiscent of Chanel, while maintaining her own typical approach, whereas the Californian designs edged exoticism towards a less radical style of celebrity dressing. In the late 1960s, young people wore kaftans on the streets; by the late 1970s, they were becoming occasion wear. Thea Porter worked largely in couture and the beauty of her work lies in her skilful use of simple, flowing, non-Western shapes. More generally, however, the hippie styles, originally synthesized from second-hand vintage, North African and Middle

Eastern styles, eventually became hackneyed when filtered down to the mass market and reproduced in cheesecloth and seersucker to be sold from market stalls.

As I wandered through the exhibition, I felt unexpectedly ambivalent about these beautiful clothes from the pre-punk era. It is always a strange experience to see what were the accoutrements of your daily life turned into a display of the past. Also, their richness – and the exoticism of the period – was intoxicating, but, like all intoxicants, it became cloying and eventually palled. It was a psychedelic display of beauty and excitement, but was based on a social moment of hoped-for liberation that could never be fully realized.

Thea Porter clothed the rich dissidents who pioneered rebellious behaviour, but seldom faced its consequences. They were a version of the 'drawing room pinks' of the 1930s or the 'champagne socialists' of the 1980s. The youth culture reaction was the fury and destructiveness of punk fashion, the very antithesis of hippie art nouveau. Vivienne Westwood and Malcolm McLaren hated that whole aesthetic and their angry style spoke for a more aggressive time and a more beleaguered generation. No one wanted to be exquisite anymore. Torn tights, shaved heads and bondage replaced beauty.

The bad behaviour of the rich can seem glamorous; the bad behaviour of the poor is criminalized. To argue for revolution from a position of privilege can seem disingenuous, self-indulgent or deluded. Those freed from the immediate necessity of finding the rent or the next meal may be better placed to think long term than those on the breadline, but it is difficult for the would-be revolutionary to convince the world of their sincerity so long as they flaunt their luxurious 'lifestyle'.

It was an experience at one remove to wander through this exhibition of a period you had lived through. What was most interesting to me was the way it captured the shift from radical to celebrity by way of Hollywood. The seam, the join was visible, as it hadn't been at the time, when behaviour slipped slyly from one mode to another so that you never noticed the change. Nowhere was this stranger than in the realm of sexuality, when, from one decade to the next, the 'spoiled identity' of queer was transformed.

7

What does a lesbian look like?

It amazes me that I ever conceived the idea of *Mirror Writing*, because I never wanted to talk about myself. I was a very 'out' lesbian, but my aggressive outness was a way of warding off both my own doubts and the interrogation of others. I was certainly not going to discuss my 'feelings' about lesbianism and the social rejection that turned it into a damaged or 'spoiled' identity. Even if I experienced inward ambivalence and disavowal, I was not going to expose my vulnerabilities. Consciousness raising – the sharing of experience and feelings – might have been a feminist practice, but I was adept at avoiding those sessions or, when I couldn't bypass them altogether, at steering myself through them without giving much away. What I've written about lesbian dress is, therefore, the history of other lesbians and particularly those whose glamour appeared to banish all thoughts of self-hatred.

As for myself, I tended to be classified as a 'femme' lesbian because of my interest in fashion and 'the world of interiors', but I found the label restricting. All I wanted to be was a *fashionable* lesbian. Also 'femme' is part of the way in which social communication operates to classify individuals and situations so as to fit them into what already

exists and to familiarize what might otherwise be experienced as
outlandish or even threatening. I have no wish to be my partner's
'wife' (why on earth reproduce a problematic heterosexual model?),
and was dismayed when, after the birth of our baby daughter, well-
meaning individuals (mostly heterosexual) tried to fit me into some
already existing role: 'you'll be her auntie'; 'you're her dad, then' (as
if). To me it was uncharted and creative territory, and my daughter
was the one who got it right when we first talked about it and she,
aged not yet three, concluded: 'you're my friend.' For friendship is
protean. There are many kinds of friendship and so the role of friend
is expansive rather than restricting and did not stop me from also
being a mother.

In 2013, 'Queer Style', at the Fashion Institute of Technology
in New York, exhibited a history of queer dressing. Over several
hundred years, this was the way women and men had moved outside
heterosexual norms to express their different selfhood. To 'appear' was
especially important for lesbians. The history of homosexuality was
mostly about men. The image of the 'mannish woman' was familiar,
but most lesbians were cloaked in invisibility. In *The Apparitional
Lesbian*, Terry Castle showed how, in both the past and today,
lesbianism has been wished away and denied. Writing soon after
the death of Greta Garbo, in 1993, she noted that almost every well-
known woman suspected of homosexuality had had her biography
'sanitized' – as was certainly true of Garbo, whose relationship with
Cecil Beaton, who was mostly gay, has aroused much more interest
than her affairs with women. (And as recently as 2020, obituaries
for the couturier, Pierre Cardin, reprised at length his six-year
relationship with Jeanne Moreau, but gave far less attention to his
much longer-lasting relationship with a male partner; the sexuality
of gay men too is often played down.)

For Terry Castle, this suppression goes further than denial. It amounts to the 'ghosting' of the lesbian – and she cites many examples of how literary descriptions of lesbians have deployed an imagery of ghosts and haunting. The lesbian was – and still is – the apparitional 'other' of the heterosexual: lesbianism actually 'haunts' mainstream culture. It isn't there, it is unreal, but it won't go away. Alarmingly, Castle found this suppression and denial of a lesbian reality not only in mainstream literature and culture, but also among the very writers and critics who have aimed to defend the lesbian's right to existence. The 'cultural feminists', notably Lillian Faderman in her *Surpassing the Love of Men*, published in 1981, questionably defended 'love between women' by playing down its sexual dimension. The post-structuralists, represented by Judith Butler, used the contorted language of 'deconstruction' to challenge the very meaning of the word 'lesbian' or of 'coming out' as a meaningful practice. For Terry Castle, the end result was a new suppression of lesbian identity by the very feminists and radicals who should have been supporting it, or claimed they were. Theirs was a different kind of denial and obliteration from those found in mainstream society, but was no less damaging, indeed perhaps even more so.

That some women dress in a mannish way to signal their sexual preference is a reminder of the importance of self-presentation, with clothes being central to that, as the 'Queer Style' exhibition vividly demonstrated. To dress differently or deviantly was to refuse to remain ghostly. 'We're here and we're queer.' The historical panorama of how that 'hereness' was expressed reveals two persistent themes. The first is that attitudes and ways of understanding sexuality, gender and emotional attraction continually change over time. The unfortunate rancour of contemporary debates might possibly be tempered if the disagreements were recognized as expressive of that moment and that they were certain to mutate within a decade or so. Fifty years ago, male homosexuality was illegal in Britain. To look back over the long term, over centuries, is to recognize permanent revolutions in the way gender and sex are understood.

Second-wave feminists, for example, hailed the seventeenth-century poet, Katherine Philips, as a poet of lesbianism. She was married yet wrote ardent verses to women friends. Whether she married for love or necessity, it seems likely that her understanding of love between women differed significantly from the way we perceive it in the twenty-first century. Along with her husband, she appears to have belonged to a group who practised and advocated platonic love among friends and, in her writings, she suggested that platonic love was more spiritually and emotionally fulfilling than carnal love. In the twenty-first century, it may be difficult to understand that that was a widespread view, for Freud has thoroughly accustomed us to the idea that physical sexual fulfilment is the touchstone and criterion of fulfilling relationships between men and women – and these days within same-sex partnerships. To us, it is so, and we therefore do not readily enter into a culture that views *eros* as a lesser or even degraded form of love by comparison with the more spiritualized and selfless *agape* of friendship.

On the other hand, the ambiguity (for us at least) of Katherine Philips's relationships with women could be interpreted as an aspect of the 'apparitional', ghostly nature of lesbian love as Castle claims it has been perceived and imagined. Or it may not be. So dominant has been the association of active sexuality with men and with the male genitals that the imagining of eroticism between women has been dismissed as an impossibility.

The second theme I identify almost contradicts the first, since it has persisted for at least two hundred years and possibly much longer. This is that many women who identified as lesbian costumed their difference and their specificity and became visible by adopting male dress. It is not very surprising that women who were erotically attracted to other women and recognized that attraction, sought to express their active sexuality in masculine garb. What they wore was meaningful in terms of how they understood their desires and indeed their identity, for whatever Katherine Philips' feelings for her women friends, by the end of the eighteenth century love relationships between women were edging into the public domain. Yet the question remains of why it was so difficult to escape the original binary of masculine and feminine and how consistently this was expressed through dress.

In the 1780s, two Anglo-Irish aristocrats, Lady Eleanor Butler and Miss Sarah Ponsonby, who 'eloped' together in flight from unwanted marriages, became celebrities of the day, known as the Ladies of Llangollen, and were visited by many famous individuals, from Byron to the Duke of Wellington. The romantic poets Robert Southey and William Wordsworth also made the pilgrimage to their cottage; they were so famous that they were represented in souvenirs such as china ornaments for sale. Eleanor kept a diary full of loving references to her friend and lifelong companion, but as there is, unsurprisingly, no mention of a sexual relationship, commentators have tended to assume there was none – another example, possibly, of the persistent tendency towards denial. Many of their visitors did at least hint of a relationship that was 'too intense'. That Eleanor did not write about sexual acts neither proves nor disproves they took place, nor does the fact that they themselves presented their union as one of celibate devotion prove that it was so – the very fact that they felt constrained to define it in this way at least implies a different possibility.

They routinely dressed in riding habits and the riding habit was classed as a masculine style of clothing. Their style aroused comment and curiosity at the time; the *Spectator* essayist Joseph Addison disapproved, feeling that it was 'absolutely necessary to keep the partition between the two sexes', but just how significant

Figure 7.1 *The Ladies of Llangollen. Courtesy Wellcome Collection London.*

their clothes were is uncertain. The late Elizabeth Mavor pointed out, in *The Ladies of Llangollen: A Study of Romantic Friendship*, that to wear a riding habit as ordinary daywear was a common practice among women living in the country, especially in Ireland, from where the Ladies originally came. Nevertheless, their decidedly masculine appearance caused much comment. The actor Charles Mathews described in 1820 how 'there was not one point to distinguish them from men'. Their well-starched neckcloths, their coats, tailored just like men's and their black beaver men's hats were all entirely masculine. They powdered their hair, cut like a man's in the (Roman) 'Titus' crop of the 1790s, although by 1820 this was very old fashioned, adding to the eccentricity of their appearance.

Anne Lister, a landowning spinster living in Yorkshire, visited the Ladies, then in their sixties, and sensed a '*je ne sais quoi*' that convinced her they were lesbians. Lister herself was quite clear where her desires lay. Extracts from her encrypted diaries were published in the 1990s and, when I first read these, I was convinced they had to be a hoax, so modern did they seem. (Terry Castle admits that, at first, she too doubted that they were genuine.) But they are authentic and had first been discovered over twenty years earlier by a researcher who read, but chose to gloss over, the explicit nature of some of the entries – another example of 'effacement', incidentally. In 2019 Lister achieved new fame when her story was sympathetically dramatized on British television.

Lister dressed in a definitely masculine way and observers noted her mannish appearance. In her portrait, she wears black with what appears to be a black cravat and the frill of a white shirt above it. Her self-presentation was carefully crafted, and she hoped that her appearance was 'not all masculine, but rather softly gentleman-like'. She mentions meeting other 'mannish women', but these were fellow adventurers in their pursuit of women rather than erotic objects for her.

She was financially independent and a significant local figure in the north of England. This enabled her to live as she pleased and her 'eccentricity' appears to have been tolerated by her family, neighbours and friends. Indeed, her social freedom and her ability to disregard the conventions may actually have been more unusual than her relationships with women. Most of those with whom she had erotic relationships were in a much more dependent position (some were married), yet still expressed their desires. Her diaries chronicle several affairs until, in 1832, she met another rich heiress, Ann Walker, with whom she lived and travelled for the rest of her not very long life – she died in 1842 at the age of forty-nine.

Terry Castle suggested that Lister was influenced in her self-presentation by Byron. As a poet of romantic doom, who had affairs with boys as well as with his half-sister, he could appeal to the idea of lesbianism as another form of forbidden yet compulsive erotic love, while, as also a notorious womanizer, he could act as role model for the masculine rake that Anne Lister sometimes seemed to consider herself to have been. Actually, Lister's style of dress seems more directly modelled on the new dandyism promoted by Beau Brummell, but fashion is always a kind of bricolage, with magpie thefts from history, from other cultures, or from other sexes, and women's fashions have regularly copied or parodied masculine styles. So, the interpretation of lesbian dress must always take into account the proposals of fashion itself and, at the end of the eighteenth century, the upheavals in fashion mirrored the political upheavals of the period and the social changes of the industrial revolution.

Beau Brummell did not just invent a new style; his strict tailoring, neutral palette and emphatic masculinity announced a rejection of the effeminacy of court fashions for men. Gone were the lace, high heels, embroidery, bright colours, powder, wigs and cosmetics, in favour of the plainly polished leather boots, sober dark coats and jackets and plain, scrupulously clean white linen of the new dandies. This was a revolutionary style, suitable for the rapidly developing new urban environment. It was also a reinforcement of a starker conception of the masculine and formed a strikingly gendered contrast to the Regency or, in France, Directoire women's fashions, which , based on a neo-classical aesthetic of simplicity, featured pale muslin with an emphasis on the natural female form and suggested lissom fragility. These fashions emphasized gender and the difference between masculine and feminine became more emphatic. So, as fashion separated the sexes more rigidly, it could more readily be deployed to suggest sexual identities.

In the pre-industrial period, lesbians may have been 'ghosted', but there were many familiar slang and other words for lesbians and lesbianism, and there is literary evidence for their existence in working-class life. There were women from the poorer ranks of society who are known to have cross-dressed, sometimes in order to join the armed forces or to become pirates. In some cases, the reasons for the adoption of male dress may have been purely practical: the desire to earn a better wage or, as a single woman, to be protected from men's advances. To dress as a man gave a woman freedom to travel unaccompanied in public in a manner that was otherwise impossible, or at least very difficult. On the other hand, some of these women did have relations with women. Some even 'married' other women, but we know much less about them than about Anne Lister and the Ladies of Llangollen.

In the early nineteenth century, new and radical ideas developed about how social life should be organized. As early as the sixteenth century, Thomas More had imagined a utopian community in which dress minimized class difference. In the 1820s and later, actual utopian communities were founded, some of which pioneered dress reform as a visible demonstration of the new life, using their clothes to signify equality between both classes and genders. Their styles incorporated a critique of restrictive fashions for women and a number of different communities tried to introduce trousers as a signal of equality. They were too much in advance of their time, but, by the mid- to late nineteenth century, changes in women's lives – the development of girls' schools in which sport had an important place, the debates about feminism, the vote and women's role, and, not least, the popularity of the bicycle – had begun slowly to modify social attitudes to gendered dress.

The adoption of masculine dress in the nineteenth century was not automatically a sign of lesbianism, but lesbian self-presentation cannot be divorced from these wider changes. For a woman to dress like a man was to invoke a variety of associations: feminism, socialism, sexual inversion – all of which were controversial and alarmed the dominant forces in society. What united them was that they all represented one thing: a rejection of male domination, male authority, 'patriarchy'. So, women in trousers challenged male power even if this could at the same time make them exposed and vulnerable. Throughout the nineteenth century, they were routinely mocked in the press, were denounced from pulpits and, even at the turn of the twentieth century, were excluded from public spaces, such as hotels. In Britain, female pioneers of cycling plus fours found themselves ridiculed and hounded. The French writer, Colette, claims that women in trousers were forbidden by law from appearing in public (although images from the period do show women in 'bifurcated garb' cycling through the Paris streets). Indeed, research into attitudes in the north of England in the 1930s suggests that rejection and ridicule of females in trousers persisted, the wearing of them being seen as immodest and as a rejection of male authority. Even during the Second World War, when women in slacks, as they were called, became a common sight, there were those, especially in rural areas, who regarded trousered women as positively ungodly. The wearing of trousers by women therefore merged and confused the various reasons for doing so. 'Mannish dress' signified a general demand for the right to power and authority. The demand for sexual autonomy implied by lesbianism was part, but not the whole of it.

The bohemian circles of the nineteenth century were social communities of another, less formally organized kind. They were inclusive; they welcomed (if ambivalently) unmarried women, lesbian or not. Sometimes a woman, excluded from polite society, often for some sexual impropriety, became the central personality in such circles. An unconventional way of life was possible, and, whereas many bohemians survived on family remittances, poverty was not a bar to the world of the café and salon. Well before the First World War, there were also groups of independent women who went further, engaging in forging a new and exclusively female lifestyle. One of the best known was the group that met at the Paris salon of the rich American heiress Natalie Clifford Barney. She was a poet and her home at 20 rue Jacob was a meeting place for literary women, although men frequented it too. It was an intellectual as well as a social centre. Barney herself was openly lesbian as were some, but not all, of her salon habituées. She was known as the 'Amazone' from her appearances on horseback in the Bois de Boulogne, dressed in the formal riding gear of bowler hat, black jacket and bow tie and white shirt, but she appears very feminine as Valerie Seymour in Radclyffe Hall's *The Well of Loneliness*.

For lesbianism could, after all, announce itself as a celebration of femininity and womanliness as much as an assertion of the independence conventionally associated with the masculine. What was more troubling, as I noted earlier, was the absence of any possibility of escaping these opposed alternatives: masculine/feminine. That did not appear to concern Natalie Barney, nor Renée Vivien, Natalie's lover before the First World War. She too was a poet, an adventurer and a traveller, addicted to drugs and anorexic; she died at the age of thirty. In a photograph, she is posed in knee breeches, a velvet jacket, striped waistcoat and lace jabot. Whether worn specifically for the photograph or in daily life, such an ensemble gestured to a kind of dandyism and theatricality that was increasingly to lift lesbian dress to a sophisticated level of what was neither parody nor transvestism, but which used fashion ironically to express a different sexuality.

In the aftermath of the 1914–18 First World War, cultural life expanded, cultural customs changed, and women appeared on the public stage more dramatically than ever. Short skirts, short hair, the obvious use of cosmetics and changed norms of behaviour in public, such as smoking, were interpreted as signifiers of women's emancipation, but the '*garçonne*' fashions – the new boyishness – did not necessarily suggest a greater tolerance for different sexualities. Nevertheless, there were now groups of artistic and intellectual women who created a privileged – although often fraught and complicated – way of life as women who loved other women.

One of the most famous of these women, the novelist Radclyffe Hall, wrote what was virtually a manifesto for a certain kind of lesbian 'mannishness' in *The Well of Loneliness*, which was banned after its publication in 1928. Dress played a pivotal role in the creation of the lesbian identity of the central character, Stephen Gordon, with detailed descriptions of her rows of folded shirts, her cuff links, her well-cut masculine suits. Her lover, Mary, plays a pallid role in the novel. Hall says little about her dress and her femininity is simply a taken-for-granted given. The novel ends tragically, in the sense that Mary eventually leaves Stephen for a 'real' man. Radclyffe Hall, on the other hand, lived for many years with Una, Lady Troubridge, who had done precisely the opposite, leaving her husband in order to be with Radclyffe Hall. As Katrina Rolley pointed out in a 1990 *Feminist Review* article, '*Cutting a Dash: The Dress of Radclyffe Hall and Una, Lady Troubridge*', the couple as a unit is crucial to the construction of this kind of double lesbian identity. It is the presence of the feminine partner at the side of her mannish companion that fixes her (the femme) as also lesbian.

Figure 7.2 *Radclyffe Hall and Una, Lady Troubridge, 1927. Photo by Fox Pictures, courtesy Getty Images.*

The Well of Loneliness depicts lesbianism as tragic and humourless, but the famous photograph of the pair in evening dress can be read as camp and almost mocking. They are costumed with what appears to be a triumphant sense of challenge. This is not self-mockery, but something closer to throwing down the gauntlet. The appearance of each of the women in the photograph, which is itself very stylized, the dual pose carefully arranged, is intentionally glamorous and mannered. Una reclines on a leopard skin rug, wearing a silk evening dress, while Radclyffe Hall stands behind her in dinner jacket and satin skirt, cigarette in hand. It is also deeply fashionable. Radclyffe Hall does not just look 'mannish'; the kiss curl lacquered to her cheek, the languid pose, the dinner jacket are camp, artificial and, above all, of the moment, while her partner's languorous pose and downcast gaze borrow from Hollywood.

Yet the lesbian artist, Romaine Brooks, painted Una in an outfit as masculine as any worn by her partner, and, after Radclyffe Hall's death, her lover took to wearing the novelist's wardrobe. (In the early 1950s I once caught sight of her in Harrods. Slight and slender, she cut a curiously archaic and ghostly appearance in the flashy 1950s, complete with monocle and striped trousers – an apparitional lesbian, indeed, yet at the same time, startlingly noticeable.) Her oscillation between feminine and masculine suggests the element of masquerade in lesbian dress, but, in any case, the 1920s loved theatricality and dressing-up. Newspaper gossip writers filled their columns with reports of the fancy dress parties of the upper class. 'Lesbian' was yet one more daring 'appearance'.

In those years between the wars, what was effectively an international coterie of creative women, involved in different ways with the arts, used costume and masquerade to express the originality of which their sexuality was a part. Mercedes de Acosta was one of the most flamboyant. Socially well connected, she mixed in New York society and a world of artists, the theatre and celebrity. She is best known for her time as a screenwriter in Hollywood, where she became the lover first of Garbo and then of Marlene Dietrich, who apparently called Mercedes '*mon grand amour*' in spite of the fact that Dietrich was simultaneously conducting an affair with the British tennis star, Fred Perry.

A number of female stars, directors and writers in 1930s Hollywood were known to have had erotic relationships with women. Dietrich, who had many affairs with men, as well as some with women, was celebrated in the Berlin Museum of Cinema as a lesbian icon (or was at least when I visited it in 2007), but that is unusual. The museum also has archive footage of Mercedes running down the beach in California, combing back her hair with butch élan as she goes, dressed in the sort of one-piece bathing costume worn by men of that period: a vest attached to very short shorts in a contrasting colour. But when not on the beach, she had devised a kind of uniform for herself, consisting of a black Directoire redingote, a long coat with exaggerated lapels, nipped-in waist and wide skirt. In a paparazzo photograph, in which she is walking down the street with Garbo, she carries white gloves and wears a white skullcap. A less-than-admiring observer thought she looked like Dracula.

One speculative interpretation of these theatrical outfits could be that they visibly expressed the idea of the 'third sex'. Magnus Hirschfeld, the German sexologist, whose institute and papers were burnt by the Nazis in 1933, had developed the concept of the third sex as the way to freedom from the constraints of gender. By the 1970s, this had been rejected as too biological and damned as 'essentialist' (that is, assuming inborn, essential qualities that differentiate men and women). Yet a woman I knew, who had moved in bohemian circles in London in the 1930s, assured me that the idea of the third sex had been very popular with gay men and lesbians before the Second World War. It was wonderful, she insisted, because it removed you completely from heterosexual norms. She expressed dismay (this conversation took place in the mid-1980s) that lesbians were now having babies ('we wanted to get away from all that'). What seems reactionary and outdated at one time could function as liberating at another.

Travesty could also play out ironically. One of the most famous and popular of the many perennially popular images of Marlene Dietrich is from the film *Morocco*. Dressed in top hat and tails, she flirts with and kisses the female singer in a nightclub. The thrill is in the ambiguity, for this sort of travesty always suggests something beyond mere male and female – the 'undecidable'. It is an appeal to the imagination and as such must always be more seductive than mere depiction or reinforcement of more obvious gender stereotypes. The image is, of course, doubly ironic for those in the know in its playful reference to Dietrich's own bisexuality; disappointingly, the film ends in a reassertion of the heterosexual norm as Dietrich traipses off into the desert in the wake of her indifferent lover, Gary Cooper.

Whether membership of a mythical third sex enabled lesbians to escape the dual codes of masculine and feminine or not, there were many lesbians who tried to do so by devising imaginative ways of dressing. We do not know how seriously Mercedes de Acosta or her contemporaries took Hirschfeld's ideas or were even familiar with them. They certainly dressed in an original way, and it may be that lesbianism was to them as much a way of simply standing out from the crowd as of rejecting women's secondary place in society.

The women who frequented Natalie Barney's salon in the 1920s and 1930s wore startling hats and original outfits and accessories that signalled that they were *fashionable*. Janet Flanner, a successful journalist who lived in Paris for many years in an open relationship with her partner, Solita Solano, always looked smart and elegant, reported their friend the photographer Berenice Abbott, in the knowledge that a professional woman had to dress well and must never be dowdy. Flanner was described as often wearing a huge seal coat trimmed with black skunk, stockings with a gold stripe, and a black cloche hat. When relaxing at home, she wore rose-pink flannel Oxford bags made by her tailor, and she was photographed by Abbott in a top hat, black velvet jacket and striped trousers. An admiring younger woman in the expatriate American circles of the time remembered how striking they looked: Flanner, Solano and Nancy Cunard seated at the Café de Flore, dressed in black tailored suits and white gloves, sipping martinis at the cocktail hour.

This circle of women took a lesbian way of dressing to its ultimate level. It was daring and aesthetically exciting and spoke of their sexuality in a sophisticated, yet usually discreet way. Each had her own style. Evelyn Wyld, for example, who worked with the designer Eileen Gray, created her own distinctive appearance, consisting of beautifully cut trousers, Byronic silk shirts and wide, embroidered belts.

This is not to assume that these women devoted their whole lives to their appearance. On the contrary, they had successful careers as creative individuals. They were professionals, whose first allegiance was to their work. But the special and outstanding originality and elegance of this generation of lesbians between the two world wars was undoubtedly connected to the fact that they either had independent means or the contacts and professional success that allowed them to mix in exceptional circles. Afterwards, lesbian elegance would never be quite the same again.

They were – or so we tend to assume – living in a different world from the lesbians photographed by Brassaï in the famous lesbian nightclub, Le Monocle, in Paris. Brassaï's images show them as invariably either strongly butch or femme, but we know little or nothing of how they experienced this difference or what it meant to them – or whether the Flanner circle ever visited Le Monocle. Many of Brassaï's images invoke the underworld of prostitutes and working-class life more generally, but we also do not know where the habituées of Le Monocle came from, whether they were working class or included well-off women, possibly 'slumming'.

Fashion has always been considered trivial and that is still the case today, despite – or perhaps because of – its greater visibility in the popular press and the attention devoted to it in the context of celebrity culture. What this easy dismissal forgets is the crucial role it has played in modernity and modernism. 'The modern' explores a world that is uncoupled from the natural. Whether in abstract, non-representational art or in the exploration of an urban world of machines and industrial and scientific invention, modernist art 'makes strange' the world of modernity it observes.

Charles Baudelaire, poet of nineteenth-century modernity, disdained the natural. For him, artifice was the hallmark of civilization. He wrote of the dandy as not only a dissident, whose pose was 'an expression of outlaw and revolt', but as an individual who recreated himself as a work of art. Dandyism was the highest form of masquerade and recognized its own artificiality. It is therefore not surprising that dandyism appealed to queers of all descriptions. Sex has often been positioned as the last refuge of the natural. This may partly explain why there is so much hostility to those who love their own sex. Yet paradoxically they are the standard bearers of the knowledge that nothing in civilization is 'natural', and certainly not sex and sexual behaviour.

Fashion, even more than the other arts, is the handmaid of the artificial, so it is no wonder that its world should have provided gay men and lesbians with a sphere of influence in which love of artifice was an asset. Two women, lovers, were more or less the creators of British *Vogue* for a short period in the 1920s: Madge Garland and Dorothy Todd. Garland was a refugee from a wealthy but oppressive father, who was a textile manufacturer and clothing importer, but, although she had little education and no training, somehow she managed to establish herself as a paid journalist on the staff of the then-fledgling British edition of Condé Nast's *Vogue*. In those days, the publication contained little original material, although Oscar Wilde's niece, Dorothy Wilde, also a lesbian, was working on the magazine, as was the writer Aldous Huxley.

In 1923, Dorothy (Dody) Todd became *Vogue* editor in London and together the two women – at home in Bloomsbury Group circles and with contacts in New York and Paris – transformed the magazine into a significant cultural enterprise. Under their direction, it flourished with a combination of high fashion, high art and journalism. Virginia Woolf and Edith Sitwell contributed; Cocteau and Le Corbusier featured in its pages.

Todd and Garland were obviously a couple. Virginia Woolf records in her diary how Dorothy Todd had 'a shimmer of dash and "chic" even'. In *All We Know: Three Lives*, Garland's biographer, Lisa Cohen, describes Todd as small and heavy. She had dark hair in an Eton crop and her daily uniform was a jacket with a velvet collar and a matching skirt. She moved, as Cohen describes it, 'in an aura of expensive perfume' and she had 'a commanding, pleasing voice and a plummy accent'. Madge was simply, brilliantly fashionable. All her friends and other commentators throughout her life mentioned her exquisite clothes and how beautifully she carried them off on her slim figure.

The American firm, Condé Nast, not only owned *Vogue* but insisted that the British edition followed the American to a large extent. It was therefore not very surprising that, by 1926, the American headquarters had had enough of the intellectual magazine British *Vogue* had become and were worried by the dubious reputation of the women who ran it. Todd and Garland were sacked, to be replaced by Alison Settle, as elegant as Garland, but safely widowed. Dody Todd went rapidly downhill, and the couple were in a desperate state when, two years later, Virginia Woolf visited them at their 'incredibly louche' ménage. Todd was wearing spongebag (check) trousers, Garland was in pearls and silk; 'both rather raddled and on their beam ends.'

Before long, the couple separated. Dorothy Todd sank into alcoholism, but Garland was clearly a survivor. After a period of poverty in Paris and the south of France, she managed to resume her career as a fashion journalist. In 1934, she was even invited to return to *Vogue*. During the Second World War, she worked for the London department store, Bourne and Hollingsworth, and assisted the Board of Trade with its Utility programme (the production of garments that conformed to clothes rationing and the scarcity of textiles yet were nevertheless well designed and fashionable). She became an influential figure in the British commercial fashion scene and in 1948 was appointed as the first professor of fashion and principal of the School of Fashion at the Royal College of Art, founded in that year. For the next thirty years, she was one of the most important individuals in the British fashion world.

Madge Garland was just one woman in the international circle of independent, artistic and creative women, many of whom were lesbians, in the interwar period. She is of particular interest in the context of lesbian style precisely because she was equally at the heart of the 'straight' fashion world, that is to say, she recognized and promoted the idea of dress and fashion and the art of creating a perfected appearance: the very masquerade that might be said to be at the heart of presentation of self and which is so especially important to the individual in search of a deviant or 'queer' style.

After the Second World War, the rarefied fashion world which occurred between the wars no longer existed in the same way. In the 1920s and 1930s, as Madge Garland pointed out, being a fashionable woman had been a full-time job. After 1945, there were few women who were either able or willing to devote their whole lives to making a fashionable appearance. Fashion, however, survived, not least with the help of Madge Garland, by moving into the mainstream and becoming accessible to much wider classes of women.

The 'second-wave' feminist movement of the 1970s and 1980s made lesbians and lesbianism highly visible after a period in which gay men especially, but also lesbians, had had a difficult time. The Cold War atmosphere of the early post-war period, on both sides of the Atlantic, delegitimized and even demonized same-sex love, which was associated with spying and traitors. A conservative interpretation of Freudian psychoanalysis defined heterosexual marriage as the only mature form of love and eroticism. Even if, as the power of theology diminished, homosexuality was now less likely to be seen as a sin, scientists and medical men took over and turned it into a disease instead. This was hardly an improvement, since the cures for this sickness, such as electric shock treatment, were as cruel as they were ineffectual. In most countries, lesbianism was not actually illegal (unlike sex between men) and therefore lesbians could theoretically avoid interference from the state and psychiatry. In practice, however, the stifling conformity of the period made lesbianism almost as socially disastrous as male homosexuality. Films, novels and journalism, if they addressed lesbianism at all, made clear it was at best tragic, as in, to take one example,

The Children's Hour, a film based on Lillian Hellman's play, in which deviation from the norm destroys lives and the lesbian has to commit suicide. Yet the film expressed the most progressive attitude available, as the audience was invited to pity rather than condemn.

In spite of post-war cultural conservatism, some lesbians proclaimed their sexuality in a style that signified their sexual preference. This time has retrospectively been characterized as the heyday of 'butch' and 'femme' dressing, because these were the decades when women who preferred other women were becoming defiantly visible, in spite of everything. Public, even if covert, spaces developed, typically bars and clubs, where they could meet. They were no longer confined to private salons – and anyway the salon had normally been a space known only to relatively privileged women.

A class divide remained. One study of lesbian life in Buffalo, NY in the forties and fifties describes how the butch/femme code of dress and the roles associated with it testified to a flourishing independent lesbian culture. The majority of the butch women were working class, as were their femme partners. Middle-class women then and later preferred a less rigid, more androgynous and – perhaps most importantly – less recognizable style. This may largely have reflected the different types of work undertaken by women at different levels of society. A butch woman could get work in institutions where a uniform with trousers was worn – as a bus driver or, more likely in the 1950s, bus conductress, for example, or in a factory, as a janitor. Middle-class lesbians usually worked in white-collar jobs, as schoolteachers, in the public sector as administrators and secretaries and, less often, in the professions, where skirts were compulsory.

In the 1950s, a well-known British lesbian journalist, Nancy Spain, wrote a newspaper article about how she managed to get herself smuggled into the dining room of The Ritz, although she was wearing trousers. This was presented as a piece of madcap daring – Nancy Spain was not quite 'out' – but, until the 1970s or later, trousered women were taboo in many public situations. Women lawyers in Britain, for example, were not permitted to appear in court wearing trousers until the 1980s.

In the 1960s, the pioneering British lesbian magazine *Arena Three* published an article advising its readers how to dress. Better to err on the conservative side, because this looks much better than looking like 'a send-up of a male impersonator'. It is always better to look female than funny. What to wear during working hours depends enormously, of course, on what you do for a living. The writer advises women in a professional or executive job or those who frequently come into contact with the public to stick to convention. A good suit and a classic overcoat might be expensive but are 'always right and never let you down'.

For the majority of lesbians, the watchword had to be discretion. Their 'wardrobe', that is, the clothes they wore, did not necessarily express their sexuality. Although the butch/femme modes of the lesbian 1950s were important, the normal style for most lesbians then would have been the wardrobe, that is, the closet, itself; in other words, discretion and invisibility. They were again ghosts – or more accurately, apparitions. For a ghost is someone who has died but has returned; an apparition is an entity who has perhaps never existed, but is a threatening terror created by society. Yet they did exist and, in the late 1960s, by which time fashions and social behaviour had been transformed, queers, including lesbians, emerged blinking into the sunlight.

Since my teens, fashion had provided me with an essential emotional resource and in the 1980s became part of what I did for a living, but long before that it was a way of exploring my off-kilter sexuality and it may be that this bore a relationship to my affinity with the artificial, the offbeat, the strange – the Surrealists, de Chirico, Baudelaire. In the mid-1970s, the late Jack Babuscio introduced the idea of a 'gay sensibility'. The political circles I moved in decided there couldn't be such a thing as a gay sensibility because it wasn't a Marxist concept, yet, as I look back, I believe it did make sense, for that generation at least. The 'gay sensibility' was the queer gaze from the margins and was in some obscure way related to the marginal subject of dress. Queers could not but be self-conscious about the way in which they presented themselves to the world. Their achievement was to turn it into a weapon.

In her manifesto, *Towards a Recognition of Androgyny,* the feminist writer Carolyn Heilbrun called for the rejection of the cultural stereotypes that associated 'compassion', 'caring' and other emotional qualities exclusively with women and called for a reassessment of what it meant to be masculine or feminine, arguing for 'androgyny' in a wider sense. This fitted with the fashions of the period, when androgyny, known as 'unisex', became the norm. Men grew their hair and women cut theirs off in order to look like the famous fashion model, Twiggy, who looked like a boyish waif. The stick-thin rock star, Mick Jagger, was the masculine ideal.

Yet within a few short years, feminists, activists and researchers rediscovered the 'butch' and 'femme' mode of dressing and the lesbian bar culture of the 1950s, along with the pulp novels of the period, which had described this culture. Feminist androgyny fell out of fashion, dismissed by some as sexless and as another way of downplaying the sexual dimension of relations between women. The American writer, Joan Nestle, led the charge with her passionate defence of butch and femme as an authentic expression of sexuality between women. Far from being an imitation or failed man, a butch woman was a specific entity, a different kind of woman. Her style of dress signalled her ability to 'take sexual responsibility', while the femme, because she was dressing to attract a woman rather than a man was also freed from oppressive stereotypes and was actively seeking her own sexual pleasure rather than submitting to that of a man. Butch/femme was celebrated as an expression of working-class culture and, in the United States, was rediscovered as part of lesbian Afro-American culture. This was a celebration of 'out' identity, playing with at one level, yet also taking seriously established components of masculine and feminine. It was also a performance.

The idea that gender is a performance is not new. Simone de Beauvoir wrote as far back as 1949 that 'one is not born, but rather

Figure 7.3 *Author's outfit for Gay Liberation Ball. Courtesy Victoria and Albert Museum.*

becomes a woman'. In the 1980s, Judith Butler developed her concept of 'performativity': the individual performs a culturally scripted identity, which is created and reinforced by repetition. Hers is the uncompromising view that any biological or physiological component is irrelevant, since reality is a socio-linguistic performance. In the twenty-first century, 'queer', 'gender fluid' and 'non-binary' can express an embodiment in practice of transgression and subversion, yet can also express the sense of an essential self.

Queer is attractively inclusive in its simple statement of being against the norm in whatever way the performer proposes. In one version, 'queer' doesn't pretend to be anything more than a one-off assumption of travesty, a pop-up shop of identity. Ironic and playful, it acknowledges the transience of pose. Yet as queer erects an umbrella under which all subversives can shelter, it can deny queer actors their own differences from one another. In this respect, it rather resembles the old idea of 'bohemianism': the bohemian subcultures of the nineteenth and early twentieth centuries included gays, lesbians, individuals of different ethnicity and even eccentrics of all kinds.

There is a value in the idea of deviance from the norm. To be marginal might be the best place to be, because from that position you see the world differently and are freed to explore ideas and fields that others have disregarded or simply not noticed. Yet belief in queer as a transgressive identity has become harder to sustain as lesbians, like gay men, have been increasingly visible and, superficially at least, increasingly accepted. That this should have continued in an ever more conservative climate and in the face of the triumph of neo-liberal economics seems unexpected and might lead us to ask just how transgressive it is to be queer, but its apparent acceptance may at least partly result simply from the expansion of individualism and the decline of social solidarity.

Queer could even be interpreted as an expression of the inherent amorality of capitalism. In the twentieth century, those in power realized that they did not need to enforce strict forms of morality in order to extend growth and profit; on the contrary, the more individuals wanted to express their individuality, in no matter how bizarre a way, the more they were likely to spend. The gay/lesbian identity itself came to be discussed as a lifestyle choice rather than a permanently fixed orientation. In the twenty-first century, the lesbian may find it difficult to keep her footing in the slippery, liquid flux and flow of changeable identities and virtual reality. In a world of self-revelation there may cease to be a need for covert sartorial signals denoting sexual preference. To be 'queer' – in 1950s Britain, a damning and dangerous epithet – can still thrill with originality and celebrate itself, but today it can also be a statement of normality: we're just like everyone else. When queers cease to be hidden, when they exit the closet, that is, their wardrobe of seclusion and invisibility, disappointingly they may be tempted to fit in and just end up costumed in a new sort of anonymity.

The Queer Style exhibition and conference in 2013 certainly did not suggest that; it was a celebration – of gay, lesbian, trans and queer apparel in all its glory across decades and centuries. Yet the need for perennial vigilance remains. In the years since that exhibition, there has been a disturbing persistence of prejudice and intolerance, even in those Western societies that seemed to have embraced liberal values. In many other parts of the world, gays are persecuted, attacked and hunted down by religious fundamentalists and authoritarian dictators and are tortured and murdered. It should never be assumed that minorities and non-conformists are safe. They could at any time be returned to their former invisible status. For that reason, dress and the costuming of dissent still matters and is still meaningful.

Historically, queerness was judged to be false (like fashion). Tainted love: it was linked to theatricality and sinister forms of make-believe. The heterosexual majority dismissed it as essentially unreal, at best 'a phase', at worst a crime, but actually it exposed what heterosexual privilege was able to deny: that there is no existence without 'appearance' and all appearances are constructed. Identity is artifice. Heterosexual desire is oversimplified as a spontaneous inclination, as nature, not culture, but its social enactment is as much a construct as 'gayness'. (Men weren't born shooting their cuffs or smoothing their shaved cheek.) We make our world, although not under circumstances of our own choosing.

It seems somehow appropriate to conclude with Madge Garland. Here was a woman who devoted her working and private life to an aesthetic of fashion that linked it to the arts. She was ambivalent, because fashion was considered trivial, yet fiercely devoted. She was a lesbian who dressed like a fashion plate, which could itself be interpreted as a form of disavowal. Ambivalence and disavowal have haunted lesbians – as much as they have haunted many forms of dissidence. Fashion, however, is one medium whereby modern subjects define, construct and live out a way of being in the world. That such an iconic fashion leader should have been a lesbian paradoxically suggests how very queer it can be to seem straight and that, for a transgressive woman, extreme elegance could be the queerest thing of all.

8

Writing feminism

The Hours Before Dawn, by Celia Fremlin, originally published in 1958 as a crime novel, is actually a feminist protest before its time. It begins: 'I'd give anything – *anything* – for a night's sleep', the angry and despairing reaction of the heroine, Louise, to a life of continual drudgery. Working-class women were familiar with heavy housework, but it was a new experience for middle-class wives, who could no longer rely on domestic help. Louise spends all day, every day, scrubbing floors, making beds, polishing furniture, washing up and looking after her baby, who then torments her by yelling all night. Her husband shouts at her too, to 'make the brat shut up', but otherwise ignores the infant and, completely indifferent to his wife's exhaustions, complains because her cooking has gone downhill.

Fremlin's account of a middle-class woman's domestic role in the 1950s is grim. The message, immediately after 1945, was that the war had shown women to be the equal of men; they therefore no longer had to prove a point. Vindicated, they could – and should – now return to the home. In the 1950s, those with a voice – men – seemed to assume that women's problems had been solved by the arrival of washing machines and vacuum cleaners, when the reality was that many households still lacked indoor lavatories, let alone labour-saving devices.

Celia Fremlin portrayed in stark terms the undercurrent of frustration and discontent that persisted as the promised equality proved elusive. Sometimes, this burst out in unexpected places, yet the resurgence of feminism was slow. As I struggled to find fulfilling work, it was discouraging to meet up with a former university friend, a graduate, who told me that, now she was married, all she wanted was to be a housewife and mother. It was startling when my bank manager said I shouldn't worry about a pension as some man was sure to snap me up. Contemporary feminists have sometimes criticized second-wave activists for failing to challenge men who behaved inappropriately, but inappropriate behaviour was so ubiquitous that, if you'd complained every time a man touched your knee, patted your bottom or made a suggestive remark, you would never have had time to do anything else. Worse in a way was the complacency of middle-class men, expressed in patronizing assumptions. Years later, one of my fellow students on the LSE mental health course met a friend of mine and, when my name came up, he said: 'oh yes, she was a very bright little girl.' But I wasn't a little girl; I was twenty-five. Taken individually, such attitudes were trivial, yet en masse created a stifling miasma, difficult to combat openly. To protest was like protesting about the weather.

But then the weather changed. The expansion of higher education in the 1960s sent more girls to university and new horizons were opened up by the liberal atmosphere of the decade. When women finally started to protest, it was partly the result of these women's expectations having been raised but not fulfilled. Complacency was further shattered when women rebelled against the 1960s image of 'dolly birds' and a sexual freedom that delivered primarily for men.

I am afraid that I was not very sympathetic to the women's movement to begin with. At first sight, the new feminists seemed to be women with children, complaining about their lot and my initial reaction was: why did they have children, if they don't like them? It was gay liberation that first aroused me to protest, but soon I met women from the feminist groups that were springing up. Lesbians, women from ethnic minorities and working-class women prioritized different aspects of the general oppression that affected all of them and there were continual tensions, but the more feminism was mocked and vilified, the more women came together to protest and demonstrate. Feminism in the early seventies rode in on a wave of frustration and pent-up anger.

New movements burst into public consciousness. Their challenge was to ways of being as much as to changes in the law. Liberation movements brought together incompatible ideas about what the revolution of everyday life was about and how liberation was to be propelled into reality, because liberation was not about incremental change, it was about rebirth. There was a Dada impulse. Liberation was a performance, a theatrical demonstration of rage, madness and ecstasy and the human body was central to this reinvention of the self. Drag, for example, was a challenge to the normality that spread like a sludge across Britain. Conformity was the enemy of revolution. This was on a completely different plane from rational programmes of gradual improvement, yet at times the coincidence of reform and revolution resulted in one of those moments of cultural upheaval known as a paradigm shift – a fundamental alteration in intellectual assumptions and understandings – as when a kaleidoscope is turned to produce a completely different pattern. At the beginning of the 1970s, there was just such a shift.

So feminism was almost two movements in one. There was the feminism that aimed to revolutionize everyday life and transform the world, and there was a more bread-and-butter kind of feminism, involving traditional demonstrations, single-issue organizations, writing leaflets, petitioning MPs and even membership of political parties, all with the aim of incremental change. The combination of the two created a movement that was a world unto itself and was the world I lived in throughout the seventies.

In those days, no one, apart from the 'women's libbers' themselves, admitted to being a feminist. Anyone who spoke in favour of any reform for the sake of the interests of women had to preface their support with 'I'm not a feminist, but . . .'. Today, by contrast, everyone claims to be a feminist, but this can, oddly, be just as dismissive. You can say you're a feminist as a way of not thinking about it anymore. It becomes a taken-for-granted given that then needs no further investigation. 'We're all feminists now' kicks the whole thing into the long grass. Token acceptance of an idea can operate as an alternative to action; more, it can suffocate and even retard real change.

Of course, there have been improvements for women and women are certainly in a different place from where they were forty years ago, yet in 2020 domestic violence and rape are at levels as high as in the 1970s – every three days a woman is murdered by her male partner. Women still earn, on average, less than men. Men are still more likely to hold positions of power. In many parts of the world, authoritarian regimes and dictators, religious or secular (but religion is a major culprit) have stalled or rolled back women's rights. We no longer live in a time when liberal progress can be assumed. I was one of the lucky ones who benefitted from new attitudes and new freedoms, and I don't dismiss those as unimportant, but, unfortunately – and predictably – it is the poorest and least-privileged women who have benefitted least.

Protest in the 1970s was not confined to marches and strikes. Women wrote.

I read the new feminist literature that began to roll off the presses and, at the same time, discovered many forgotten classics of women's writing, republished by Virago in the 1970s. I also finally began to see my own writing in print. My first political articles appeared in 'underground' publications. I thought of myself as a polemicist, embattled against the 'establishment'. I didn't notice that the expanding academic institutions and the publishing industry were eager to take up the new ideas. It was partly the broadening of education that brought those ideas into wider discussion.

So it happened that when my first book, *Women and the Welfare State,* was published, I found that, without intending it, I'd become an 'academic' writer. As I mentioned earlier, I was happy to be published and to be part of a research community (or several of them), and yet was uneasy, because my writing was meant to be engaged and argumentative; I was suspicious of the detachment implied by 'academic'. I longed to share my ideas with a wide audience. There were feminist publications that became bestsellers, but the welfare state

Figure 8.1 *Ursula Owen, director, Virago Press, with Julia Naish, Michele Barrett and myself, members of the* Feminist Review *editorial collective. Author's photograph.*

was a specialized subject. I became part of an important intellectual movement, which was to find theoretical, causal explanations for what had gone wrong in society. Researchers were active in fields from education to the media, industrial relations and beyond, exposing the existence of massive inequalities; but it wasn't enough to describe the situation. The left-wing surge of the late 1960s expressed not just a need for social change, but also for a greater understanding of the social and economic world and crucially of how change could be made to happen. A new generation getting involved in politics felt that this change could only come about when a theory was developed to explain what was preventing change and how to overcome the inertia of the everyday. That theory was Marxism. I joined a lively Capital reading group led by David (now Lord) Triesman, although my understanding of Marxism never went beyond the basic.

Powerful left-of-centre forces still existed: political parties and trade unions, with their own responses to these urgent issues. All at least agreed that capitalism had to change, but they were not united; Trotskyists, communists and social democrats fought for the revolutionary high ground, and there were many doctrinal disputes over strategy and tactics, for sectarianism has seemed always to haunt 'the left'. The struggle to bring about change and to overturn entrenched power structures is difficult and it shouldn't surprise anyone that there are different ideas about how to do it. Theoretical disputes in those days could be passionate (a feminist example was the dispute over whether women should receive 'wages for housework', which was very controversial). Sectarianism was an enjoyable and even addictive vice. In the end, it is destructive, but it is a defence against weakness. It is easier to argue about some tactical difference of opinion or theoretical nicety than to confront the very real power of largely male legislators and politicians. To have the right strategy is important, but disputes about it could degenerate into a displacement activity – or, as in the 1980s, atrophy into arid obscurity. Right-wing parties and groups have an easier time of it. All they have to do is hang on by any means necessary to the power they already enjoy.

Meanwhile, university expansion meant more courses and courses in new subjects. Sociology, hated by conservatives, was flourishing; women's studies and the study of popular culture became legitimate academic subjects. Subjects once considered trivial were now recognized as sources of 'ideology'. Ideology was the label for a view of the world that worked to keep people in their place by its support for backward ideas, but popular culture was not uniformly backward. It could contain the seeds of the new.

The combination of low or vulgar subject matter with sophisticated theory was the basis for 'postmodernism'. Actually, it all went back to Andy Warhol – or even further back, to William Burroughs – but this was not really acknowledged, as aspects of popular culture, topics previously considered unworthy of serious attention, were now intellectually analysed. These new subjects could be anything from advertising to soap opera and all of what Freud referred to as 'the refuse of everyday life'. Warhol had lived postmodernism. Now intellectuals thought and wrote about it. They claimed that 'postmodernism' liberated hidden histories of women, ethnic groups and gays, which had previously been ignored and suppressed by the dominance of the white Western male. Sadly, the message was too often stifled in arcane language. A reaction to this willed obscurity may have led in the end to a move away from theory, into history or to eclectic approaches, with writers using bits of theory as convenient in a kind of bricolage. There were fashions in theory as in everything else. At some point in the eighties, a friend said to me: 'My publisher tells me the bottom's fallen out of the Marxism market.' Theoretical Marxism was supplanted by newer, shinier ideas. Marxist theories of how to bring about political progress had depended on the existence of an industrial proletariat, large bodies of workers in mines, factories and docks. No one had anticipated that these would be atomized and even disappear, to be replaced by fragmented and precarious forms of work devoid of solidarity. When Marx was influential, it was often said that he'd got many things right, but that one thing he hadn't got right was his prediction that classes would become more and more polarized by widening inequalities in wealth. In fact, that was exactly what he did get right, as we see so clearly today.

Groups within the women's movement worked hard to influence social policy and this reflected its campaigning and pragmatic side, but when women's studies and then the hybrid, cultural studies, offered new subject matter, I began my slide away from policy into the arts, history and film, which really interested me more, even if I feared being an intellectual butterfly. I wrote a book about women in post-war Britain, *Only Halfway to Paradise*. This covered the period of my childhood and youth, but I never thought to bring my own experience into it. Like *Mirror Writing*, it was life writing at a distance.

For me, as I now understand it, my research interests had roots in my personal life, but the category of academic separated the two. This segregation of abstract thought (or even empirically detailed material) was a weapon for the forces of backwardness and the status quo. Intellectuals could be dismissed as out-of-touch elitists who didn't understand the raw, red-blooded experience of ordinary people. This was my unease with the label of academic: that it could seem to fence-off writing about ideas into a special field, signposted as difficult. It was philistine, I felt, to assume that 'ordinary people' couldn't cope with ideas. It didn't occur to me that a wider public might not be interested in some of the ideas that excited me. Perhaps Surrealism was never going to be a mass movement. Could Proust vie in popularity with *Harry Potter*? (When Charles Nicholl was researching the life of the French poet, Arthur Rimbaud, in North

Africa, no one had heard of him and thought Nicholl was talking about Rambo.)

I found patronizing the suggestion that ideas were somehow the opposite of 'common sense' and a kind of luxury available only to 'the privileged' (people like me), while common sense was the wisdom of the silent majority. Common sense was supposed to refer to down-to-earth and reasonable behaviour, but in practice more often than not consisted of a mish-mash of opinions and propositions, such as 'you can't change human nature', 'know your place' and so on, laced with a mixture of cynicism and inertia.

The Italian Marxist, Antonio Gramsci, who had died in one of Mussolini's prisons, was a hero of the left in the 1970s, after his *Prison Notebooks* were published and translated. He exposed common sense as essentially the ideology of the ruling class, boiled down into complacency and clichés. It wasn't a way of thinking about things, but a way of stopping you from thinking. He believed it to be the task of thinkers, intellectuals or scholars, however you wanted to label them, not just to challenge that common-sense ideology, but to make their arguments for change available beyond highly educated circles. That was easier said than done in 1980s Britain, when 'common sense' was defined by Margaret Thatcher.

The election of the conservative government she headed defined the changed mood of the new decade. There were monumental political struggles, notably the miners' strike of 1984–5 and Thatcher's triumphs influenced academic thinking, defeat leading to a move away from a Marxism considered too crude. The old left-wing certainties were under scrutiny. This was another reason for seeking different theories and new subjects of interest.

One such – unlikely – subject was fashion. It was a central plank of popular culture. Celebrated in the 1960s as an aspect of sexual liberation and an exciting form of self-expression, in the 1970s it was denounced by feminists. Fashion objectified women and women now refused 'objectification'. They refused any longer to be valued only for their beauty and sexual desirability.

I accepted the argument but didn't apply it to my own behaviour and my rounds of the fashion boutiques of the period Biba, Bus Stop, Granny Takes a Trip and Quorum (very expensive) were as frequent as ever. And in practice most British feminists dressed as I did in the hippie style of the period, poetic pre-Raphaelite gowns, trailing sleeves, velvet trousers, crochet shawls, macramé belts, William Morris prints and floppy hats (a whole style recycled soon after the millennium as 'boho' or 'indie'). This was finessed as an alternative way of dressing, although it soon became well established commercially. More challenging styles included punk trash style and the army surplus greatcoat, a must for leftists, and I loved mine, bought from Laurence Corner in the Hampstead Road. It was khaki and was one of the best coats I ever had, because it fitted closely and was lined with Viyella, a cotton and wool mixture, which made it exceptionally warm. I'm sure my mother must have been mortified when I paid her a visit in a private hospital after a routine operation. My straggly hennaed curls and the coat, worn with high-heeled boots, got some odd looks from the staff, but, existing as I did in a semi-alternative universe, I was heedlessly unaware of how outlandish I must have appeared.

I have described fashion as my prop, providing me with (always shaky) self-confidence. Its magic didn't always work, because the pursuit of fashionable perfection was not only time consuming, but also involved thinking more rather than less about myself. Nor did the way I dressed always help me to escape the crippling confines of an awkward personality. If the outfit didn't work, or if I'd mistaken the occasion and turned up either over-dressed or too casual, self-confidence was gone and self-hatred returned.

At dinner with friends in the early 1980s, I met the then-editor of the *Guardian* women's page, Frances Cairncross. It surprised her to encounter a feminist who was prepared to defend fashion and she asked me to write an article about it. The article became a book. It turned out to have been a subject whose moment had arrived. And in researching and writing about fashion, I escaped the prison of the self. My research reflected my obsession, but it was no longer all about me. In pursuing my passion, I was paradoxically set free of the self-scrutiny that had started it off in the first place.

It was paradoxical that fashion as a serious subject should have come to the fore in the context of feminism. One of the longest-lasting and still lively debates is that between feminism and fashion. Feminism became an established political movement in the nineteenth century. Many of those Victorian feminists, encumbered by the excesses of crinolines, corsets and bustles, saw fashion as central to their oppression. One argument deployed was that men were forcing them into elaborate outfits that crippled their bodies and restricted their movements, so that fashionable dress was a direct instrument of male power.

Many medical men sided with the feminists, but often for conservative reasons: tight lacing, for example, was dangerous because it interfered with women's capacity to bear children, damaging their function as mothers, rather than as independent beings. Some women found corsets protective, but the crinoline and the bustle, using yards of fabric draped over metal supports, were serious encumbrances. Some feminists pioneered trousers for women, at first with little success. 'Bifurcated dress', as it was called, was just too radical. Others, members of the Aesthetic Movement, wanted to wear flowing pre-Raphaelite garments, considering them more beautiful than the stifling elaboration of mainstream fashions. The American economist and sociologist, Thorstein Veblen, gave the movement theoretical heft by arguing that women were dressed up as chattels in order to display the wealth and importance of their husbands in a form of conspicuous consumption.

After the First World War, feminism lost its intensity. A pioneer of the cosmetic industry, Helena Rubinstein, built an empire based on the belief that beauty empowered women and that beauty culture was an essential tool in that empowerment. As with so many aspects of women's lives, this was double-edged. Short hair might be daring and even controversial. On the other hand, 1920s fashions demanded a higher standard of beauty and grooming. It was hard work to be beautiful, feminine and fashionable. Femininity was more than ever a masquerade. Women wanted to put their best face forward, but the call to be beautiful could become a chore and a new duty for women. Rubinstein herself was a powerful example of how individualism could succeed as a kind of feminism, but her wealth and celebrity were founded on an ambiguous message.

Feminism in the 1970s rejected that message, but postmodernism in the 1980s partly reflected the astounding and ever-expanding power of consumerism. There was a reaction against the heavy-handed Marxists, who had denounced the seductions of mass culture. This was in part a caricature but gave permission for a new interest in pleasure. Fashion and self-adornment found a place in the debate. The idea that dress was a legitimate source of pleasure gained traction. It could also become a subject for research. It was no longer confined to museum-based costume history. It could expand and flourish in a new intellectual climate and a changing world of relative aesthetic values, when popular culture was winning out over classical art. There was no more highbrow and lowbrow; instead, everyone thirsted for style.

There was a move away from the traditional parade of fashion in linear time. Traditional dress historians, who studied garments as objects, as other specialists studied ceramics or furniture, were joined by sociologists and culturalists who opened up new ways of thinking about clothes and about fashion as an aspect of human behaviour. At first, dress historians didn't entirely welcome this, but I learned a lot from them. The word 'fashion' originates from the Latin *'facere'*, to make. Dress historians concentrated on this making and on clothes as both craft and art. Yet clothes are more than inert objects. The peculiarity about them is that they have to be worn in order to become themselves. They are intimately related to the body and therefore to the individual self. Dress has many layers of social and psychological meaning, and is part of the way in which we make or 'fashion' ourselves and our world. The combination and collaboration of dress history with sociology and psychology resulted in a new field and new subject matter. Dress was about much more than the latest fashion, but it was also about much more than haute couture. By the 1990s, both fashion and feminism, once poor relations of the cultural mainstream, were taken seriously and appeared as subjects to be studied on university courses and discussed throughout the media.

The word 'dress' was to be preferred over 'fashion' because fashion defines its subject narrowly – and ultimately negatively. In common speech, it usually refers to an idea of the modern fashion industry, central to consumer society, as a system obsessed with glamour, celebrity and newness. On the surface, it is about pleasure, but in Western thought, 'surface' implies superficiality and the idea of 'fashion' contains a vein of latent cultural hostility to a trivial obsession with how we look. Whether we recognize it or not, ambivalence towards 'fashion' represents a hierarchy of values deeply embedded in the Christian legacy and found in different forms in other parts of the world and in other religions as well. Everyone gets dressed, but high-minded people rise above fashion, for fashion is concerned with mere outer form rather than inner truth. According to this view the body is but a casing for the soul, an outer husk to contain the spirit. Clothing is even more inferior as the covering of a body that is already denigrated. We should be thinking about the purity of our thoughts and actions, about saving our souls, not about a new pair of trousers.

'Fashion', then, is a word with negative implications. 'Dress', by contrast, locates what we wear firmly in everyday life. 'Dress' even includes uniforms, and the different clothes worn for different callings. Changes in nurses' outfits over the years, for example, tells us much about social change as well as about changes in medical practise. The same is true of army uniforms. Dress, as Virginia Woolf pointed out, includes the costumes worn by judges, the police and others in power. Their uniforms represent their power. Dress matters and the study of dress takes it seriously. It challenges our prejudices in order to shed light on the deep meaning of the apparently superficial. Just as the pattern on a vase or the shape of a chair tells us about the society that produced it, so dress reveals our world. It was partly because fashion was so often (and so often negatively) linked to women that feminists needed to address it.

Beyond all that, dress was a universal category. Fashion was associated with Western societies. I myself wrote of the fashion system as a Western phenomenon. By contrast, dress could include all cultures. Most importantly of all, dress was political. In the 1980s, it could become both a symbol of the triumph of capitalism and a weapon against it.

9

Bad decade

'The Eighties': this was the Reagan/Thatcher era of greed triumphant, when glamour replaced the grunge of politics and trade unionists were yesterday's men. Dressing-up was the new art form. Sadomasochism was the new sex. Now it was right-wing radicalism that made the music, no longer the tired ditties of the left. The Big Bang and the bonfire of regulations freed the city boys to call the shots and thrusting yuppies disco-danced the night away, while AIDS victims were reviled, and demonstrators truncheoned to the ground.

The decade broke from the post-war Keynesian consensus and put in place a new and harsher neo-liberal settlement. Today, that too is broken yet remains the only game in town. With the pandemic dominant and the final act of Brexit accomplished (allegedly), no-one is harking back to the eighties, but the timely publication of two books in 2018, *Tina Brown's Diaries of the 1980s* and Paul Gorman's *The Story of the Face*, suggested that perhaps we should. This is no nostalgia trip: immersion in two different yet related versions of the bling decade might show us how the 1980s changed the tune. It might even give us the courage to pull another switch and move onto a different track.

Magazines were still important in the 1980s, before the internet came along. They defined the trends. They covered much more than style and, Dylan Jones felt, 'became the culture itself'. Paul Gorman, author of *The Story of the Face*, believes that, in flattening cultural boundaries – dissolving the distinction between pop and 'high culture' – they prefigured the digital space of today.

Tina Brown's diaries of the 1980s relive the turbo-charged immediacy of her stellar success as editor of *Vanity Fair* in New York; Paul Gorman's weighty tome reproduces the revolutionary graphics and images of his subject, accompanied by an exhaustive, year-on-year account of the magazine's development and production, its changes in personnel, office moves, attitudes to advertising and modes of distribution. The texts are very different, yet each eventually produces a similar sensation of gluttony, of having guzzled too long on the excess of unrelenting novelty, which eventually palls as endless consumerism.

A friend who had known Tina Brown at St Anne's College, Oxford, when it was still an all-women's institution, once told me that, as an undergraduate, the future media mogul never appeared in public without full make-up, even at breakfast. This anecdote, whether true or not, captures the faint sense of ridicule that accompanied Brown's early fame in London, when she won the heart of Harold Evans (then, as editor of *The Times,* locked in mortal battle with Rupert Murdoch), but it also hints at her perfectionism and determination. Taken seriously or not, she transformed the moribund *Tatler* into a sparkling, must-have style Bible. Condé Nast noticed her faultless touch and enticed her to New York. There, she revitalized *Vanity Fair,* another shaky publication with a long pedigree. In its new form, it became a journalistic sensation, its content, its style and its images defining the decade.

Her diaries of those years relive a period hysterical with glamour. Tina Brown's stunning blonde looks must have helped, but she clearly had a genius for mainlining on what she calls the 'Zeitgeist', mixing up the moods of the moment into a lethal cocktail. The diary format of her book captures the energy of the 1980s and her own energy surges off the pages. She tells us not to expect heavy ruminations on the social consequences of trickle-down economics. On the contrary, she spent those years with the super-rich Manhattan elite in what she describes as 'the overheated bubble of the world's glitziest, most glamour-focused publishing company'. She retells the story of those years with unrepentant gusto.

Recalling the 1980s by reading her diaries at breakneck speed, I understood something that had escaped me at the time: Tina Brown personifies the cultural change that overtook her generation. As a student in the 1970s she – and we – experienced the crumbling of social democracy as politicians were faced with demands for progressive economic and cultural change when economies were tanking. Those demands were eventually unsuccessful. Instead, Margaret Thatcher's abrasive politics made the weather. They drew fierce opposition, but they also opened the door to once-taboo ideas of radical individualism and thrusting competition. Those transgressive views eventually became the new normal. They did it, I now saw, by making selfishness exciting and coating it in glamour.

For yes – the 1980s were all about welfare cuts, attacks on trade unions and poll tax riots. But here the other side of it is revealed: the iconoclastic glee of flouting the gentler assumptions of clapped-out compassion. No more Mr Nice Guy! No more modesty and careful spending, tasteful clothes and quiet lives. No more Love and Peace. It was an era of temptations, of incitement to spend, the era when the consumer society finally arrived fully formed, or rather matured into a thrusting adult without excuses or apologies. These ideas were to find their cultural expression a decade later in *Sex and the City*.

Tina Brown frankly acknowledges the decadence and destruction beneath the surface of this money-mad society. Yet, it is the very decadence and greed that allows her to make *Vanity Fair* the triumph it becomes, as she exploits her readers' craving for novelty and excitement. She understands and cunningly exploits its cultural cross-breeding, treating intellectuals like film stars and socialites like geniuses. This multiplies the fascination and creates new and unexpected forms of outrage in a thrilling clash of pop and haute culture.

The triumph of obtaining permission to reproduce an image of Ronald and Nancy Reagan dancing together on a *Vanity Fair* cover sums up the attitude. Brown didn't 'much like' Reagan, but the picture spelled 'pure optimism' and she admired the president's gift for 'instinctive collusion between imagery and national mood'. That, then, was what mattered for Tina Brown: to grab the mood, to pin down the butterfly of the moment in an image, for which she was prepared to (mis)use her talents to endorse a man whose politics she probably despised. She knows that in New York 'money gets in the blood like a disease', but more telling than that is the unending *thrill* of the place, where 'crassness and need' are metastasized into the heady intoxication of being iconoclastic in that special way that only the really rich can really be.

There were friends all around dying of AIDS and there were sinister tales of murder in the towers of the wealthy. Even those, though, could become part of the *Vanity Fair* mix, part of its seductive transgression. So the flaw was the crazed double consciousness, the disavowal that made it possible to transform the ugly and politically indefensible into aesthetic thrill.

The Face was not the British version of *Vanity Fair*; on the contrary, it could be positioned as its opposite. There were points of contact. The presence of *The Face* in Manhattan was in part due to James Thurman, who knew Si Newburg, CEO of Condé Nast, and thus Tina Brown's boss (as *Vanity Fair* was under the Condé Nast umbrella), and it would oversimplify to set up a stark contrast between Manhattan glamour and the downbeat alternative eccentricity of London style in shabby 1980s

Britain. Both Tina Brown and the inventor of *The Face*, Nick Logan, understood that the message of the new, the exciting and the shocking must be delivered through the prism of style. However, *Vanity Fair* sought big names, whereas *The Face*, on the other hand, sought the unknowns waiting to be discovered in the basement clubs of urban Britain.

Yet *The Face* was also the last incarnation of the twentieth-century avant garde. It emerged from the defiance of punk and the music scene of the late 1970s, a time when music fused with fashion, and each was challenging boundaries. So it brought men's fashions to the fore and promoted new bands, but it also featured the photography of Cindy Sherman, Robert Mapplethorpe and Bruce Weber, whose work explored taboos in innovative forms.

The avant-garde sensibility of *The Face* in the 1980s (in the 1990s it became more interested in the mainstream and eventually succumbed to commercialism) was mirrored in the academic world and politics. 'Transgression' was a buzzword in cultural studies circles and 'subversion' replaced 'revolution'.

Even the then-Marxist Martin Jacques translated the seduction of emerging forms of capitalism into the 'New Times Project', launched by *Marxism Today*, the theoretical organ of the British Communist Party. In attacking trade unions and public services as sclerotic, the 'project' meant to promote more radical forms of democracy, yet ended up endorsing Thatcherite assumptions. The radical chic of promoting right-wing politicians and 'right-wing' ideas in a left-wing magazine became a self-defeating triumph of style over content.

It would be easy enough to dismiss *The Face* as merely a puerile example of thinking that style actually mattered, when it was nothing more than froth on the egos of the Thatcher generation. But what that misses is one absolutely vital point: the 'great moving right show' was clad in the costumes of the latest fashion. Style was the spoonful of sugar that made the revanchist medicine go down.

10

The vulgar
Fashion redefined

To revisit the past can be an unexpected experience. Each time I have
returned to the 1980s, they have changed a little more. When I lived
through those years, it was an angry, contested time. Thatcherism was
trashing thirty years of progress. Militant activists expended a lot of
energy in unsuccessfully trying to halt that process. I experienced it
as a right-wing decade.

Each succeeding trip down memory lane, however, has made
the 1980s look more radical and the present more enfeebled. It feels
as if oppositional forces, even though they failed, were then much
stronger than they have since become, but the failures were draining.
Now, after years of bashing the poor, the erosion of the welfare state
and the decay of the social fabric – years when cheap, processed food
and fashions from Chinese sweat shops have been workers' reward
for zero-hours contracts and austerity – radical institutions have
decayed, and the culture has become more punitive. Opposition
swells and sinks back in the face of a triumphalist return to a past
that didn't exist. Thatcher's 1980s has come to seem quite hopeful
and resistance far more focused than it is today, when movements of
protest – #Me Too, Black Lives Matter, the Climate Emergency – have

not, so far, cohered into one radical project. Which is not surprising, yet the causal connections are there to be made.

The exhibition, 'The Vulgar', curated by Adam Phillips and Judith Clark, on display at the Barbican from 2016 to 2017, revived these split memories of a past that the future has changed. It was not focused on the 1980s, but vulgarity was an essential component – denounced and celebrated – of that decade. Now, it was laid out on the exhibition table to be dissected.

To take an abstract noun as the subject of an exhibition is unusual. Every exhibition must first define its subject, and this may often be less straightforward than appears, even when based, for example, on historical periods. It might be possible to argue that 'the Georgian Period' continued into the Regency; or that the 'short twentieth century' only saw the light of day in 1914 – following on from the 'long nineteenth century', beginning in 1789. The problem of definition is even trickier in the case of an abstract noun, because then an epithet condenses an assortment of theories and assumptions into a single shorthand. Also, the producer – in this case, the curator – shapes any cultural project, and an exhibition based on an idea provides the perfect opportunity for the development of their preoccupations. Well, that, of course, is the point.

Adam Phillips is a psychoanalyst whose work has often explored commonly used words and popular clichés, sensitive to their slippery and shifting meanings. His definitions and explorations of 'the vulgar' and words associated with it, acted as a running commentary throughout this exhibition, reproduced in the lavish pink and gold catalogue. As co-curator, Judith Clark created a rich display of ensembles to illustrate many aspects of the contentious word, and the end result was a testament to creative co-operation.

The stated aim was to interrogate 'the vulgar'. The exhibition posed questions of fashion itself by exhibiting exclusive haute couture designs that have challenged their own elitism by taking on board a wide variety of potentially 'vulgar' themes: 'quotations' from popular culture, (e.g. Mickey Mouse); explicit sex; and the untrammelled display of the gold and glitter associated with excess.

In an interview, Phillips expanded on his own relationship with the word, as someone of Jewish descent who is aware that vulgarity has often (in Western societies at least, and certainly in Britain) been associated with Jewish flamboyance and the lavish display of wealth – and perhaps I should here declare my own investment in the subject. Growing up in a downwardly mobile family in one of the most constipated sections of the bourgeoisie, I was intensely aware of the danger of vulgarity – and despite decades of rebellion against this family phobia, I can still never utter the word 'toilet' without a tiny wince of agony. I may have dressed more gaudily at some periods of my life, but today at least my minimalist taste in dress again echoes the restraint of the Hardy Amies years (although missing the wonderful, strict tailoring); and my grandmother's most frequent piece of advice, 'don't make an exhibition of yourself', still echoes in my ears if I am ever tempted by some excessive garment. I simply can't get rid of the fear of vulgarity that Phillips so boldly confronted.

I'm not sure how much this ingrained, although disavowed, prejudice influenced my response to the exhibition, which was not quite what I'd expected. The double-storey Barbican gallery permits a view of exhibits below from the walkway above and, seen from this position, some of the most dramatic garments were viewed in splendid, static isolation, but the majority were grouped, sometimes in rows, at others in side-rooms, always with plenty of space between each figure. The low lighting and black walls created a cathedral-like atmosphere far removed from any hint of the subject of the display. Visitors and mannequins alike were wrapped in silence. There was thus a weird dissonance between the utterly restrained way in which the garments were displayed, conservatively, on headless mannequins, and the subject of the exhibition.

A second surprise came with the first exhibits, a fifteenth-century chasuble and an evening robe by Elsa Schiaparelli, both made of gold cloth. In spite of their metallic sheen, they did not noticeably gleam or sparkle, but, on the contrary, appeared sombre and restrained. Gold may be a signifier of vulgarity, but this gold suggested hierarchy and an exclusivity far removed from bling. Next came white 'grecian' or 'classical' robes by the French designer Madeleine Vionnet, who flourished in the early twentieth century. Adjacent were two Lagerfeld Chloé designs from the 1980s, also based on and to some extent parodying Cretan or Greek dress. These introduced the opening meditation on 'the vulgar': the idea that vulgarity is about copying and recycling, about the insertion of new or retrieved ideas, but also about pretending to be what you are not and can't be.

This neatly related to the idea that fashion itself is – possibly – vulgar, because it is commercial, is caught up in continual change and innovation and can therefore never be, as the 'grecian' pastiche falsely claims, a 'classical' rather than a 'fashionable' style. This in turn raises a question about whether fashion garments should ever even be displayed in a building devoted to high art. In 1983, the Metropolitan Museum of New York made the controversial move to stage the first-ever exhibition to be dedicated to a fashion designer: Yves St Laurent. Some critics doubted that a commercial fashion enterprise had any place in the museum, for the museum was seen as a cathedral, dedicated to art and therefore above and removed from commerce. (That may have been why Margaret Thatcher didn't like museums. I believe she dismissed them as 'dead places'.)

In the Vulgar exhibition, this controversy was referenced by St Laurent's famous Mondrian dress, several versions of which were on display. The dress itself – a mini shift printed with a Mondrian painting of red, yellow and blue squares, oblongs and black lines – queried the relationship between art and fashion in a directly visible way. It may have been intended to raise the status of fashion to that of creativity and art, but arguably did more to align fashion with tourist scarves or tote bags printed with an image of, say, the Mona Lisa. It certainly didn't settle the question of whether fashion can ever rise to the status of art. That question remains controversial forty years later, even if the museum fashion exhibition is by now well established – partly because it is so popular and commercially successful and therefore perhaps inescapably vulgar.

The Vulgar exhibition identified the growth of vulgarity from the beginnings of the consumer society in the eighteenth century, when an increasingly confident bourgeoisie began to grasp for the luxury and lifestyle enjoyed by the aristocracy. In response to this, manufacturers produced cheaper copies of originally exclusive wares. Wedgewood, for example, with its production of china ware and ceramics, rose to success on this wave. These commercial changes led to enhanced definitions of the difference between good taste and bad taste as the rich and powerful strove to create new social and cultural barriers between themselves and the upstarts. Taste became a weapon in the class war.

Dress was a key factor in the display of taste and the curators chose a magnificently embroidered mantua or overgown for court wear, its skirt fully three feet wide, to symbolize this assertion of rank. A woman could barely have moved in such a dress, but it demonstrated social power and wealth, albeit of the woman's family and husband, rather than herself. It was so static by comparison with modern fashions and so hieratic that it seemed closer to the Catholic chasuble at the entrance to the exhibition than to consumerism of any kind and didn't visually endorse the idea of luxury consumption (although it was a valuable luxury item) but seemed beyond or prior to that in its monumental rigidity. To me, it spoke of rank rather than wealth. Nor was it 'vulgar' in any way I could understand that term. Its beautiful textile was subtly embroidered, not showy. I wondered if the woman who had worn it had felt empowered by its hooped skirts and train. You would surely feel like a somebody when wearing that dress, but I am not sure that a statement of social power is the same as vulgarity, unless any such straightforward assertion is automatically vulgar. The direction of the argument being developed within the exhibition suggested that 'the vulgar' is subversive of authoritarian modes of being, whereas the Georgian dress seemed to endorse it.

Vulgarity certainly, however, challenges the policing of 'good taste'. This is because it is exaggerated: 'too much', according to Adam Phillips. As I moved through the exhibition, a series of contemporary avant-garde ensembles by Viktor and Rolf, Galliano and others illustrated this, yet because their excess was deliberate, they seemed to miss the unintentional aspect of vulgarity. The designer Jean Paul Gaultier referred obliquely to fashion 'mistakes' when he said that it was the badly dressed people who were the most interesting. Perhaps he was implying that bad taste or vulgarity was inadvertently revealing of the individual's hidden aspirations or desires, for a woman criticized for looking vulgar or over-dressed has usually not deliberately tried to be vulgar. She may have wanted to be noticed, but positively. She probably did not intend to 'make an exhibition' of herself, although she may have intended to 'show off' and showing off is another aspect of vulgarity.

Even when vulgarity is rejected, it has, for Phillips, a way of being the repressed that returns. Puritanism was one of the 'Others' of vulgarity which the exhibition explores, represented in a black dress with elaborate white lace collar and cuffs designed by the 'hedonistic' John Galliano, but Phillips claimed that this garment, too, is vulgar.

The whiteness of the collar was its vulgarity, in that it demonstrated the wearer's purity too blatantly.

The power of black as a statement could have been further explored than this exhibition chose to do. In different guises, it can speak of virtue, modesty and religiosity. The aggression of black, whether worn by a Nazi, a seventeenth-century Puritan or an Islamist, demonstrates the wearer's ideological purity, but the logic of Phillips's argument implies that a woman wearing a niqab could be vulgar by demonstrating her faith too blatantly. In the end, this suggests that anything can be defined as vulgar and, in having it both ways, Phillips came close to abolishing his own subject of enquiry.

The secular purity of fashionista black, especially in the 1980s, or of minimalism in general is also subject to this argument. In the 1920s, Chanel introduced a studiedly downbeat aesthetic, dressing the female half of the *beau monde* in housemaids' frocks, handmade in exquisite materials. Even before that, some of the artists of pre-war Paris had renounced flamboyantly 'bohemian' dress in favour of workwear or sober suiting. This illustrates how taste – and not only in the field of fashion – is a perennial pendulum swing, with new ideas invariably in conversation with or reacting against what was previously 'in'. There is therefore a risk in the focus on what is actually one-half of an equation: that nothing will seem vulgar when there is no restraint to set it against.

A section in the exhibition was devoted to the appropriation by haute couture of the most ubiquitous workwear textile of all, denim, but these ensembles seemed unconvincing, in no way vulgar or 'common'. Unlike the assertiveness of the classic jeans, they lacked confidence in themselves and stood there as curious hybrids. But perhaps that was the intention: to illustrate the way in which the appropriation of the everyday by high style deprives it of vitality.

A related section showed the traditional textiles and costume of the Arles area of Provence, a key inspiration to the couturier Christian Lacroix, and this was an interesting example of the way in which 'folk' traditions can survive largely as 'high style', since women in the south of France no longer dress as the traditional Arlésiennes. Yet, although 'traditional' dress was 'popular', I do not think it was usually thought of as vulgar but had more to do with a different divergent meaning of 'vulgar', to mean simply 'of the common people', everyday rather than ostentatious, simply a local style.

A different dimension of vulgarity is the whole visual and kinetic array of popular culture. Images from film, pop art and everyday visual discourse have been incorporated into high fashion time and again, referencing the suspicion of mass culture by the arbiters of high taste at the same time as avant-garde artists have reworked it. The symbiotic relationship between mass and high culture was lavishly illustrated in this exhibition. Many allusive and associative ideas were explored through the medium of dress, such as a Mickey Mouse handbag or a dress based on Warhol's soup cans, for example (the latter being a weird double appropriation).

At the heart of the exhibition, sexuality and the body defined vulgarity. Western fashion has repeatedly explored the boundaries of the permissible and forbidden in the exposure and concealment of the body. Transparent clothing and semi-nudity were on display here and the 1960s were identified as a turning point in giving permission for the greater display of uncovered skin. A parodic commentary on this was the fake nudity of Walter Van Beirendonck's body garment piece: an entirely naked, idealized male body worn under transparent trousers, a visual demonstration of the disavowal and double nature of fashion and its relationship to the human body.

Phillips suggests that we wouldn't know who we are without vulgarity. This claims it as a definition to dispute, a boundary to transgress. He was clear that it is a powerful and repressive marker of class as well as ethnicity, but, even more importantly, it polices sexual pleasure. He wondered if vulgarity could even be the precondition for excitement and whether vulgar people were having more fun and more pleasure than 'we' were. Erotic vulgarity is the opposite of admiration and respect. 'It encodes and carries our disowned pleasures and fears.'

In the section devoted to the 'baroque', there was an acknowledgement of the way in which standards of taste that had dominated since the eighteenth century have been undermined, partly by mass media, partly by a superficial understanding of what is 'democratic' on the one hand and 'elitist' on the other. The curators suggested that there may be no more 'high' and 'low' in fashion. In that case, what they referred to as 'baroque fashion' was the creation of ensembles that 'assume that a desire for excess is the norm . . . without the norm of established taste'.

I'm not convinced that a desire for excess is the norm, given the drab 'athleisure' uniforms of our daily lives. Vulgarity may be, perhaps, a norm in the desire for spectacle and virtual or vicarious excitement, relished, for example, in the reality TV of the Kardashian family. Nevertheless, there is, I suspect, as much hostility as empathy in the audience for such excessive lives and, while Adam Phillips was right to celebrate the vitality of vulgarity, an acknowledgement of its sadistic side was missing.

'Vulgar' behaviour can be aggressive and intimidating, rather than life affirming. It can be interpreted as the opposite of polite behaviour, not in the sense of conforming to rituals, but rather in the sense of consideration for other people's feelings. It becomes hostile, even a threat. The great thing about vulgarity is its liveliness, fun and sense of humour as opposed to the often-anaemic nature of conventional good taste, and Phillips makes a convincing case for vulgarity as a spirited kind of standing-up for yourself and refusing to be bullied. But it can also become the tyranny of the majority and itself be a form of bullying, a two-fingers up to the idea that anything could be more complicated and subtle.

'The Vulgar' provided a fascinating and suggestive opportunity to explore an idea in a new way, with the aid of its visual expression. Yet, as I walked round the exhibition, I realized that something was missing. My image of vulgarity had been all the fun of the fair, a seaside Luna Park with tinny carousel music, the shrieking 'trippers' on the roller coaster, the clamour of the dodgem cars and shots from the rifle range. (Of course, there was a sinister side to all that too, demonstrated in *Strangers on a Train* and *Brighton Rock,* that sleaziest of post-war movies.)

At the Barbican, sepulchral silence reigned. If vulgarity is 'in your face', this definitely was not. The conventions of the fashion exhibition somehow overrode its subject. The over-the-top-ness of some of the contemporary designs seemed intellectual rather than visceral, some of those from the past mild rather than rambunctious. A Charles James dress printed with multiple images of Snow White appeared not as vulgar, but as an understated, slightly drab (in the way I like), 1940s frock. A creation by Iris van Herpen, classified as baroque, was, indeed, baroque. Made from Japanese hand-pleated material stiffened with wire, it was sculpted into shell-like shapes reminiscent of a Jurassic reptile, bizarre but hardly vulgar, if vulgar implies ease of access and readily understood. The very emphasis on haute couture and its experimental exaggerations removed the experience from the 'common'. It was far more interesting and suggestive than a display of items from UNIQLO or Primark would have been, but the result was a rarefied, rather than a vulgar atmosphere.

'The Vulgar' claimed to interrogate the idea of the fashion exhibition as well as fashion itself, but I'm not sure how successfully.

It is a huge creative task to represent an idea in visual terms. This fashion show made a great attempt and, if the experience it provided was of quiet contemplation rather than raucous enjoyment, it was nevertheless thought provoking and an opportunity to examine where high fashion appeared to be going. If its direction was opaque, that would appear to accurately represent the general turmoil of the zeitgeist.

I visited the exhibition in the autumn of 2016, a few months after the EU Referendum. I think my reaction was influenced by this, and especially because I'd recently returned from a group holiday in Albania. The majority of my fellow tourists on this trip had voted to remain, but a trio of aggressive Brexiteers launched a furious attack on Europe, immigrants and, above all, us 'citizens of nowhere', such that the group nearly came to blows in the middle of a spectacular thunderstorm. The oldest couple in the party, two distinguished retired journalists, gazed on appalled as forked lightning split the night sky and the three Faragists denounced Poles, bureaucrats and Brussels with a bewildering fury not that far from actual threat. These were not the 'left behind' from an ex-mining northern town; they were middle-class men from the southern counties and the most puzzling aspect of their outburst was that they had won – Britain had just voted to leave the European Union – yet they were so angry, whereas the rest of us couldn't rise above the feebly forlorn.

Later in the holiday, we visited a war memorial to the fallen partisans of the Second World War. The simple monument in cream concrete unleashed a further outburst of fury from the Brexit trio. They perceived it as mean and inadequate, a typical communist insult to heroic war heroes. I saw an elegant example of restrained modernist minimalism. The referendum may not have created, but had certainly exposed a split society, a split expressed as much in culture and taste as in economics or politics.

The Vulgar exhibition came too late. A few years earlier, the contrasts explored by Adam Philips had still made sense, but not anymore. I'm not sure where the vulgar locates itself, or rather, where we locate it, in a split society. From Adam Philip's point of view, stark minimalism might be judged vulgar in its exaggerated refusal of display, its disavowed claim to superiority. Perhaps the three Brexiteers felt that a war memorial ought to be more extravagant in its triumphalism, ought to show its heart on its sleeve and that the refusal to give way to emotion was a form of contempt, like the dandy's blasé aloofness and indifference to other people.

Modernism and minimalism come with a set of characteristics usually considered masculine. Functional, clean and spare, ornament is alien to them. They are styles of control, analytic and intellectual, a disavowal of feeling and the irrational. That denial of emotion can be experienced as a claim to superiority.

In *Baroque Between the Wars,* the historian Jane Stevenson championed what she terms the alternative twentieth-century 'baroque' style of the 1920s and 1930s. This modern baroque was a critique of modernism and had links to Surrealism. The Surrealists were avant garde but loved certain aspects of popular culture. They attached great importance to disregarded things, to the cheap and the kitsch and the poignancy of objects that were becoming outmoded. They believed that a 'profane illumination' inhered in such things. They were materialists who sought to grasp the mystery of life, yet recognized that it must always remain intangible.

The 'baroque' style of the 1920s and 1930s was playful, exaggerated, loved the style of the fairground, mass culture, personal souvenirs, the Tarot cards. The style, as Stevenson claims, was created by women and gay men who worked in the 'minor' arts of interior decoration, photography and textiles at the time. It was essentially a queer style. Also, it was 'vulgar', in the original meaning of that word, because it connected up with what ordinary people like. For me, Stevenson presents too stereotyped a contrast between masculine and feminine, high art and low camp, elite taste and the taste of that undefined and undefinable category, the 'ordinary people'. Taste was and is a vehicle for snobbery and elitism, but cannot be read off simply from a class position. IKEA, for example, has changed everyone, with its command to 'chuck out the chintz', and modernism is now a popular style.

Jane Stevenson's point, however, is that between-the-wars baroque was inclusive and humanistic as modernism was not. Its embrace of style oddities, of strange found objects, of the ephemeral and cheap, its eclecticism in fact, testified to the importance of personal feeling in relation to objects and our surroundings. This 'baroque' was quirky and jolly, but it also embraced the supernatural and the frightening; all those emotions that modernism tried to eliminate with the purity of its white walls.

In the post-Brexit political climate, elitism became a rude word, so perhaps Adam Philip's defence of vulgarity's vitality had been unnecessary. More likely, I think, is that the very concept of vulgarity as he defined it has largely disappeared. There is too much information. As Jean Baudrillard wrote as long ago as 1981, 'there is more and more information and less and less meaning.' In such a world, there are no more binaries, simply an overload of choices that hardly last long enough to solidify into a taste, still less a movement.

11

Fashion as fetish

In the 1990s, I read a lot of Surrealist literature, in the hope that it would explain the fascination of the past, first as revealed in fashion, then in urban life and the world of city streets. It's just a subjective impression, but the bureaucrats of modern education seemed often to dismiss a love of history as nostalgia, of little relevance to the present day. The Surrealists, by contrast, were interested in just those subjects that rationalists dismissed as essentially backward, superstitious or actually meaningless.

Elsa Schiaparelli knew and was influenced by the Surrealists and expressed their ideas visually in the clothes she designed. Her career started when an American friend visited her, wearing a sweater that was 'different from any I had yet seen'. She described it as 'definitely ugly in colour and in shape', but, intrigued by its tight, twisted texture, she visited the Armenian couple who had made the garment and they knitted one to Schiaparelli's own design: she created a Surrealist trompe l'oeil sweater with a fake white bow knitted into the front. This launched her career as a fashion designer.

Perhaps the sweater was successful because it is witty. Its effect is tongue-in-cheek. It hints at the artifice of all dress and that may have been what its wearers liked about it; or perhaps they felt empowered by owning an article that was unusual and slightly avant garde. They may not have even known quite why they were drawn to it, for a garment's appeal can be quite elusive. For each of us, there are one or two garments that have come into our lives and have some special quality, so that they are worn and treasured until they are literally worn out. Yet the source of their power may never be clear. Perhaps you wore the special dress to a fateful event, where you met someone who changed your life.

Part of the mystery of fashion's appeal seems to have to do with the relationship between garments and the body they cover. This relationship is profound and meaningful. It is also paradoxical because Western culture has traditionally dismissed fashionable dress, one of its own most important cultural forms, as superficial, trivial and unworthy of serious consideration. As I suggested earlier, Christianity is still embedded in our largely secular culture, so that we continue to be influenced by the belief that it is the inner, not the outer, that matters.

The French poet and bohemian Charles Baudelaire analysed how changing fashions played a central role in modern society, the nineteenth-century world of the rapidly growing cities. It was the continual, restless changes of fashion that best expressed the zeitgeist and the passion for the new that characterized consumer society. In reflecting on the way fashion changed, he was at pains to understand how an aesthetic of one period can be superseded, or how aesthetic tastes can change, yet he insisted that it can still create a beauty with eternal appeal.

Western fashion has used garments to change the shape of the body, emphasizing one or other part of it, sometimes distorting it, or fetishizing a single part, whether breasts, back or legs. There are also other cultures in which the body itself has been modified, for example with foot binding, or lengthening of the neck or earlobes, but this is not true of all civilizations. The Japanese kimono does not exaggerate the shape of the body but fashions a cocoon around it. The shape remained unchanged for centuries. The kimono is a flat surface, a vehicle for extravagant, elaborate and elegant designs. Kimonos could be works of art in their own right, but nudity or semi-nudity, the concealment and revealing of the body or the body's own kinetic shape, was not part of the kimono's appeal. (In Edo period's Japanese erotic prints, while both male and female sexual parts were shown, the nude body seemed rather unimportant, and couples were shown having sex without bothering to get undressed.) Perhaps the kimono endured because for 300 years Japan was a closed society; perhaps on the other hand, Europe was the outlier in fetishizing stylistic – and bodily – change. Globalization has created a stylistic world in which 'tradition' and 'fashion' are in creative friction, resulting in a third way of style mash-ups and contradictions.

Yohji Yamamoto's designs exemplified this possibility, since his designs drew on both Western and Japanese traditions. Wim Wenders's 1993 film, *A Notebook on Cities and Clothes*, explored Yamamoto's work, partly by means of a series of interviews with the designer. In one of these, Yamamoto insisted that he wanted clothes not to be ephemeral, but to last, and even more importantly, he was preoccupied with finding the 'essence' of the shirt, the shoulder, the jacket. In describing his ideal garment, he implied that the ephemeral itself could describe something more permanent. He spoke, for example, of a thick coat for a person who really needs it in the depth of winter: in this way, you wear the reality, 'the coat is so beautiful because . . . you cannot make a life without this coat, it looks like your friend or your family'. Even when you saw the clothes themselves on the floor or hung on the wall, you would recognize the owner and think: 'this is John, or Tom, this is yourself.' An individual's most 'successful' clothes become part of that person's identity. The garment and the wearer work together to create a third entity: one's 'appearance'.

Schiaparelli agreed, writing that a dress could never just hang like a painting on the wall, or like an object, such as a book or a vase, remaining intact and unchanged throughout its life. A dress has no life of its own. It only comes alive when it is worn, and as soon as this happens another personality takes over. The dress, originally the designer's creation, is appropriated and animated by the person who wears it. They may succeed in making it look wonderful, but there is also the risk that, by not wearing it well, they ruin the impression of beauty it aimed to create. Sadly, Schiaparelli concluded, the beautifully designed dress then becomes an indifferent object, or even a painful caricature of the dream or the expression the designer (and the wearer) had wanted it to be.

Her comment about the nothingness of garments on a hanger is sometimes borne out by the experience of visiting exhibitions in which lifeless garments are displayed as objects – although the kimono is again an exception, since kimonos can stand alone as works of art. But there is often something creepy about the mute presence of untenanted clothes, as if they were ghosts of their possible wearers. There is also something disturbing about the idea that the frock's creator could take the wearer over once they have put on the garment. It suggests that the power of the garment might not always be benign. The other side of this coin is that the injection of a designer's creativity could infuse its strength into the wearer.

These ideas of embodiment and possession have been explored more often in fiction and myth than in theory and analysis. Hans Christian Andersen took the idea of the power of the garment to its logical conclusion in his tale of the Red Shoes. Once the dancer put them on, the ballet pumps took possession of her and forced her to dance until she died of exhaustion. In the ancient Greek legend of Nessus' shirt, this was a poisoned garment, which clung to the body of the wearer and destroyed him. (The Tudors used poisoned garments to murder their enemies and the method is alive and well today; the Russian dissident, Alexei Navalny, was poisoned by his contaminated underpants.) These powerful stories and some legends of the supernatural imbue clothing with a sense of the dangerous, but clothes do not have to be supernatural to be powerful. Military uniforms, priests' chasubles and judges' robes directly signify power. There is nothing other-worldly about the awe they can invoke.

The power of dress arises from several different sources. There is the social power given it by rules and norms; there is its psychological power as expressive of the individual self. There is its uncanny power, a power that has to do with the importance of objects in human culture, with the close relationship between body and clothing, and thus a boundary between animate and inanimate. The magic garments that Schiaparelli and Yamamoto allude to develop properties that go well beyond their utility. They become talismanic. A garment can become a fetish.

I became interested in the idea of the fetish in Western culture when I read a series of articles by the intellectual historian William Pietz. In them, he excavated the intercultural origin and meanings of the term and how these developed in Western thought. He does not address the meaning of fetish in African cultures, but his focus of interest is legitimate, given the centrality of the fetish to two of the most important theorists in Western thought, Freud and Marx. The Pietz articles set out the complex development of 'the fetish' as a Western concept in some detail and, although the articles are clearly written, his analysis might be taken as an example of how 'theory' is too 'difficult' and too complicated for general readers or 'ordinary people'. Isn't it too rarefied; doesn't it take us away from day-to-day existence and the important things in life, such as love, family, earning a living? Also, we crave certainty and answers, but theoretical explanations tend to send a message that 'it is more complicated than that' and that answers are not simple. Yet to explore the idea of the fetish is to approach a brute fact about humanity: human beings are irrational, but, in their irrationality, they search for meaning. The fragment of colonial history explored by Pietz is therefore highly significant, as, apart from its inherent interest, it clarifies aspects of consumerism and contemporary daily life.

The Western idea of the fetish has at least three distinct meanings, from three different traditions: anthropology, psychoanalysis and Marxism. Anthropology is concerned with religious and cultural aspects, psychoanalysis with sexual beliefs and behaviour and Marxism with commodities and the economic significance of objects. The idea of the fetish arose in what Pietz describes as 'a space created by the . . . trade between cultures so radically different as to be mutually incomprehensible'. This space belonged neither to West African nor to Christian European culture. The term originates from the Portuguese and from the early slave trade period when Portuguese traders were active on the West African coast. There, they encountered unfamiliar cultural practices and objects. They interpreted these in terms of concepts derived from their Roman Catholicism (witchcraft, superstition and idolatry), but, while they rejected them, it seems likely, or at least possible, that Africans incorporated certain aspects of Christian cult motifs into their fetish objects. Nails driven into wooden figures, for example, may have been assimilated from the Crucifixion.

In the seventeenth century, the Portuguese Catholics were ousted by Dutch Protestants, and Pietz suggests that, for the latter, the African fetish and related phenomena introduced irrational and therefore chaotic elements into the trading situation. The Dutch lived by mercantile ideas concerning rational behaviour as enlightened self-interest in the pursuit of wealth (although this is my simplification of Pietz's argument). For them, the fetishes valued by the Africans were close to what they regarded as the Popish and idolatrous practices of Roman Catholicism. That is to say that they tried to understand them on their own cultural terms, yet at the same time, from this perspective, African fetish objects were, like Africans themselves, outside what the Western traders understood as civilization – or understood at all.

All this added up to a complex cultural encounter involving Western and non-Western civilizations. It led eventually to the Enlightenment view of the fetish as an example of false values and superstitious delusions, which blocked natural reason and misunderstood the causal origin of events of a material and explicable nature. This modern idea of the fetish emerges in the same period as the development of the commodity form and a new form of the economy: capitalism.

The fetish was different from an idol in that it was a material object often worn on an individual's body; in it was condensed some magical or religious power arising from the – possibly chance – circumstances in which it was first acquired. Pietz defines it as a material object that has been invested with religious or psychological meaning. An object can become a fetish as the result of a singular event. This event could be almost anything: the offer of a job, the confirmation of a longed-for pregnancy, a sporting victory, but the creation of the fetish occurs when the event is associated with an object, such as the ring you wore that day, the strange piece of stone you found or the trinket you picked up in a junk shop. The coincidence of object meeting event may begin as chance, but then takes on symbolic meaning. The power of the fetish exists in that it replaces chance with fate. The object had no particular significance until it was connected to an event.

Pietz's sophisticated analysis attempts to explain how something actually valueless and originally arbitrary comes to acquire an emotional value and achieve an apparent power. This is more than a kind of false consciousness; it condenses a complex cultural encounter into a single object. Its purpose is to both express and to ward off the fear the encounter arouses, or to promise success in one's endeavours. This is the role of the fetish object in Western societies. Key for Pietz is the cultural cross-fertilization involved. Cultural appropriation has recently become the focus of challenge and condemnation, but surely the idea that cultural styles belong only to one particular nation or group within a sealed cultural space is a flawed view. The 2013 Silk Road exhibition at the Metropolitan Museum of Art, for example, demonstrated in great detail that so-called appropriation had existed for centuries. Also, rather than being seen through a paranoid lens as a theft of one culture by another, it is more likely to result in the enrichment of both.

In the nineteenth century, the Western idea of the fetish was taken up by two of the most influential figures in the thought – and practice – of that century and the next. In his work on political economy, Karl Marx developed the concept of commodity fetishism to describe and explain the way in which an inanimate human product acquires a life of its own, but there is an important difference between this and the earlier meaning. In anthropological fetishism, the fetish bestows power (real or imagined) on the owner or wearer. By contrast, in Marx the fetishization of the commodity involves the disempowerment and alienation of the human workers whose labour made it. A shirt, for example, is the outcome of the labour of the worker who put it together, but the shirt then takes on a life of its own in a market economy, because it is exchanged for money. The actual labour of the worker has disappeared from view. The human relationship – the human connection between worker and capitalist employer or between worker and purchaser – has also disappeared, transformed into a relationship between things, that is, object and money. The object becomes a fetish in the sense that it has acquired a symbolic power over and above, or even quite distinct, from its material existence. It now expresses something beyond itself and over and above its usefulness. It has acquired economic value.

At the turn of the twentieth century, Sigmund Freud used the term 'fetish' to explore sexual obsessions. Some concerned items of clothing, as, for example, when the presence of some item, such as a shoe or a corset, is necessary for the actors, or one of them, to achieve sexual satisfaction. This developed into whole subcultures, in which sexual fetishes, notably in sadomasochism, were differentiated and costumed in specific garments, such as leather or rubber. When the sight or wearing of a high-heeled boot becomes erotically arousing, the link has been established between the (originally) unrelated object and the individual's sensations and obsessions. Both Freud and Marx dwelt on the malign dimension of fetishistic thought. A sexual fetish, for Freud, distorted and limited the ability of the individual in thrall to it to experience pleasure. Marx argued that what he called commodity fetishization misrepresented capitalist relations and concealed the actual exploitation of workers.

Scepticism cannot destroy the perennial fascination of the relationship between chance and what is 'meant to be'. In supposedly rational societies, dominated by scientific thought, the idea of luck is as widespread as it ever was, both attached to and separate from religious views. A dress, for example, develops a metaphorical meaning when, in the consciousness of its wearer, it comes to symbolize or stand in for a notion of empowerment, or one of modesty or one of conformity or nonconformity. Then this dress, if associated with success of whatever kind, can become a 'lucky' dress, and at this point it has taken on a life of its own and become a fetish. The wearer can then start to half-believe that it was because of the dress that she got the job or pulled the guy.

Sigmund Freud used the term 'disavowal' to describe a form of unrealistic thinking. By attributing certain powers to the fetish, its owner manages to believe the false while also knowing that it cannot be true. In other words, disavowal is a mechanism that permits one to believe both of two incompatible propositions; for example: 'I do not believe in ghosts' and 'I saw a ghost last night.' Here, the person believes they are a modern person with no time for absurd superstitions, but at the same time take pleasure in the creepy but exciting possibility that they might have actually seen a ghost. They have achieved the impossible: believing and not believing at one and the same moment.

In the modern and supposedly secular world, disavowal is a common process. We go about our lives with our conscious minds resembling Freud's description of dreams and the unconscious, where mutually incompatible events and beliefs can coexist in perfect harmony, and inanimate objects are endowed with a power they cannot objectively have. People read their horoscopes avidly while knowing somewhere in the recesses of their brains that there is no evidential basis for the accuracy of such forecasts. (It is just 'a bit of fun' and yet maybe . . .) A sceptic might go further and argue that the mighty edifices of the major organized religions are simply disavowal writ large and that 'faith' itself is a massive trade-off between hope and reality. Belief in irrational propositions that are not sanctioned by official religions are referred to as superstition. Superstition is defined as beliefs based on fear and ignorance. Officially, they are simply not true, because they are not sanctioned by the pope or any other religious authority. Yet they bubble up and flourish (encouraged since the millennium by the power of the internet).

Rightly or wrongly, the thinkers of the Enlightenment have been criticized for their over-valuation of Reason and their disdain for emotion and mysticism, 'enthusiasm' as it was named. The

Romantic movement was a response and a challenge to this, as was psychoanalysis. However, no clear alternative to religion emerged out of the turmoil of the industrial revolution. No new mental scheme for the expression of thoughts and feelings that go beyond the rational and mundane gained traction. The result in contemporary society is that innumerable beliefs compete in a largely unregulated market of ideas. Among these are common attitudes to dress. The rage aroused by the original Punks, and more recently Goths, for example, is irrational, as is the inflated importance given to school uniforms in the UK, that is, the idea that they actually improve students' behaviour. Evidence doesn't matter. The garments are symbolic.

Performers such as actors, dancers and sportspersons have seemed especially prone to what we call superstition. This is not surprising, because their bodies are their instruments, and their skills often depend on split-second decisions and movements that can easily go wrong. Accidents are always waiting to happen in the worlds of sport, dance and the circus. Tennis star Billie Jean King had a lucky dress, which she continued to wear for big matches long after its style went out of fashion. A more eccentric example was the 2001 Wimbledon champion, the Croatian Goran Ivanišević, whose collection of superstitions included 'having' to watch the children's TV programme '*Teletubbies*' every morning. This led to a second-order fetishism, when his fans attended his matches dressed in Teletubby costumes.

Ivanišević stripped off his shirt after every match, to display his sportsman's torso. Because the body is central to many performers (hence their preoccupation with injuries), what they wear becomes infused with magical meaning because of the close relationship between dress and body. One rational psychological explanation for the rituals of luck is that the player uses them as a way of 'magically' controlling the uncontrollable – the weather and the opponent's form, in the case of tennis. It may be that the 'lucky' dress subjectively gives its power to the player; but equally, and in reverse, perhaps the body seems to add to the meaning and power of the garment. The question that can never be answered, of course, is whether Billie Jean would have won her Wimbledon titles if she hadn't worn the dress or whether Ivanišević would have achieved his only Wimbledon title without the Teletubbies' help.

At the end of the nineteenth century, Max Weber wrote pessimistically of modernity as involving a waning of the magical. A real loss was involved, he felt. Yet, life did not become more rational, and the contemporary era is as romantically irrational as the early nineteenth century of gothic romance and Byronic discontent. The Surrealists were unusual in viewing the idea of the fetish and of the irrational in positive terms. For the Enlightenment, the fetish signalled error, excess, difference and deviation; it was one of many phantoms that haunted Reason. The Surrealists felt otherwise. They used fetishism in order to subvert utilitarian and humdrum values. For them, the fetish and the fetishist escaped the confines of the drab, everyday world into a poetic and different reality; Surrealist art displayed a preoccupation with the human body, with clothing in the exploration of these ideas and with the uncanny and uncertain boundary between the animate and the inanimate.

Caroline Evans has written of the way in which many of Schiaparelli's designs investigated, in a playful and, yet at the same time, serious way, the ambiguity between the inside and the outside of the body. This acted as a means of exploring what we now call the decentred self, that is, the self that is not pure consciousness or purely rationalist, but which has an unconscious. Schiaparelli explored the body/garment interface, for example in her gloves with veins or nails embroidered or appliquéd onto them. This strangely echoes the description of the gloves of the dandy, Beau Brummell, which, says the French writer Jules Barbey d'Aurevilly, 'moulded his hands like wet muslin, . . . [showing] the contours of his fingernails as does flesh itself'. In the grey linen jacket Schiaparelli designed, she included a trompe l'oeil figure of part of a woman, almost a second self, with yellow hair cascading down one arm, while another (third) that is, embroidered arm is folded across the waist. The 'tear' dress is another example. Slits that looked like open wounds slashed the garment and suggested at the way in which the body of the individual and the garment can almost become one. The garment is not itself a fetish, but it deploys the Surrealist preoccupation with the relation of inanimate to animate, which a fetish also expresses. These designs hover always on the border between the comic and the sinister.

In so many ways, in other words, the relationship between dress and the idea of the fetish undercuts rational perceptions of fashion. It questions the assumption that we live in a hedonistic society, rationally dedicated to pleasure. It suggests that as soon as we delve into what attracts us to the practices, entertainments and pastimes that preoccupy us, we discover a foreign country haunted by the lingering afterlife of long-gone gods and discarded beliefs. The sacred lies in wait in unexpected quarters, and solid reality will always be haunted by its ephemeral opposite.

12

Haunting

The Celtic belief that the spirits of those we have lost are held captive in some lower being, in an animal, in a plant, in some inanimate object and so are effectively lost to us until the day . . . when we happen to pass by the tree or to obtain possession of the object which forms their prison. Then they start and tremble, they call us by our name and . . . the spell is broken.

MARCEL PROUST, À la recherche du temps perdu: Du Côté de Chez Swann

The dressed individual creates an 'appearance'. Ghosts 'appear'. Another word for ghost is 'apparition' – an appearance, a making visible. I often felt like a ghost as I wandered along the aisles of West End department stores, searching for garments that would give me a presence. Later on, I became interested in ghosts and haunting generally. I wanted to understand why ghost stories and haunted houses continue to compel in a supposedly secular age, in which the existence of ghosts is officially dismissed as irrational. Faith is more powerful than reason and religious beliefs are almost as powerful as ever, but the vaguely secular world lives in a state of disavowal or what Theodor Adorno referred to, in the context of astrology, as 'disorientated agnosticism', a very good phrase. Modern individuals read horoscopes, listen to ghost stories and generate conspiracy theories in a terminally undecided state of mind. Scientific rationalism is the official ideology, yet has not won the day.

The ghost story feeds this uncertainty. It is essential that the story remains ambiguous to the end, and that the reader is left unnervingly undecided as to whether the ghosts were 'real' or imaginary. I thought it would be interesting to write a history of ghosts, and even embarked on a fictional ghost story, and taught a course on The Uncanny at the Architectural Association, but my interest remained shallow, because I don't 'believe in' ghosts. I am essentially too ambivalent to take any such project seriously enough, and, as a tutor at LSE once pronounced, ambivalence is incurable. Possibly ambivalence is addictive. Perhaps it is related to disavowal, allowing belief and scepticism to coexist, while at the same time doubting both, whereas, with another twist, wanting to believe.

In a book of essays, *Cultural Passions*, published in 2011, I explored the will to believe, in a brief essay on the Tarot. I justified my interest in psychotherapeutic terms: telling the cards was a way of thinking about your problems and preoccupations of the moment; it was another kind of therapy or therapeutic technique. The coloured Arts and Crafts 'Golden Dawn' pack stimulated the imagination and drew out emotional responses. The way the cards turned up might seem random, but everything has a meaning, just as the peculiar events that take place in dreams must have a message, however confused. I told the cards in order to raise funds at feminist and school jumble sales, but it disturbed me that more than once a 'client' asked to consult me again, privately, and I was surprised when a friend told me she had consulted the late Henrietta Llewelyn Davies, a psychic astrologer, who had been the guru of some well-known feminists and professional women.

In the lexicon of modern-day beliefs, ghosts and the supernatural do not exist, but they have not relinquished their hold on the contemporary imagination. Fantasy fictions, from *The Lord of the Rings* to Philip Pullman's *His Dark Materials*, and from *Star Trek* to *Game of Thrones* and *Harry Potter*, are proof of a continuing human desire to believe in the existence of superhuman and supernatural powers and to yearn for something 'beyond', both to cling to the mystery and to desire its solution. Popular culture has long fed this desire. In the nineteenth century, spiritualism, conjurers and eventually film explored the possibilities of magic, the continued existence of the dead in an invisible realm and of fiction as a ghostly parade of alternative realities drifting across a screen.

'Superstition' has its roots in very old beliefs, as the Proust reference to Celtic culture in the epigraph of this chapter suggests. The wily priests of the early Christian era incorporated remnants of paganism into their new religion as a way of keeping converts on side. Pre-Christian beliefs were demoted to the status of mere superstition, but they never disappeared. In *Cultural Passions*, I also wrote about visiting the three Hawksmoor churches in the East End: Christ Church, Spitalfields, St George's in Shadwell and St Anne's, Limehouse. For the psycho-geographers, Iain Sinclair and Peter Ackroyd, these were sites of 'occult London', but I was never sure whether those writers believed that the three churches were really connected by occult ley lines, remnants of the 'old religion', or whether they simply liked the poetry of the idea – or indeed whether I thought that myself. If the 'old religion' was a form of animism, then it was potentially close to beliefs about climate change – and paganism still exists and does have resonance with the green agenda.

My daughter and I discussed this. Neither of us has any religious beliefs, although she inclines slightly in the direction of Buddhism. (Once as she returned home in the very early hours of the morning from an evening's partying, a stranger she passed in the road knelt before her and said she had the most beautiful aura he'd ever encountered.) We agreed that, whereas we reject organized religion, we shared that common desire for meaning (Why are we here? What is out there?). We wanted there to be some kind of transcendence, yet in the end agreed that it was the mystery itself, the unknowingness, that was valuable. It wasn't ambivalence so much as uncertainty. Uncertainty, indeterminacy, ambiguity were good. We embraced the Mystery.

The nineteenth-century gothic revival was a direct response to Enlightenment thought and an irruption of everything that rationalism had suppressed: madness, sensation, feeling and the feminine. It was the 'Other' of the age of reason – a kind of revenant (a corpse which returns from the dead) itself. Fears about hell and damnation waned paradoxically when industrial development emerged as a new hell-on-earth and the romantic imagination created new terrors in Dracula, vampires and Frankenstein. There was nothing new in the tendency to infuse inanimate objects with life. The Celts had once believed that trees, plants and stones contained spirits; now, with the Romantic movement, the significance and location of apparitions changed. For fear has a location, and as once-wild places – moors, forests and marshes – had instilled terror, in an urbanizing world this fear migrated to the built environment.

Gothic romances appeared at the beginning of the industrial age. The neo-gothic sensibility was linked to architecture. Decaying mansions formed the backdrop for gothic horror. The camp revivalism of Robert Walpole's house, Strawberry Hill, was a critique of the cold beauty of the neo-classical; it was an architectural folly, poised somewhere between the hysterical and the farcical, the refined and the kitsch. Walpole wrote a gothic novel, *The Castle of Otranto*. Like his house, it was not too seriously intended; on the other hand, Edgar Allen Poe's tale, *The Fall of the House of Usher*, written seventy-five years later, was in deadly earnest.

The story of Roderick Usher's decline and death is told by his friend and opens with a description of this gloomy dwelling, surrounded by decaying vegetation. The sight makes the approaching friend feel as if he were recovering from an opium hangover; the house is the opposite of the sublime; it does not inspire awe but drags him down into a sickening mood of gloom and apprehension and speaks of the malign power of the inanimate. There is an inherent potential horror in the inertness of objects that are not alive, but which nevertheless exist so powerfully and solidly. To endow the inanimate with life results in a blurring of boundaries between the lifeless and the living, experienced as disturbing and even horrific. One expression of this is the haunted house.

The idea that a house can have malignant feelings or intent differs from the fear that a medieval castle or, in modern times, the grim sublime of the prison might realistically inspire. A temple or cathedral might also give rise to awe, a mixture of fear and exaltation, but there was nothing grand or spiritual about the haunted house.

It was a modern and secular fear. The classic location of the haunted house might be the countryside and often an isolated and sinister spot, but, to generations accustomed to crowded streets and massed terraced houses, the very existence of a country mansion standing alone in grandeur and solitude could seem overburdened with meaning. Perhaps it was a reminder of a former social order that might be vengeful and threatening. The ghost (in French a *revenant*, one who returns) has not finished with us, but reminds us how the past haunts the present. The aristocrats, whose power and land the people seized (even if in Britain they didn't) would return to wreak vengeance in the end.

Haunting and the haunted interior could as tellingly express bourgeois fears. The German literary critic Walter Benjamin played with this idea in describing the nineteenth-century middle-class interior as the ideal location for murder. Its furnishings suggest 'the horror of apartments'. The rooms are overcrowded with gigantic sideboards distended with carvings, sunlight finds it impossible to penetrate through palms and aspidistra, while long corridors, lit only with hissing gas, provide the perfect stage for crime fiction and the detective novel, and seem fit only to lead to the corpse. 'On this sofa the aunt cannot but be murdered.' The overbearing presence of too much furniture is a new version of Poe's description of how inanimate matter has an evil power that suffocates human life – and at the same time is more alive than the corpse – and, like Poe, Benjamin felt the crushing 'opium hangover' of the bourgeoisie, represented by its overpoweringly vulgar taste.

So too much furniture becomes uncanny. The uncanny is the presence of something that ought not to be there – as when his sofas and cabinets intrude on and take over the space that should have belonged to human beings. At the same time, the emptiness of rooms (empty of living persons, that is) produces eeriness: the sense of emptiness when something that should be present is not.

A house should always be inhabited, filled with life and families. An empty house is inherently eerie, while at the same time the presence in it of inanimate things that seem to take on 'a life of their own' is uncanny. The house can therefore be both eerie (too empty) and uncanny (too full) simultaneously. How familiar is the scene in a movie when someone moves from room to empty room to find: nothing. The eerie emptiness of the house becomes uncanny at the suggestion that something might be there. The uncertainty of absence/presence is unsettling, but, in the end, it is this vacancy, the absence of a ghost, the absence of anything, that provokes a kind of horror. The lonely individual advancing through the house must feel that behind every shut door, but also beyond every gaping open door, they may find some horror, even if it is only the horror of vacuity, but actually, even if nothing is visible, there is something there. Perhaps the horror of the empty house can reflect the horror of one's own nothingness.

Especially if one is a woman. In Poe's story, Roderick Usher's twin sister, Madeline, played a central role, buried alive but returning to destroy her brother as well as herself and representing almost too neatly the return of the feminine repressed. Family relations were at the heart of this and many horror stories as Freud demonstrates in his famous article, '*The Uncanny*'. The article typically begins as though it may turn out to be a short story; Freud describes how he got lost in an unfamiliar city and kept finding he had somehow returned to the red-light district. Prostitution is the illegitimate 'Other' of the family, but Freud chooses not to develop this louche side of the story. Instead, he goes on to discover that the bourgeois family is embedded in the word 'uncanny' itself. Having escaped the threat of loose women, through the rest of the essay he carefully unpicks the German word, *unheimlich*, usually translated in English as 'uncanny'. He eventually traces the word back to its complete opposite, *heimlich*. And *heimlich* begins by meaning homely, comfortable, secure – homelike, as belonging to the home, place of ultimate security and safety. Yet gradually this very word, by being associated first with the private and then 'that which is concealed', comes to have an entirely different set of meanings: first as hidden, then mysterious and possibly occult, obscure, then unconscious, until ultimately the uncanny is 'the familiar making a disquieting return' – memories that can't be indefinitely repressed or buried family secrets.

The unhomely home houses the Freudian family with all its secrets, forbidden desires and murderous impulses. This family then becomes associated with and represented by the house itself – the home – the building in which the family dwells; to an extent, the home is the family, standing in for and symbolizing it. This leads to the unsurprising, indeed banal, conclusion that the haunted house is haunted by family secrets. Not all ghost or haunted house stories place fear of the feminine at their centre. The stories of M. R. James, while they explore the horror of the inanimate, usually concern unattached men, but more typical is Henry James's novella, *The Turn of the Screw*, which, with its central ambivalence – whether the governess really saw ghosts or whether they were the product of her disordered and hysterical state of mind – illustrates the danger presented by the unattached woman.

A key figure in Victorian fiction (and life), the governess is a victim of misfortune, a woman without a dowry or a husband. Sometimès, she is an orphan, at others she has a widowed mother and perhaps sisters, but no father, in either case economically without means of support other than through her own efforts in a restricted field where most paid work was closed to middle-class women. Yet, in her victimhood, she is also dangerous in the way that the weak can be dangerous because of her ambiguous place in the social hierarchy. She is neither married nor eligible.

She is inserted into a family yet is not of it and this is the situation in which James's unnamed heroine finds herself. It is her first attempt to earn her own living. She meets and is charmed by the uncle of the orphaned children who are to be placed in her care, but she is merely exploited and tantalized by the unattainable prospect of a wealthy and attractive husband, since, no sooner has she met him, than the uncle removes himself from the situation. Yet she has been 'carried away' by him and it is of him she thinks when she first sees the ghost of a man who is not he.

The tale plays itself out in an environment that James explicitly states is not sinister or alarming, or at least not at first. The house, Bly, is no stereotypical haunted house. On the contrary, the governess is delighted by what she sees on her arrival. Having expected something 'dreary', she is delighted by the broad façade of the house with its open windows and fresh curtains, and by the garden with its lawn and bright flowers. It is true, though, that she first 'sees' the ghost of the valet, Quint, as he stands on a tower, 'one of a pair – square, incongruous, crenellated structures – that . . . flanked opposite ends of the house and were probably architectural absurdities . . . dating in their gingerbread antiquity, from a romantic revival that was already a respectable past'. The description comes close to mocking the exaggerations of the romantic gothic and slyly hints at the fakery of ghosts, but, as the new governess explores the great house with her little charges, the extent of it, the 'empty chambers', 'dull corridors' and 'crooked staircases' becomes mysterious, uncertain and oppressive. It is only a 'big, ugly antique but convenient house, embodying a few features of a building still older, half displaced and half utilised', yet the young woman starts to feel 'almost as lost as . . . on a great drifting ship'.

Jack Clayton's film version, *The Innocents* (1961), differs from the novella because from the beginning it relies on the eeriness of the house to create fear and tension. The very lake that the governess passes on her first approach to the house is unnaturally still. The interior of the house is disorienting. The governess in her crinoline is continually impeded by bulky furniture (like that in Walter Benjamin's bourgeois apartment) and awkward corridors, and Clayton uses familiar ploys of billowing curtains, shadows and crooked stairways, creating a place of uncertainty and ambiguity, and, as the film develops, the governess's fearful and sometimes panic-stricken movements through darkened corridors at night represent visually her developing emotional state.

The film also diverges from the book in siding with the governess and her perception that the house really is haunted by the malign presence of the previous governess, Miss Jessel, who died in mysterious circumstances, and Quint, the valet, her lover. The audience, as well as the governess, sees the apparitions. It also quickly becomes clear that the young woman – still a girl, really – cannot control Miles and Flora, the children in her care. And the orphans are not normal; their behaviour is secretive, knowing and subtly defiant – another typical feature of horror and haunting: the evil child.

This is a deviant family: children looked after by servants, the housekeeper, Mrs Grose, and the inexperienced governess (and formerly by the valet as well). The family is abnormal because the family as an institution is the location (the only sanctioned location) of sexual love, but this family is sexless. Sexuality resides outside marital relations, in the illicit liaison that, the new governess learns, took place between Miss Jessel and Quint – a relation transgressive on social and moral grounds. That both are now dead is certain, but how they died is not. Miss Jessel may have drowned herself, she may have tried to procure an abortion; Quint is rumoured to have had an accident on the way home after an evening's drinking, but he may have been murdered, possibly even by Miles.

At the climax of the story, the governess is left alone in the great house with Miles, the child she believes has been delivered up to evil by Quint, and the child and the woman confront the unseen ghost. But Miles dies and the governess is left entirely alone. The film does not tell us what happened to her afterwards. We know from James's narrator that she survived, for he met her years later and described her as a wonderful and admirable woman, although, he gives no reason for his admiration. The story remains incomplete and unresolved', as ghost stories must. It is the uncertainty that is the pleasure.

From an analytical point of view, the empty house, no longer a sanctuary, combines with the unattached and therefore unstable woman to create a dangerous space, ripe for the expansion of fear and evil. 'Those who walk there, walk alone' states a disembodied voice at the close of another horror movie, *The Haunting*, adapted from the novel *The Haunting of Hill House* by Shirley Jackson and, like *The Turn of the Screw*, made into a successful film in the early 1960s. Those who walked alone were women.

It was not just lesbians, as Terry Castle suggested, that haunt society. It is all unattached women, perhaps even all women. Women are essentially deviant in departing from the masculine norm and especially when the irruption of the feminine and of feeling and irrational emotion disturb the cold, male world of reason. Unattached women are particularly dangerous and share one thing with M. R. James's desiccated bachelors: their loneliness. To be unattached, and unimbedded in a family, to be outside the norms of social organization, is the most dangerous thing of all, to yourself and to those around you. André Breton opens his 'novel', *Nadja*, with the words, 'Who am I?' Whom does he haunt? The word, he feels, refers to 'what I must have ceased to be in order to be who I am' – as if past (failed) selves are always threatening to return. And perhaps the present self is weak, shallow, fragile. In empty rooms, we are haunted by ourselves and even by our own solitude – the fear of being unanchored, not belonging anywhere, having no place in the world.

Homelessness has a different, brutal and concrete meaning in today's society. I first encountered serious homelessness in the 1980s when I drove down into an underground car park late at night and was shocked as people I hadn't known were there rose up like ghosts, disturbed by my arrival. Since then, homelessness has spread onto the streets. Tents, mattresses and duvets occupy the recesses in front of shop windows, in traffic tunnels and on bits of wasteland. They were even spread along the Broad (Broad Street) on my last visit to Oxford and somehow there they were even more shocking, as they suggested

Figure 12.1 *Rough sleeper in 'the Broad'. Author's photograph.*

a direct challenge to the picturesque fantasy Oxford, the myth I wrote of earlier as they contradicted the complacency of the beautiful street. There they were, planted alongside Trinity College and Balliol, but pedestrians passed them by as though they didn't exist, as though they too were ghosts.

The cultural expression of ghostliness contains all our bad dreams, congealed into claustrophobia, but the homeless haunt us in another way. Part of that haunting was the mismatch between my life, organized around cultural preoccupations, and the reality of the social fabric all around as the nation sank into a nastier kind of capitalism. To write was also a kind of haunting, as it could never perfectly realize what I wanted to say (if I even knew what that was). I searched for some other form that would express my diffuse obsessions better and investigated the past in crime novels that were never quite crime novels but aimed to understand how Britain had gone from winning the Second World War to where we were now, a grandiose plan impossible to achieve.

13

Nostalgia mode

To watch one of those old films is to slip back decades into the past.

There is the Past once more, as if in a dream: the shabby streets of London after the war. In memory, that London will always be a monochrome – black and white, like the films themselves – a vista of bomb sites, rain-swept alleyways and broken dreams, and in the darkness of the cinema you can almost penetrate the membrane between past and present and re-enter that world of austerity as the infinite regress of memory propels you into a time where melancholy constitutes its promise. Films, like reading, offer an exit from reality into a world that can only exist in the imagination.

The war had rubbed away the sharp edges of things. Bricks and stones were cracked and scabbed. In that London, you could cross an invisible frontier, where the safe, middle-class world of West London bled into something vaguer, more uncertain and ambiguous. To wander around the streets was to get inside what Iris Murdoch called the interstices of existence, labyrinths, where on the edge of districts, as Claude Lévi-Strauss felt in 1940s Manhattan, 'the web of the urban tissue was astonishingly slack'. Walter Benjamin thought that, beyond the class frontier (of Berlin, in his case), sexual experience awaited – or perhaps eerie nothingness.

In Paddington, you could find yourself passing the leprous façades of once-grand stucco terraces. Afro-Caribbean children tumbled up and down the front steps and adults sat watching and waiting, as if beyond the grey streets their gaze caught sight of the tropical island they had left behind. They might not have been thinking about the Caribbean at all, but it was a fact that the consciousness of streets stretching endlessly away in all directions produced an indefinable mood of nameless potential mingled with disappointment, as if your hopes were dashed before they'd even taken shape, but yet persisted in a city whose recovery from war had scarcely begun. Things seemed more provisional. London was supine like the mangy old lions who lay in torpid resignation behind the bars of their narrow cages at the Zoo. It was just this negative capability that paradoxically created the expectation of finding, if not an island paradise, at least a secret garden at the end of an alley, a haunted house behind an ancient façade or a scavenger's pickings along the neglected banks of the Thames at Rotherhithe.

There was a poverty of surface: the strangers treading the pavements wore class uniforms. Men in hats, for men wore hats in those days: bowler hats, homburg hats, trilby hats, the latter when worn with suede shoes suggesting something a little more daring – a refugee from the racecourse, an ex-RAF officer, a con man perhaps. Women in headscarves and shapeless coats shuffled along the street markets in worn-out shoes to buy vegetables from costermongers in flat caps and white scarves. Younger women were still wearing strict wartime suit jackets, often over printed frocks, with bare legs and socks set off precociously with platform or wedge shoes. Fashions lasted longer then. In another dimension, women in fur coats swam alongside the glass counters of department stores, those hushed temples of consumption.

When styles so closely conformed to class distinctions, the task of transforming yourself in clothes that might signal some form of as-yet only vaguely conceived dissidence was rather baffling. The acres of carpeted space in art deco dress salons offered only humiliating encounters with sales assistants, who would insist on accompanying you into an enormous fitting room to offer a running commentary on everything tried on. Blue jeans existed, but where to buy them was a puzzle. In any case, jeans hardly represented the kind of appearance I aspired to. I'd heard of Existentialists and the Left Bank and, instead of jeans, I appropriated my grandmother's black lisle stockings or wore Black Watch tartan trousers, cutting edge since Juliet Gréco, the existentialist chanteuse, had appeared in them.

The dark, dusty jazz clubs promised an opportunity to make a splash in an 'arty' outfit, for 'arty' seemed to be the only word to describe some alternative mode of dressing. A black polo neck sweater, perhaps, or possibly a dirndl skirt could be assembled to advertise the fact that you were a rebel. The skirt, along with embroidered Magyar blouses, harked back to some garbled idea of 'peasant dress' worn to demonstrate solidarity with Russian and Polish allies in the immediate post-war period, when the Soviet Union was still a friend, before the Cold War was declared.

En route through Soho to hear Humphrey Lyttleton's trad jazz band at the 100 Club in Oxford Street, you couldn't fail to notice that the women who stood on every corner still wore the fashions of a decade earlier: platform shoes with ankle straps and suits with military shoulder pads. Whether this was because they were too poor to afford new clothes or it was an informal tarts' uniform, to show off legs at a time when most women's pins were muffled in yards of voluminous material or hobbled into pencil skirts, was unclear.

The streetwalkers signalled what they were, and youth was keen to signal its rebellions, but London's strangeness, or perhaps it is the strangeness of any big city, was its secretiveness. Every pedestrian could be a refugee from any of the hidden social worlds that lay beneath the uncompromising façades and dour panorama of trudging crowds. Incognito was the true urban uniform. Even the class markers might be deceptive.

When the noise of traffic faded as you found yourself an intruder in some backwater, some road or square that became eerie simply by being uninhabited, your awareness of hidden lives intensified, and perhaps this sense of hidden worlds was stronger in London at a time when there were so few cafés or public spaces, when life was lived behind closed doors, in private places, as was not the case in Paris or Athens, not that I had visited those cities then. They were just exotic names.

London was, or seemed, a secretive place, but for that very reason dress played an important role. It gave off signals of belonging to those imagined mysterious worlds; it played an essential part in the panorama. But sometimes the signals themselves were so covert as to be invisible to all but the initiated. When I asked a gay friend about the clothes he'd worn in queer fifties London to announce his sexual identity back then, he was hard put to think of anything. Eventually he offered, doubtfully, 'perhaps a green corduroy jacket?' – the uniforms of those who were then beyond the pale had to be almost as hidden as the circles to which they gestured. There were those, like Quentin Crisp, who flaunted their defiance, wore make-up and camped up their abjection, but it was safer to remain anonymous.

Aged fourteen, fifteen, sixteen, I was searching for a hidden world that didn't exist, that was really nothing more than my own future adulthood, when, simply by growing older, I would sooner or later find an open door, even if it was not the door my mother would have wanted me to open and may not even have been the one I wanted to open myself, but in my teens I was always searching, never finding. The melancholy of city streets seeped into my own melancholy mood or reflected it. It was almost like a kind of nostalgia for the present, the sense that there was some alternative reality just beyond the walls and blind alleys that stretched out, mile after mile.

Nostalgia has never had a good press. Richard Hoggart suggested it was memory gone sticky. It was sickly sweet, a cloying sentimental distortion. Socialists always wanted to move into a bright future and get away from a backward past. Nostalgia was nothing more than false consciousness.

There were British films to express progressive aspirations. *Hue and Cry* told the story of a group of kids who foiled a gang of robbers, the climax a chase played out against a backdrop of council houses rising from the rubble, but for the most part it wasn't until the 1950s that comedies like *The Lavender Hill Mob* reflected a new mood of optimism, in which crime was parodied into cheerful fun. *The Fallen Idol* and *The Shop at Sly Corner* were more typical of the late 1940s in linking crime darkly to personal trauma and thwarted passion, as did *The Third Man*, most famous of British post-war films. This, like *The Fallen Idol*, was a collaboration between Graham Greene, Carol Reed and the producer, Alexander Korda. It is often included in the film noir canon, but it is not a true film noir, because it has a clear ethical framework. The American journalist in occupied Vienna is naïve and out of his depth, but he is not the typical weak and morally dubious film noir anti-hero, whereas the stiff-upper-lip British officer, played by Trevor Howard, states, and personifies, however cynically, the moral compass of the film – or the period. Stark, black and white photography underlines the contrast of the defeated city, partly destroyed, yet still standing amid its own ruin. The soundtrack, with its inspired use of a limited instrument, the zither, expresses perfectly the jarring mood of momentary jauntiness and grotesque comedy combined with unbearable melancholy. All combine to produce a powerful noir mood of loss and then elevate this mood into stoicism. The present seems hopeless to the tragic heroine, but she strides defiantly away from the American who, just as hopelessly, loves her and tried to save her from her destiny in the Soviet sector of the city. If there is nostalgia, it is not looking back, but searching for an alternative reality, a present time that was not a heartless prison. A less romantic sense of the tragic haunted *Brighton Rock* or *The Shop at Sly Corner*. In each of those films, unselfish love, of father for daughter or girlfriend for psychopathic lover, foundered against the harsh reality of crimes having consequences, with death the final destination.

The mood of these films was even gloomier than the grey London streets, but everywhere there was a sense of faded expectations. It was less a sense of wanting to travel backwards than of being stuck in an unwelcome present. In the light of this, the gaze backwards into the past is less a sentimental longing than the appalled stare of Walter Benjamin's angel of history; the backward gaze of the subject being blasted forward by the gale of what is to come: This wind irresistibly propels him into the future to which his back is turned, while the pile of debris before him grows skyward. 'This storm is what we call progress.' In *The Third Man*, the present is a knife-edge and the human protagonists are poised forever on this, the tightrope between past and future.

As the pandemic crisis lengthens, I am beginning to sense a mood that sometimes seems similar to the atmosphere of exhausted acceptance characteristic of those films. There is still a sense of people keeping their heads down and stoically plodding on, not lifting their eyes to the horizon, of just putting up with things. The times are very different. Emotions are less stifled. Anger is more openly expressed. The austerity period was also different in that Britain had won a war, yet that moment of exhilaration quickly faded because the population was exhausted. From 1945 to 1950 and beyond was the aftermath. At least the war had brought excitement, even if it had been much too exciting, yet afterwards normality must have seemed like a shrivelled, pricked balloon, shortages without passion, endurance without glory. The stifling cloud of the Cold War settled overhead. Insidious new fears menaced: of communists, espionage and atomic annihilation. Fear was no longer a rocket from the sky. It lurked in the shadows. Gruesome murders testified to an atmosphere of psychotic repression. Bomb sites disfigured the bleak streets of shabby, war-torn London. In retrospect, it could be understood as a period of recovery, but the convalescence was slow.

The Labour government battled to push through a radical agenda in the face of bankruptcy, strikes and hostility. My mother lived in fear that Prime Minister Clement Atlee was personally determined to 'requisition' our house and hand it over to squatters, and she regarded rationing and ration books as a punishment for the middle classes.

The 'Establishment', represented by the law and the church, tried to return women to their subordinate pre-war status, but ultimately failed. In the meantime, my mother pointed out with real dislike the slovenly dress of the women loitering at the wrong end of the Fulham Road, whose style flouted so many rules of appropriate self-presentation. Never mind about shortages and coupons; for a lady not to wear stockings in the street was to sink close to the status of streetwalker. I was more interested in the New Look, with its bouffant skirts, nipped-in waists and immensely artificial version of the feminine.

To absorb yourself in those post-war films is not to indulge in sentimentality, but to engage in a process of re-evaluation, both of the time and of the self you could never be again. Seen in retrospect, the passions acted out on celluloid have a certainty the period lacked when it was real. The present may be a knife-edge, but, when actually happening, it doesn't seem sharp at all. When you look back, you see what happened next, but at the time you were unsure, hesitating on the brink of what might be your life.

It took at least ten years for that post-war mood of austerity to shift, but by the time I reached university, a brighter, newer, more modern world was opening out and I plunged into the shiny freedoms, the Foale and Tuffin dresses and the exploding world of pop design. Before long, though, nostalgia returned in the shape of 'vintage' and, by the millennium, culture was saturated with pastiche, forward to the past, retro eclectic interiors, recycled modernism and the sixties reborn in a phantasmagoria of repetition. Austerity seems quite pure by comparison.

In the 1990s, I taught a course on film noir. Most of the films I discussed with students were American: the famous ones, *Double Indemnity* and *Cat People*, and the obscure, with terrific titles, such as *I Wake Up Screaming* and *Sorry, Wrong Number*. There were British examples: *Night and the City* and *The Shop at Sly Corner*, which, when I saw it, aged eleven, featured music I'd never heard before, namely Mendelssohn's violin concerto.

There was a fascination in the films' weak heroes and cheapskate *femmes fatales* and the moral ambiguity of their stories: of temptation succumbed to, love betrayed and failure. The black and white photography created a world of disconcerting angles, shadows and eerie vistas. Mendelssohn's music, though, suggested a different future, of possibility and hope. The films, some famous, but many neglected or forgotten, not a few made as 'B' films on small budgets, were and remain strange, haunting works of art and they were a further inspiration for my four novels.

So, the drab façades of bombed-out London paradoxically seemed to offer an alternative and thrilling hidden world. But of course if it ever were to become possible actually to revisit that past, I know that I should only long to get away.

14

Cracks in the pavement

It was in the cities that the Western fashion system developed. It might have started in the medieval royal courts, but with the rise of capitalism and the middle class, it migrated to the growing urban centres. These formed a theatre or stage for the production of individual performances and those performances were costumed. In the 1940s, for example, the bowler-hatted office worker was playing a role as much as the flat-capped men in the football crowd or the lady in evening dress at the opera. It therefore seemed quite natural to me to slide from the study of fashion to the exploration of urban life. Mine was a romantic view of the city in the culture of modernity, as of everything else. I had little time for those who romanticized the countryside and denounced cities as immoral and artificial. On the contrary, artificiality was the whole point – and possibly immorality too.

This was at the end of the 1980s, when the old Cold War certainties were breaking up and there no longer seemed any solid ground for socialism. Thought broke free from the straitjacket of theory. As, astonishingly, the Soviet Union disintegrated, the Berlin Wall was breached and Margaret Thatcher was defenestrated from office, the space for identity politics expanded in what seemed for a while a more carefree world. Celebrity culture forced itself on everyone's attention, creating a confusing atmosphere. Politicians began to appear on comedy programmes. Young women were presented as sexually free and equal with men, but at the same time unbridled sexism ran riot.

'Lad culture' shared the stage with the Spice Girls in a bewildering *mêlée* of raunch and self-assertion. In this atmosphere, feminism struggled, in danger of being suffocated in shallow forms of apparent acceptance. People were tired of hearing about the same old issues of exploitation, oppression and violence. These were as pressing as ever, but it was more enjoyable to riff about lipstick lesbians and admire Madonna's love of Frida Kahlo's art.

One of the last theoretical discussions of the 1980s concerned the essentially urban character of the *flâneur*, a fascinating, ambiguous figure. The *flâneur* emerged as a response to urbanization in the early nineteenth century, when the growth of immense cities of a new kind was part of a monumental upheaval, transforming economic and social life and customs. The nineteenth-century metropolis, strange and alien as it seemed at first, provided the conditions for a new mentality. This the *flâneur* personified and, as a writer, described.

The origins of the term are uncertain. The nineteenth-century *Encyclopaedia Larousse* suggested that *flâneur* may be derived from an Irish word for 'libertine' and defined the character as someone who sauntered through the streets, observing people and society and frittering away his time. He could exist only in the big city; provincial towns offered a stage too restricted for his promenades and a field too narrow for his observations. He was probably first identified in a pamphlet published in 1806. In it, the characteristics of a typical *flâneur* were already outlined fully fashioned, although the word was not used. The anonymous author of the pamphlet portrayed a man of independent means, 'Monsieur Bonhomme', who was free to roam Paris at will and spent most of his day observing the urban spectacle. Fascinated by the surface of city life, he inspected new inventions and watched the many building works in progress, went shopping or window shopping, looking at books, new fashions, hats, jewellery and novelties, and he was highly sensitive to dress as a vital component of street life.

When not doing the rounds of the shops, he spent time in cafés and restaurants, choosing the ones favoured by actors, writers, journalists and painters, which suggested he was interested in the world of entertainment and the arts. In these places – equally a feature of the new and changing city – he could pick up gossip about new plays, rivalries in the art world and projected publications, and could discuss the seasonal Salon art exhibitions. He was also a voyeur who loved to watch the lower ranks of society, observing soldiers, workers and 'grisettes' (seamstresses of 'easy morals') as they went about their work or amused themselves at open-air dances and fairs. He appeared as an essentially asexual character (as often also was the related figure of the dandy); women barely featured in his life, appearing only as bit-part players – the manageress of a restaurant, a street vendor, a prostitute.

'M. Bonhomme' was, in fact, an early example of the species of 'consumer', yet he was more than that. He resolved to keep a diary to record all the curious things he observed during his wanderings, and this hinted at the literary role the future *flâneur* would occupy, in particular as the inventor of a new kind of writing: personal, idiosyncratic and semi-autobiographical. The *flâneur* was a shape-shifter who embodied two related yet separate ways of understanding and defining the world the metropolis offered: the shopper and the writer, those eager figures exploring this new urban life and its diverse possibilities. He represented the possibilities of urban leisure, but also signalled an emerging class of literary innovators living on their wits; at the same time, he was perhaps a literary creation himself, a symbolic or even allegorical representative of the new kinds of life it was possible to live in the metropolis.

Where were women in all this? Nineteenth-century great cities created an environment in which the status of women was uncertain. Women factory workers were detached from the family economy and operated as individuals. They might also work as street traders and in the new kinds of shops, especially, by the mid-nineteenth century, the department store. Their independence, however limited, represented a challenge to patriarchal assumptions. The masculine order perceived unattached women on their own as a threat to men. They challenged the status quo of male dominance and at the same time tempted them to sin. In other words, the Victorians associated unaccompanied women with prostitution.

Prostitution was both a social threat and a metaphor for general disorder. It symbolized the overturning of natural hierarchies and social institutions. The focus on prostitution symbolized, but also masked the wider issue of women in the public sphere. The prostitute was perceived as a 'public woman', but the fear in nineteenth-century urban life was that every woman in the new, disordered world of the metropolis – abroad alone and unaccompanied by a man on pavements and in cafés and theatres – was a 'public woman', in other words, a prostitute. The idea behind this was and still is that women are rightfully the property of men. It follows that a woman not attached to one man is not an independent being but is the exact opposite: she has become the property of all men. It has been impossible to eradicate this belief and there continue to be many societies in the twenty-first century where the belief still holds, and men behave accordingly. Even in London and other capital cities, where women are theoretically free to travel around on their own, they still do not inhabit the streets on the same terms as men.

Janet Wolff launched a debate on women's presence in cities in her essay, 'The Invisible *Flâneuse*'. She argued that there could never be a female *flâneur*. The *flâneur*'s freedom to wander at will through the city was a masculine prerogative and therefore the concept of the *flâneur* was a gendered one. Women by contrast were imprisoned by an ideology that confined them to the home, even if they did actually venture onto the streets. Additionally, the *flâneur* could be seen as a metaphor for the 'male gaze': men's visual and voyeuristic mastery over women. The theory of the 'male gaze', developed by another feminist writer, Laura Mulvey, and based on a form of psychoanalysis, implied that a woman had no 'gaze' of her own; she was not a subject in charge of her destiny, but was exclusively a passive object, existing only as someone to be looked at by men. To me, it seemed and still seems counter-intuitive that such a disempowering theory should have found such popularity among feminists. Perhaps it expressed at a gut level the sense women had, and have, of being continually looked at and judged; but while it recognized the phenomenon, it did little to help women escape it, in fact appearing to deny any such possibility.

I absolutely recognized female oppression, but I took issue with Janet Wolff, because it seemed to me that she developed too unrelenting and pessimistic a conception of women as completely imprisoned in ideology. In my rather turgid riposte, I attempted to demonstrate that urban life, even if women remained unequal, which they did, offered them more opportunities for independence, however limited, than their confinement to the rural family economy. In city life, there were 'cracks in the pavement' that offered spaces and opportunities for assertion and empowerment, however partial. I rejected the idea that the iron law of 'ideology' (restrictive theories or assertions of what and how women should be and were) completely dominated and defined women. I suggested instead that actual experience, women's lived lives, retrieved through historical research, could be inconsistent and contradictory. Actual lived existence did not always match what ideology said ought to happen. The more pessimistic feminist view I objected to dwelled by contrast on the oppression of women and the seamless power of theory. So, my reply to Janet Wolff was partly an expression of frustration at what I read as a conservative feminism that dwelt too exclusively on oppression and said too little about the possibilities of protest and escape.

The prostitute was often falsely romanticized (by men), but the original male *flâneur* was also romanticized and he too, I suggested, was a marginal figure rather than a symbol of power. To perceive him as a masterful voyeur was to underplay the financial and psychological insecurity of the role. The *flâneur* was often actually working as he loitered along the pavement or delved into the underworld of street survivors, searching for the material he could convert into writing for sale. He was also a lonely and unattached figure – a forerunner of Raymond Chandler's private eye as much as of future bohemians and hipsters. Walter Benjamin went so far as to argue that the *flâneur's* repetitive saunterings represented stagnation and ultimately impotence, and that he was far from being an embodiment of male domination. On the contrary, he was a marginal and often isolated victim of urban anomie.

The *flâneur/flâneuse* has continued to interest writers because, on the one hand, they were a symbolic representation of 'the writer' as a distinct type of person, whereas, on the other, they rescued consumption from false consciousness and transformed it into something creative. The *flâneur* contributed to the image of a certain kind of person and a certain form of lifestyle, running right through the bohemian and the beatnik, and surviving as the 'hipster' even since the millennium. At first glance strictly colourless observers, they were actually presenting themselves as a possible model for a way of life.

As I look back on this debate now, I believe that possibly the *flâneur's* popularity at the end of the twentieth century was itself a romantic attachment to a mythical figure (for he was a kind of myth about freelance intellectuals in the metropolis). In the twilight of the twentieth century, researchers – myself absolutely included – saw a glamourized version of themselves in this independent individual, just at the point when academic life was becoming increasingly bureaucratic and rule-bound. It was a long time since the unattached writer living on their wits had morphed into a salaried journalist or academic; now, as universities became businesses, the illusion of the free-floating intellectual was hard to sustain. The *flâneur* perhaps represented, among other things, nostalgia for a life less regulated by managerial interference.

When I was writing about the *flâneur/flâneuse*, I made no connection with my own youthful sorties into unfamiliar parts of London. London is so extensive that there are still districts unknown to me, especially those ambiguous, in-between places on the edge of the capital. I have failed to achieve what Iain Sinclair recorded in *Lights Out for the Territory* and *London* Orbital, extending his *flânerie* to those mysterious regions, half suburb, half wasteland – Erith and Crays, the far distant edges of Bromley – and that may partly be because, as a woman, I am warier of exploring potentially hostile territory. The threatening figure of Dicken's Abel Magwitch had come from those sinister marshes and, in myth at least, they were where gangsters in concrete wellies disappear. Similarly, when I read François Maspero's *Roissy Express*, his account of a journey through the new Paris suburbs (also explored in the French TV series, *Spiral*), I resolved to explore this other Paris beyond the *péripherique* but have never quite dared to venture into those twilight regions.

Since the era of the *flâneur* debate, the existence of a female gaze, a queer gaze, a non-Western gaze has been recognized. It is acknowledged that women do have at least agency, yet perhaps this is largely lip service, for women continue to be menaced on the streets, at best their right to be there is questioned, at worst they are physically attacked. Feminist debate has shifted away from ideology to target the actual behaviour of men in public and in private. There is more emphasis on personal pain, on the vulnerable nature of identity and of personal experience and feeling as subjective truth and less on the theoretical causes of male aggression, so that the situation today is less abstract than the more academic debates of the 1980s. What remains the same is that the potential of empowerment seems always to be overshadowed by the dangers women face. Today these dangers seem more threatening than ever. We can still ask Janet Wolff's question: Can there be such a woman as a *flâneuse*?

Rather than answering this question, recent books about living in cities have taken a different route. The early *flâneurs* described the social scene around them as detached observers, sociologists of a kind, rather than autobiographers. Later, some, such as Louis Aragon in *Paris Peasant*, combined description with subjective reflection. Describing how he privileged chance in his wanderings through 1920s Paris, Aragon felt that old certainties, old gods, had lost their power and that he lived in a world – this world he was exploring – prey to completely new obsessions, but at first he failed to recognize 'the gods in the street', because he was so weighed down by his precarious truth, in other words his own theoretical preconceptions. During his wanderings as a *flâneur*, however, instead of looking for certainties in abstract thought, he found 'the face of the infinite' in the concrete forms that surrounded him. The streets were a source of enlightenment and, at the same time, of transcendent mystery.

Less subjectively, Iain Sinclair and François Maspero incorporated history, especially political history, into their accounts of, respectively, London and Paris. The post-war Situationists had developed the idea of the *dérive*, or drifting, as a process that was part-playful, but could encourage insight and enlightenment. In their explorations, Sinclair and Maspero extended the idea of the *dérive* or an extended walk without a fixed destination, but not without a purpose.

Lately, writers have seemed readier to experience the city at one remove. Matthew Beaumont's *Night Walking* revealed the history of walking and, among other things, its relationship to the development of streets lit at night. In his latest book, *The Walker: On Finding and Losing Yourself in the Modern City*, a concluding chapter discusses the paranoid nature of much contemporary architecture, and uses, as I have done, Freud's idea of the uncanny to get at the often-ambivalent relationship of human beings to the cities that have arisen around them. Most chapters in his book, however, analyse what it means to be a contemporary pedestrian by exploring the fiction of G. K. Chesterton, H. G. Wells and Virginia Woolf, among others. This is also the method used by Olivia Laing in *The Lonely City: Adventures in the Art of Being Alone*, in which she wrote about artists who were working in New York at the height of the AIDS epidemic, framing these discussions in brief reflections on her own loneliness in Manhattan. In *The Flâneuse: Women Walk the City in Paris, New York, Tokyo, Venice and London*, Lauren Elkin acknowledged her independent existence as a woman who can enjoy the freedom of the streets without becoming a woman who 'walks the streets', yet bypassed issues that are still so relevant and menacing, and rather than describing her own experience, approaches her chosen cities largely through literary figures and artists. This is fine, except that it is not really *flânerie*. To be a *flâneur/se* implies a direct exploration, a real encounter with the streets, and I wondered why these writers had not included more of their own experience. Might it have seemed narcissistic? Or did the contemporary landscape offer too little in the way of eccentricity and the picturesque? Or was there, as Maspero felt, no middle ground between city centres, that had been cosmeticized into pastiches of themselves, and dangerous outer regions given over to crime and violence?

It was disappointing that Lauren Elkin chose the Bloomsbury Group to represent *flânerie* in London. This circle of writers and artists is an important part of early-twentieth-century British culture, but I can never quite understand why its members have come to feature so prominently as leading representatives of our bohemian heritage. For all their experiments in sexual relationships, its members maintained a bourgeois lifestyle and had comfortable incomes. Both before and after them, there were individuals who led far edgier lives and took greater emotional and financial risks. There were women painters and writers whose work was arguably more original and interesting. The bohemian women of the Second World War, described by D. J. Taylor in *Lost Girls,* experienced penury and abortions, and in their male-dominated circles were routinely belittled and disregarded, battling through, often at permanent cost to their own talents, as they devoted themselves to ungrateful, neurotic men, while running the enterprises the men were theoretically in charge of.

By contrast, Vita Sackville-West's elopement with Violet Trefusis was doomed to failure because neither woman had any idea of how to be self-supporting, and they were economically dependent on their respective husbands. I find it rather perverse that Vita has come to be seen as one of the great lesbian lovers, especially given that in the earlier part of the twentieth century there were numerous less-well-known women artists who were far more fiercely independent, quite a number of whom lived with women partners, even if they might not have wished to be labelled as lesbian. Some specialized in textiles and design and did not write about their unconventional lives, but those living in London negotiated the city just as a man would do and, unlike Virginia Woolf, were never economically dependent on a man: Enid Marx, the designer, for example, whose designs were used for the upholstered seats in the Tube rail network for decades.

Elkin's chapter on London ends on an elegiac note, suggesting that since there are few people left (if there are any, they must be well over ninety years old) who remember the London that Virginia Woolf described, we have to reconstruct it through our reading of her books. Then Elkin adds, in a contradictory reverse, 'Or we could put on our shoes and go out [of] the door.' I wonder why she did not take her own advice. A contemporary *flâneuse* who saw her role as a detached observer, could have 'gone out the door' of the British Library –

and walked into the surrounding streets. She could, for example, have travelled a few hundred yards north into Euston's Bangladeshi community. She could have explored the thriving playground of Granary Square, north of King's Cross railway station, where, on hot summer days, small children from nearby public housing dance in the low-rise fountains in front of the Granary building. On those summer days this building, home to Central Saint Martins, part of the University of the Arts, looks out on a sort of urban *plage* with picnicking families; during one Wimbledon, a giant screen relayed matches to anyone who cared to watch from the ease of a deckchair. In the evenings of one hot summer, students and visitors sat about on the steps leading up from the side of the canal and watched the Japanese horror movies being shown.

Alternatively, she could have started in the British Library itself and wondered if the tourists filling its cafés are – or are not – the

Figure 14.1 *St Pancras Old Church. Author's photograph.*

Figure 14.2 *Crick Institute, St Pancras. Author's photograph.*

flâneurs of the twenty-first century. She could have admired the bulbously swollen Crick Institute, an enormous dinosauric toad squatting magnificently opposite St Pancras station and dauntingly dedicated to research into disease. (Nearby residents were fearful that ebola or other killer viruses might escape from the carapace of its walls.) She could have visited the sinister little Old St Pancras Church, where the architect John Soane and the transgender the Chevalier d'Éon are buried, and where there is a memorial tomb to Mary Wollstonecraft and William Godwin (though their remains rest elsewhere). She could have wandered through the station itself, with its shopping galleries and champagne bar and tourists decanted from Eurostar every thirty minutes (perhaps less often after Brexit).

She could have crossed the Euston Road into central Bloomsbury, where the area immediately to the east of Gower Street is no longer residential as it was when the Woolfs lived there, but, with three universities – University College (UC) London, Birkbeck College and SOAS University of London – has become effectively a university campus in the middle of the city. The monumental UC Library – a modernist building often used in period TV crime dramas such as *Foyles War* and Agatha Christie's *Hercule Poirot* – rises above Georgian terraces (George Dance the Younger, the architect of Bath, lived in Gower Street) that march elegantly eastwards and across Southampton Row, beyond which they alternate with formidable nineteenth-century mansion flats and post-1945 social housing.

Partial gentrification has altered the atmosphere of the area. Until the 1980s, Argyle Street was lined with sordid hotels, used by the prostitutes who haunted the roads around the two major railway stations late at night, standing alone and vulnerable at points along the roads north, hardly *flâneuses*. Today, they have vanished, or, rather, gone online. Students and families saunter beneath the magnificent plane trees in Brunswick Square and the hotels have been smartened up. Across the street, the modernist Brunswick Centre, at one time a shady haunt of drug dealers, has been transformed by shops, cafés and a cinema and bar, and in 2021 a café, unique in selling alcohol (a continental rather than a British idea), was granted a liquor licence. Bloomsbury is a part of inner London that, while continually threatened with privatization and rising rents, still has a mixed population and diverse life. Many famous and infamous individuals have lived in Bloomsbury, their histories sometimes surviving in its bricks and mortar, while the buildings themselves provide a whole history of architecture, from the magnificent neo-classical Mecklenburgh Square to the insane exuberance of the

Figure 14.3 *Brunswick Centre, Bloomsbury. Author's photograph.*

Russell Hotel and the blocks of social housing at the eastern edge of the district. There is always something new to find. On a recent visit, I discovered in a flower bed a stone plaque in memory of some Jacobites who were executed in 1745. My observations are hardly original, yet to me the history and geography of the district are all much more interesting than yet another encounter with the over-exposed Bloomsbury Group. I acknowledge, though, that mine is the privileged perception of a woman who does feel able to wander these streets. It would be more revealing, perhaps, to see those same streets from the perspective of a young Bangladeshi woman living in one of the crowded flats towards the Gray's Inn Road.

The *flâneur/flâneuse* has continued to interest writers because on the one hand they were a symbolic representation of 'the writer' as a distinct type of person, on the other, they rescued consumption from false consciousness and transformed it into something creative. The *flâneur* contributed to the image of a certain kind of person and a certain form of lifestyle, running right through the bohemian and the beatnik and surviving even since the millennium. At first glance strictly colourless observers, they were actually presenting themselves as a possible model for a way of life. The *flâneurs* fascinated because they were always 'lonely in the city'. The figure expressed the strangeness of street life in which the solitary pedestrian is (as often as not) completely alone among crowds of thousands. Georg Simmel concluded that each individual walking the thronged pavements had to develop a 'blasé attitude' to protect themselves from being overwhelmed, but perhaps there is another side to it; perhaps there is a release, even an exhilaration, in letting go and simply drifting or sauntering along among strangers towards whom you have no obligation. This does not mean there is no connection. On the contrary, there may be glimpses of individuals who capture your attention, even as they hurry past. This was the theme of Baudelaire's poem '*To a Passerby*' and it was significant that he chose a woman as the fascinating stranger, not simply because she represented the possibility of an erotic encounter that was tantalizing because it could not be fulfilled, but because, whether Baudelaire himself recognized it or not, her presence was more of an irruption, the crowds of men forming the backdrop against which she stood out.

Lauren Elkin's optimism about women's possession of the streets seems at odds with recent renewed fury and outrage following the murder of a young woman in South London in 2021. In spite of that – or even because of it – it matters to hang on to some kind of optimism, to a sense that things can be different, that there are still 'cracks in the pavement'. In just such a spirit of optimism, Elkin uses an illuminating discovery, when she discusses a famous photograph by Ruth Orkin. This captures the situation of a beautiful young woman running the gauntlet of men's stares and leers in a stony Italian street. The famous image has usually been interpreted as a classic example of the male gaze and of women's unfreedom in public, but Elkin discovered an interview with the woman in the photograph, whose description of having a wonderful time with Orkin in Florence in 1951 completely contradicted the apparent meaning of the image. The photograph, the woman said, had been meant to capture the sense of triumph and freedom she and Ruth Orkin were experiencing. They had been neither lonely nor fearful, and the photo was a celebration of their independence and inspiration.

When I looked again at the image after reading this unexpected interpretation, I could still see none of that triumph. The young woman hurrying along a short stretch of pavement appears trapped by the gaze of no less than fourteen men, one of whom seems to be trying to physically block her way. As she clutches her stole and bag around her, her eyelids are lowered and the look on her face expresses endurance, the expression I remember well, that says: 'I am not noticing this, I am ignoring it and I am behaving as though it isn't happening.'

There may be no one 'true' reading of the photograph. It may be that the men were playing up to the camera. Perhaps Ruth Orkin and her unnamed friend sat down for a drink with some of them. Perhaps – in fact, almost certainly – the woman's defiance and the men's intrusiveness are both true. Perhaps the image reproduces faithfully the atmospheric combination on the street, when intimacy jostles with alienation, when there is both fear and desire, the possibility of an encounter and its refusal. Perhaps Ruth Orkin was the true *flâneuse* of this encounter, recording incompatible realities in one image, as if one has overlaid the other, in a double exposure, capturing a world that has long since gone.

15

In search of lost streets

Everything we believe imperishable tends towards destruction; a worldly position, like everything else, is not created once and for all, but just like imperial power, is reconstructed moment by moment by a sort of perpetual continuous creation.

MARCEL PROUST, À la recherche du temps perdu: Albertine disparue

The 1990s was a period of my life when I travelled to other universities in other cities, as external examiner to courses and higher degrees or as speaker at conferences. Wherever I was, Glasgow, Antwerp, Amsterdam, New York, Bologna, I tried to slip away to explore unfamiliar urban landscapes, art galleries and museums and above all just life on streets that were different from London, yet familiar even in their difference. I got to know Glasgow well, because a colleague, Harvie Ferguson, took me everywhere, introducing me to unexpected dimensions of the dark, northern metropolis and the sobriety of Hillhead's sombre tenements and dignified streets, the postmodernism of its new shopping centre and the raw, high-rise tenements. It was a city that appeared forbidding, but its vitality flowed below the surface and suggested possibilities of mood and discovery, remaining in that respect indeterminate and open-ended. The Scottish city bore a resemblance in my imagination to the Berlin of the 1920s, and Berlin in turn seemed the template of all blackened northern cities of the early twentieth century. This was not the Weimar Berlin of cabaret shows and gender bending, but a metropolis scarred by working-class struggle, crime and destitution, threateningly alive, the city of Döblin's *Berlin Alexanderplatz*. Contemporary Glasgow, quieter, fading into the dusk of a misty autumn afternoon, seemed, for all its solid presence, 'transitory, fugitive and contingent', the words used by Charles Baudelaire to describe modernity itself.

Modernity was a slippery concept. David Frisby also taught at Glasgow and, in a pioneering study, *Fragments of Modernity*, he aimed, through an examination of three German writers of the early twentieth century, to explore modernity as a new way of experiencing the social world and what it meant to be modern. The trio, Georg Simmel, Siegfried Kracauer and Walter Benjamin, explored a daily life that was fragmentary, unfixed, insecure and fleeting. The slow time of the past was replaced by fast time, in which 'all that is solid melts into air'. It followed that the truth of modernity was to be found in an investigation of the surfaces, the passing moments, the brief encounters, the outward appearances of things.

Kracauer and Benjamin had explored the daily life of Berlin's city streets in the 1920s and I found their work reassuring, for, if the study of detail and the evanescent provided a key to modernity, then my own work on fashion, cafés and eccentric personalities was after all not as frivolous – or 'naughty' as the sociologist Paul Hirst once expressed it – as some of my colleagues seemed to believe. Actually, I could cope with their scepticism. Worse than their doubt was my own corrosive uncertainty. I always felt anxious about my work, fearful that others might see me as little more than a dilettante butterfly floating between dubious research subjects, and I feared that that was what perhaps I was, a sort of lily of the field (they toil not, neither do they spin) of academia.

It was particularly exhilarating to be introduced to the work of Siegfried Kracauer, until then unknown to me. Kracauer's fascination with disregarded aspects of the everyday world invested them with the glamour of the marginal. The subjects he wrote about – detective novels, the hotel lobby, going to the movies, chorus girls – suggested an interest in pleasure, desire and erotic adventure that had often been considered either beyond the reach of social theory or else beneath its dignity. Kracauer's work was novelistic. He did write two autobiographical novels and his work opened the possibility of a field intermediate between fiction and non-fiction.

Kracauer was also innovative in exploring popular culture, especially film. This partly explains the significance of his rediscovery in the 1980s, a time when intellectual interest, as I have described, was moving in the direction of consumer society and its mass cultural forms. It was no longer the deep structures of capitalism that kept people awake at night, but rather the significance of the 'low-brow'. My partner, Angela Weir, and I even wrote an article, turgidly titled 'The Greyhound Bus Station in the Evolution of Women's Popular Culture: Lesbian Popular Fiction in the Nineteen-Fifties', which analysed the hidden meanings of 1950s lesbian pulp fiction. Years previously, my first lover had brought a dozen of these novels home from San Francisco, after studying for two years at Berkeley. They had at first seemed illicit and almost shameful. Not that it seemed shameful to be a lesbian, but to be reading pulp fiction. Read retrospectively, however, they became quite different; sociological research into the emergence of a lesbian subculture and the beginning of the end of secrecy.

This wasn't untypical. It was the unconsidered fragments of reality and the most despised entertainments that exposed the hidden secrets of modernity and the sources of its alienation. Industrial culture produced innovative forms (montage, for example) and these forms could, more accurately than traditional art and literature, express the alienation or estrangement that defined the whole of the modern experience. An underlying consistency and pattern, clues to the nature and meaning of this modern society, could be traced in the apparently meaningless turmoil of city life and mass culture.

The sleuth's 'clue' is an essential element of detective fiction, and the detective novel was of such interest to Kracauer that he wrote an early book about it. *Der Detektiv-Roman* could be read as a rule book for the writing of any crime novel from the period between the wars or even after, but it was more than that. It was subtitled '*A philosophical tract*' and was an analysis of the alienated modernity Kracauer observed. Alienation was the product of the distorted rationalism of an Enlightenment gone to the bad, its potential for emancipation sacrificed to industrial capitalism and the bureaucratic surveillance that resulted from it. Within the framework of the novel, the private detective (Hercule Poirot being the archetype) was the embodiment of the false rationality of modernity, the very personification of Reason. The analytical beam of his laser-sharp mind was triumphalist but limited. He was a kind of god 'in a world that has forgotten God'. He was a magician whose magic is reason, an omniscient narrator who also functioned as the secular equivalent of a priest (and Kracauer noted that G. K. Chesterton's detective, Father Brown, actually was a priest) and, like a priest or a monk, he was asexual and solitary. His friendships – such as those between Sherlock Holmes and Watson and between Poirot and Captain Hastings – were not of equals but of genius and sidekick. Paradoxically, although the detective represented Order, he was also a marginal character and an outsider. Poirot was a foreigner, Sherlock Holmes, a drug addict and Miss Marple, a spinster no one noticed.

The detective novel, therefore, far from being escapism or pulp, represented and explored essential aspects of modernity. Yet Kracauer rejected the false solutions of the plot when order was restored at the conclusion. For crime fiction failed to confront the real crime, which was political: the immiseration of the working class and the social origins of crime. Instead, it simply mirrored the alienated world of modernity, reproducing the ideologies of the consumer world and its individualism. It was, therefore, sentimental and lapsed into what Kracauer called kitsch, a form of emotional falsity. Kitsch used elevated language and fake moralism but expressed itself in stylistic vulgarity and excess. Detective fiction recognized this but recoiled from revealing the underlying causes. This is what made it ideological.

Similarly, the characters in detective fiction were accentless stereotypes without inner life, merely labelled with characteristics, such as 'genial' or 'jealous'. Human personality was flattened out, just as, Kracauer believed, that photography was the perfect art form for modernity in flattening out reality and depriving it of any kind of 'aura'.

Alison Light, writing in *Forever England* of women and fiction between the wars, took issue with this kind of analysis, especially the widespread belief that Agatha Christie's novels were peopled with just such puppets. She perceived in them an affinity with the kind of rootless modernity described by Kracauer. Their identities reflected the unreliability of modernity itself, for in modernity identity is not fixed, but shifting. Outward appearances bore little relation to the hidden motivations exposed by Poirot's thought processes. The respectable spinster turned out to have been sending poison pen letters to all her neighbours; the local doctor was a murderer; the first-person narrator was the most unreliable narrator of all in Christie's *The Murder of Roger Ackroyd*.

As crime fiction has developed, its flexible form has been pushed and pulled in every direction. It has surpassed the limitations Kracauer criticized and has expanded to include sophisticated explorations of the ills of civil society. As long ago as the 1940s, the ironic cynicism and melancholy of Raymond Chandler's novels, set in the deadly sunlight of 1930s Los Angeles, described a world in which the powerful were not brought to justice. Dashiell Hammett's Sam Spade and Raymond Chandler's Philip Marlowe were less than omniscient, immersed in the fray rather than above it as they ventured down the 'mean streets' of depression-era America. They did not operate as detached brains, nor were they celibate on principle, since the lonely existence of each was interrupted by short-lived erotic encounters tinged with romanticism, but they never ceased to be loners, and lonely in the city in a way that Poirot and Sherlock Holmes never were. Contemporary sleuths come in all shapes, sizes and genders; more often than not the plot retains the traditional scaffolding of accepted notions of right and wrong, good and evil. The hard-boiled fiction of Jim Thompson is almost alone in confronting a real darkness at the heart of crime.

Kracauer noted something even more unsettling about city life than the transient individuals continually hurrying along the street: the transience of the past, the transience of the fabric of the city itself and how the two complement each other. He had trained as an architect and was sensitive to the way in which the buildings and monuments that construct the city have a double existence. On the one hand 'some street blocks seem to be created for eternity' – as are cathedrals, courts of justice and museums – while, on the other hand, 'the present day Kurfürstendamm is the embodiment of empty, flowing time in which nothing is allowed to last'. Transience soaks into the very stones of the ever-changing city. This provokes reactions in the observer, the resident, as they become aware that familiar landmarks have entirely vanished. The irony Kracauer noted – whereby buildings 'created for eternity' are pulled down, obliterated and replaced in a matter of decades – makes for a disorientating sense of continual alteration, which is built into the experience of the city and contributes to the sense of uncertainty, of shifting ground beneath one's feet. The 'homelessness' of the modernist subject is not mere irrationality or false consciousness but is a reaction to the experience of endless change. Psychologically, this was reproduced, Kracauer argued, in moral ambivalence, reflected in thrillers (and films) even as they attempted the fictional restoration of a normality that no longer existed.

I responded to Kracauer's reflections on the changing urban texture, as someone who has lived her whole life in London. It fitted with my sense of the way in which a city can embalm the sense of a disappeared past. I could walk through streets and rediscover areas altered beyond recognition, but could equally revisit districts where I once lived, a place I'd once worked or my old school, to find them utterly unchanged.

The factory, site of my first encounter with an industrial strike, surprisingly still stands, although it now functions as an office. Every morning as I walked to school along Brook Green in West London, I passed it. A warm smell of washing-up water ebbed out onto the road and its faint vapour surrounded the picket line of ETU (Electrical Trades Union) workers holding their handwritten placards. Only many years later did I discover that their protest was part of a major, landmark strike in which the left wing of the union was eventually defeated, a turning point of post-war politics during the heyday (but at the same time the slow decline) of the British Communist Party.

Such memories are typical 'kaleidoscope memories' in that they shake the past into a different pattern. To the middle-class twelve-year-old, the strikers appeared exotic and, while slightly alien, also poignant, a shabby and somehow vulnerable group with their handwritten placards outside the monumental factory; to my adult self, many years later, they retrospectively became a piece in the post-war jigsaw of labour struggles, Stalinism and anti-communism.

Today, as I didn't then, I wonder what they thought of me, the schoolgirl glancing in curiosity at inhabitants of a different world; but I don't expect they noticed me at all. Thus, two worlds could have an encounter in the street while remaining utterly sealed off from each other. Strangers remained strangers, separated by the intangible membrane of custom.

The memory of that encounter may have unconsciously been part of what led to my writing the four-period crime novels between 2007 and 2014. They were set in the decade 1945 to 1955, mostly in London, but also partly in a divided Berlin of refugees, rubble and espionage, in the sleazy Brighton of gangsters and dirty weekends, and in the colleges and bedsits of uptight 1950s Oxford. I was drawn to this, the Austerity period, as a time that seemed particularly apt for thwarted passions and sordid crimes. It seemed the perfect period for the thriller. The war had shattered 'normal life' in Britain, when the established rules of behaviour were to some extent suspended. Human decency held together for the most part, but there was a desperate side to wartime life: illicit affairs in the blackout and forbidden luxuries on the black market, as well as heroism, self-sacrifice, 'carrying on' and sudden death. Urban dwellers endured chronic danger. Many acted beyond their strength, surviving from day to day. That was their knife-edge. Hitting peaks and troughs became normality. The period afterwards was one of exhaustion and, more importantly, of psychological repression. Men and women stuffed their wartime experiences into the closet; a veil was to be drawn over affairs, loss, even crime, but the repressed returned in the shape of dubious business dealings and grotesque murders.

I decided to explore the period through fiction after I'd finished my history of bohemians and countercultures in the nineteenth and twentieth centuries. The book was published, but I found I was still attached to the flawed, deviant and romantic bohemians who created a life of defiance against a background of attics, cafés and salons. I missed these people who couldn't keep to the straight and narrow but were irresistibly drawn to the dark side and to the breaking of rules, if not downright criminality. That they expressed dissidence in works of art or sometimes in surreal forms of self-dramatization made them even more interesting to me. My side trip into novel writing was mainly an attempt to bring them to life again, to spend more time with the mad, bad and dangerous to know. More prosaically, I had spare bits of research, which could be knitted up into fiction.

I also felt, perhaps fancifully, that crime novels might be a way to explore political ideas in a more accessible way. In particular, it might be a means of explaining the erosion of left-wing ideals and hopes in the face of Stalinism and the Cold War, which was a war against socialism in any form, not just against a corrupted version of communism. By the time I was working on these novels, however, the old left was dead and buried. Communism is a forgotten episode in British politics. Today, there are probably few people who know that, in 1945, two communist MPs were elected. Communism collapsed and imploded into its own contradictions. Stalin alone is remembered. The British Communist Party, once a genuine force, disappeared as utterly as Kracauer's bulldozed buildings.

After my second novel, *War Damage*, appeared, a literary website asked me to write a short article about my favourite villainess. In a way, this piece summed up not only the imaginative hold the 1940s had over me, but also a fascination with 'going too far'. In my teens, I had tried to reject respectability. I had longed to kick over the traces and, whereas I was too cowardly to take any really lethal risks, I had thrilled to deviant personalities and wished I was like them. Therefore, my choice of villainess could not be anyone but the 1940s British film star, Margaret Lockwood, who played one of the great femmes fatales in the Gainsborough Studios melodrama, *The Wicked Lady*. She was insane with wickedness, but enjoyed every moment of it. Poaching her best friend's fiancé, the aristocratic Sir Ralph Skelton, was just the beginning. Soon bored with provincial married life, she impersonated the notorious highwayman, Captain Jerry Jackson. During a successful hold-up, she encountered Jackson himself. They became lovers, although, in the meantime, she had fallen for a handsome neighbour, Kit Locksby. Intoxicated by her double life, she murdered a guard during another ambush, poisoned a family retainer who discovered her secret, betrayed Jackson after he was unfaithful to her and was eventually killed herself, making a deathbed declaration of love to Locksby.

In *The Man in Grey*, Lockwood played a cold and heartless husband stealer and murderess (again opposite James Mason), a far cry from the exuberance of Lady Skelton, but both films perversely gave romantic passion a gothic twist. Lockwood and Mason enacted the Fallen Woman and the Fatal Man, heroine and hero of the Romantic Movement, but their love appeared as an engine of crime and betrayal, destroying those who suffered from it, rather than as a source of redemption or even just as tragic romance.

Secretive myself, I am still drawn to the idea of persons who dare to live double lives, whose motives are occult and perverse, reminding us that all lives are ultimately secret and unknowable, that each of us, to some extent, wears a mask. My first crime novel, *The Twilight Hour*, turned on an impersonation. My second, *War Damage*, featured a woman whose dubious past comes back to haunt her – always a hazard for those who lead a double life or reinvent the past – and my third, *The Girl in Berlin*, included a cameo of Anthony Blunt. And while to 'live a lie' may be immoral, it is also daring – a defiant gesture against normality.

16

A visit to Rimini

I'd never visited Rimini until I was invited to deliver the opening keynote speech at a conference on fashion. This was to be held at the town's University of Bologna outpost. Rimini to me was a seaside resort associated with the 1960s, when British workers began to enjoy foreign holidays. It was also Federico Fellini's hometown and the setting for his early film, *I Vitelloni*. That coming-of-age movie had explored a neglected provincial backwater and the group of frustrated young men who longed to get away from the place, so I was surprised to discover an elegant little city containing a Renaissance cathedral designed by Leon Battista Alberti, a magnificent fifteenth-century square (Piazza Cavour) and a Roman bridge, plus a now rather glitzy beach resort, slightly separate from the old town.

I'd hesitated before accepting the invitation to Rimini, uncertain why I felt ambivalent. The book I'd written on fashion had been published a long time ago, in 1985. Since then, I'd developed other interests. I wasn't sure what more I had to say about dress. Lately, I'd been giving talks on tennis; I was also working on the vague idea of a book about opera. To speak at a conference on fashion seemed like a return to the past, but any journey into that particular undiscovered country is less a reprise than a new and different experience, so it would be different. And anyway, after all, who would not want to visit

Figure 16.1 *Piazza Cavour, Rimini, Italy. Author's photograph.*

Italy in the spring and catch up with the colleague who'd invited me, Simona Segre-Reinach, whom I liked and admired?

In advance of the visit, I thought about the way fashion itself has changed so much since I first wrote about it. I found some of the changes – some of the styles, at least – unsympathetic and even wondered if I was falling out of love with fashion altogether. I wasn't sure one could even talk about it in the ways I was accustomed to.

According to one definition, fashion is change, but I was less interested in changing styles than in the way fashion is discussed and thought about and how that – the 'discourse' of fashion – has altered.

Once, there was a belief that fashion had a narrative. Perhaps this was always a fiction, but at least the narrative existed. This story described how one fashion evolved out of another. Women's fashion was a parade of outrageous and peculiar garments until you arrived at the rational twentieth century and suddenly clothes became comfortable, especially after the invention of Lycra. Occasionally, there would be a revolution, as with the arrival of Directoire-style dress around 1800 or the New Look in 1947, but on the whole fashion styles changed gradually. New shapes grew out of the old in an evolutionary rather than a revolutionary sequence. Hems rose and fell according to a logic that seemed obvious to all, even if one would now be hard put to explain why they brushed the ankle in 1953 and had risen to the crotch by 1967.

The fashion discourse was not exclusively descriptive. A second and related narrative linked evolving styles to social change. The miniskirt of 1967 could be explained in relation to the early 1960s, to Pierre Cardin and to Yves St Laurent's A-line, but it could just as clearly be understood in terms of changing attitudes towards sexuality and the status of women. The fashion narrative was, however, itself mutating and as it did so was losing its authority. Its decline was already beginning to be noticed in the late 1970s, when the insightful *New Yorker* fashion writer Kennedy Fraser felt that fashion had been 'atrophying for a decade or more'. Individualism increased and, instead of dictating what was fashionable in any given season, magazines began to offer a variety of 'looks'. Today, fifty years later, any belief in a linear, evolutionary-style logic has been lost. We no longer believe that changes in fashion are to be explained in their own terms.

The social context of fashion has also been turned upside down. In the early post-war years, rules and customs about what to wear were strict. When I was a social worker in the 1960s, I was thrown out of a hospital ward by the sister in charge because I was wearing a leather jacket; in 1970, there was much disapproval when I wore trousers to work. Today, many such prohibitions have broken down or simply been forgotten. British schools continue to obsess about uniform codes, but, in 2017, mothers angrily condemned the head teacher of an English primary school when she objected to their doing the school run in pyjamas. At a funeral, it might still be inappropriate to wear, say, a Hawaiian shirt and shorts, but, in Britain at least, mourners are not expected to wear black. Meanwhile, although audiences at La Scala may still dress more formally, at Covent Garden opera-goers are got up in anything and everything, from jeans to dinner jackets and from cocktail frocks to joggers.

Dress has been casualized. Leggings, jeans, 'jeggings', combat trousers, sweaters, sweatshirts and puffa jackets have provided practical and adaptable wear that can cross boundaries between work and leisure, between classes and age groups and even between the sexes, in adaptations of garments once used for athletics and skiing. Some see this casualization of dress as a kind of loss of dress etiquette, but others view it as the triumph of comfort over vanity or conspicuous consumption. Jeans at the Royal Opera House may express the music lover's rejection of the 'elitist' social baggage that comes with the music they love, but it may also suggest a lack of respect for the artists involved and all the work they have done to produce the finished performance. It may be that we have lost part of the behavioural language of dress in becoming casual. Alternatively, we may feel freed by the absence of rules (although in practice athleisure wear provides a new set of rules or markers of appropriateness).

This new uniform may be unimaginative and dull, but it has one great advantage. We live in societies in which there are shocking – and increasing – differences in income and life chances, but we dress as though we lived in a classless, ageless and even unisex society. This is the irresistible seduction of athleisure wear: that it falsely democratizes us. Just as we all call one another by our first names, so we dress to conceal obscene differences in wealth. Outrage dressing used to be worn to shock; now we conceal the outrage of inequality in Uniqlo uniforms. (The classic suit, which has persisted since the early nineteenth century, has survived as a uniform of power and has been adapted for women, but even that has begun to slightly lose its grip.) Athleisure wear is part of the great democratic lie: the false idea that we are all equal and that that is why we can all dress alike. It is as if by wearing a casual uniform we erase the inequalities of zero-hours contracts, universal credit and food banks – and it does at least have the result that the poor don't stand out in the way they used to – but if you look closely, you can tell.

The aesthetic of athleisure wear also differs radically from an earlier idea of elegance. That embodied the belief that '*il faut souffrir pour être belle*' – to be beautiful (and fashionable) involved discipline and sacrifice rather than the self-indulgence of contemporary celebrities. Furthermore, the fashionable individual dressed well not to show off so much as to display respect for others as well as themselves. The brashness of the trainer changed everything. Baroque decoration was deliberately at odds with the whole 'ensemble' – since the 'ensemble' no longer exists. The trainer draws attention to itself as a separate thing in its own right. It doesn't 'go with' anything. It is also that paradoxical thing: a statement of individualism worn by everyone. This is light years away from the stately haute couture parade of Dior and Balenciaga in the 1950s, with its trickle-down of styles into demure and carefully structured ready-to-wear versions. Haute couture may continue to produce collections, with famous designers continuing to be news, but its role has altered.

Fashion had been newsworthy for 300 years or more but has now become a mass media phenomenon in a new way. In the 1990s, *Sex and the City* brought fashion to the forefront of popular entertainment on television. It reinforced the idea of fashion as excessive, exaggerated and whacky; it portrayed women as airheads, who thought about nothing but sex and shopping, but it suited the decade. It bonded fashion tightly to television and that bond has continued to hold, in series such as *Killing Eve*. Since the millennium, social media has massively added to the circulation of fashion images with influencers who showcase fashion as part of their lifestyles. Social media reinforces the idea that fashion is a frantic conversation of random events. A logic or narrative of fashion has been displaced by multiple incidents and personalities. Any style can 'have a moment'.

In spring 2016, for example, the radical design label Vêtements sent a red and yellow DHL t-shirt, the uniform of a delivery firm, down the runway. It sold for £185 – although, on the DHL site, it cost £4.50 if you bought in bulk – but was taken up with frenzied enthusiasm and was soon all over social media. It was impossible to decide whether this was a cynical joke or a subversive trend, capitalist kitsch, cultural nihilism or a statement about the bleakness of our world. This was not even anti-fashion, which is the creation of an alternative style look that critiqued the mainstream. Vêtements' founder, Demna Gvasalia, was quoted as saying, 'if it's ugly, we like it'(and the DHL colour scheme of garish red and yellow was certainly hideous), a comment that reprised Gaultier's remark in the 1980s, when he said: 'the badly dressed people are the most interesting.'

In 2019, in a report in the journal *Fashion Theory,* Elke Gaugele described the theft by the far-right of styles until then associated with countercultures; fascism was infiltrating fashion and twisting radical protest to its own ends. The far-right American political strategist, Steve Bannon, owned a clothing firm that produced garments displaying pro-Trump slogans, while sinister enterprises in Germany inserted motifs such as 88 (code for Heil Hitler) and fascist runic symbols into their clothes. It was noted that some of the rioters who stormed Washington's Capitol in January 2021 wore sweatshirts printed with slogans that appeared to have been specifically designed for the occasion.

In the following issue of *Fashion Theory,* Charlene Lau celebrated the radical avant-garde fashion of Bernhard Wilhelm for disrupting gender stereotypes and attacking bourgeois good taste from a totally different, extreme-left perspective. So, it may be that in fashion, as in the wider politics, the 'normal' centre is attacked from both 'extremes' and it might not always be clear to the observer – or perhaps even to the wearer – to what sort of dissent a particular style or way of dressing speaks; at the same time, ideas of what is normal, conventional dress have begun to unravel. In 2017, there was even a conference in London with 'the death of fashion' as its theme. It was held in a canal-side building, which the owner was hoping to develop as an undertaker's establishment; from it, she planned to organize funeral processions by water. The conference wasn't exactly a wake for fashion, but it came to no definite conclusions. In other words, no-one was sure if fashion was dead or not. *Gilets jaunes,* prison shirts and medical wear were discussed, but whether they were statements of fashion chic or fashion nihilism remained unclear.

As the date of the Rimini conference approached, I still felt ambivalent and was unsure what I should say as I grappled with the fashion realities I have just described. I turned my attention

from what I should say to what I should wear, but the fashions of
the moment didn't improve my mood. I prefer closely fitting clothes,
but shops were inundated with enormous, billowy dresses, and on
the television screen women in public life – presenters, journalists,
women MPs – looked like surrendered Mormon wives with their
floral ankle-length tents and ubiquitous submissive ringlets. Some
commentators suggested it had something to do with the #MeToo
movement. We should all cover up now. How depressing. Even before
I left for Italy, I was out of tune with fashion or fashion was out of tune
with me.

Afterwards, I felt my lecture had been an embarrassing disaster,
clogged with old-fashioned obsessions concerning history, the
'garment as object' and sustainability. I felt mortified as soon as it
was over, for I recognized that the youthful audience, who seemed
exclusively focused on social media, on online 'influencers', life
on Instagram and the celebrity culture of the internet, were,
unsurprisingly, in a very different place from me and had found my
talk both boring and baffling.

The following day, I attended a presentation on the development
of fashion studies as an academic discipline. The speaker outlined
the work of the few nineteenth-century sociologists, such as Georg
Simmel and Thorstein Veblen, who had been the first to seriously
study the subject of fashionable dress. Then she moved on to the
amateurs, the one-off writers: the art historian, Quentin Bell, author
of *Of Human Finery*, and the psychoanalyst J. C. Flügel, who wrote
The Psychology of Clothes. Bell wrote with novelistic insight and
perceptive understanding; Flügel's eccentric work proposed that, if
we were all cured of our neuroses, we would cease to wear clothes
altogether and fashion would become redundant. Both volumes were
positioned as idiosyncratic forays into a marginal subject considered
rather trivial at the time.

Next, unexpectedly, I heard my own name placed midway in this resumé of the past. It came as a shock to find myself relegated to history. Clearly, my original instinct had been correct; I had nothing relevant to say to today's fashion specialists. I knew, naturally, that my book, while remaining a founding text, had been followed and superseded by many others, but this speaker placed me so firmly in the past in the company of long-dead sociologists that it was as if I no longer existed in real time and was no longer still alive and writing. The speaker was of course within her rights to interpret my work as she wished, but I was dismayed to be defined in this way by someone else. It wasn't how I saw myself and I was offended to be reduced to a book I'd written more than thirty years earlier. It returned me to the problem of 'brand diffusion'. In the context of the conference, I was exclusively a fashion writer, and no one had thought to read any of my other books and perceive a different pattern.

It took me a while to understand that my reaction was consistent with a *Leitmotif* of my past. It related to my wish not to be defined as 'femme' and not to be classified as my daughter's 'auntie'. It equally related to my work and to the continual effort to get away from what I'd already done, to leave social policy and pursue history, to find new subjects and follow new passions, to search untiringly for a different sort of writing and one that was unclassifiable – and therefore perhaps didn't exist.

On the return flight to London, I read Janet Malcolm's essay, '*A Girl of the Zeitgeist*'. The girl in question was Ingrid Sischy, who became editor of the influential American art journal, *Artforum,* in the 1980s. In the 1970s, *Artforum* championed minimalism in art, but, when Sischy took over, its focus changed, as she was more interested in the relationship of art to popular culture. I had no special reason to read the article, nor any particular interest in *Artforum*, its editor, or its long-forgotten culture battles, yet, as I read, the effect on me was dramatic. I was suddenly immersed once more in the whole intellectual climate of the 1980s. It wasn't that the theoretical feuds of the period still engaged me; it was rather that Malcolm's deft interviews and descriptions of her subjects actually transported me mentally to a different time. This was more than remembering what it had felt like to be in that atmosphere. Momentarily, I relived it. I felt it. I was there.

In no way am I nostalgic for academic life in 1980s Britain, yet as I read Janet Malcolm's article I was stunned by the recognition of a change in sensibility, hard to describe, yet startling. The way we think has changed and that is itself a disorienting thought. In conversation with Janet Malcolm, the painter Julian Schnabel told her as much with what she described as 'devastating carelessness': 'All that is the language of another generation,' he said. His generation didn't use language like that anymore. They were a different cohort, interested in different things. That, I thought, had been the problem when I spoke to the Rimini audience: they simply don't use that language anymore and they are just not interested in aspects of dress that used to seem vitally important. A different time involves a different sensibility. The changed sensibility produces a different language. The different language represents a different form of thought. The result of this is that time alters everything, even the past. Just as I can no longer read, say, *Middlemarch*, as I did in my twenties and therefore have a new experience on re-reading the same novel, so I inevitably reinterpret past events and even my own past, my past self, differently.

The dismay I felt that anyone should presume to define me, combined with the shock, when I read Malcolm's article, of remembering, indeed reliving, something of the way I used to think, brought me up against the brutal possibility that I might have reached an age at which I could no longer relate effectively to contemporary concerns. As a friend whose career had taken him to the top of the civil service and beyond, reflected, with gracious resignation, 'It's not our time anymore.' Our Now is past and it can be an exhausting struggle to relate to the new Now, while the new Now cannot see outside its own obsessions, just as I once couldn't see outside mine.

In retrospect, it seems ironic that the arrival of dress studies in the 1980s coincided with the decay of the fashion narrative and the gradual entropy of the old haute couture idea of the fashion system. It found itself in the vanguard of a more general cultural re-evaluation. The *Artforum* shift of emphasis from minimalism to mass culture was just one example. Fashion studies developed alongside courses on media, film and even celebrity. My own schoolgirl education had covered classical music, gothic architecture, Renaissance oil paintings, Elizabethan poets and Victorian novels. I had read *The Great Tradition,* in which F. R. Leavis argued that the nineteenth- and early-twentieth-century novels of George Eliot, Henry James and Joseph Conrad were the touchstones of moral seriousness and expressed universal moral values. Today, Shakespeare survives, as do Dickens and Jane Austen, not least in their translation to film and television, but they now share the stage with James Bond, *Star Trek* and *Strictly Come Dancing.* Mass culture has won the contest between highbrow and lowbrow. The terms themselves have fallen out of use.

The progressive idea embedded in what came to be called postmodernism was that the universal ideal expressed by Leavis was not really universal at all but was in fact the discourse of the 'white, Western male', blind to the indignities, particularly of race and gender. New forms of culture have shown more vitality, have advanced new ideas and have seemed often to have been viewed as natural vehicles for liberal and forward-looking ideas, yet the balance has arguably shifted too far when *Harry Potter* is taken seriously as great literature and *Game of Thrones* as relevant to the current political scene (even if there are still plenty of political dinosaurs around). Classical music has become almost a niche interest; in 2021, when the conductor Sir Simon Rattle announced his departure from the London Symphony

Orchestra, he suggested that there was an indifference to classical music in Britain that went right to the top of society. I hadn't thought, when I became involved in fashion studies, that I would end up appearing to endorse a cultural populism that, whatever its valuable aspects, has arguably thrown out the baby with the bathwater.

My visit to Rimini reminded me of the past in another, different way; my own fashion past. I was really no different from the Rimini millennials working to present their perfect selves on Instagram, trying to create an 'appearance'. In fact, I concluded that they were just as insecure as I had been and that the way they idolized celebrities (most of whom seemed to me to be at best vacuous, at worst boring, ugly and rude) was an index of their own search for 'the way to be'.

My visit had been more emotionally significant for me than I'd expected. It was by coincidence that I'd seen *I Vitelloni* shortly before my visit, but it was a resonant coincidence. Confronted by the elegant millennial chic of Rimini in 2018, compared with its shabby on-screen past, I'd been forcefully reminded of the relentlessness of change and the pathos of memory. In the stagnant world of *I Vitelloni*, made in 1953, custom and tradition no longer worked, yet outworn norms of behaviour still constricted everyone. The protagonists were innocently unaware that all they were rebelling against was within a few years to be ruthlessly swept away by consumer society, which created new configurations without solving anything, but at least presented different problems.

To briefly relive in 2019 the disappeared intellectual climate of the 1980s and simultaneously to recall the lost world of the 1950s had reminded me that reality continually transforms, but that (as in fashion) now is always the normal and the right way to be. Upmarket Rimini had obliterated Fellini's backward provincial world. 'Now' passes relentlessly into history. Yet the past, as Freud knew, is never really forgotten. There is always a return of the repressed.

17

Returning to Queen's Club

There was a return of the past, and perhaps of the repressed, when I decided to write about the only sport that interests me: tennis. My plan was to treat it as an aspect of consumer culture, a spectacle akin to opera, soap opera and dance. I was determined to avoid the usual boosterist approach to sport as expressing nationalism, competition and a flawed notion of heroism. The footballer Marcus Rashford became a true British hero when in 2020 he used his clout as a star to persuade the British government to perform a U-turn and provide free school meals for children outside term time, but the more general elevation of sports personalities into demi-gods is at best exaggerated and at its worst transforms the vices of aggression, competition and venomous rivalry into virtues. When an opinion survey (admittedly it was a straw poll of little significance) found that those questioned regarded Roger Federer as second only to Nelson Mandela in terms of heroism, this seemed at some fundamental level perverse and absurd. Federer may be a supreme tennis player, perhaps the best ever, but it seemed simply inappropriate to place him in the same category as the revolutionary who fought apartheid. Sport has filled a vacuum created by disillusionment with politics and politicians.

Tennis, however, is not a typical sport. The atmosphere of an English tennis tournament, made up of rain, weak sunshine, the smell of grass, the ringing call of the score and the thock of ball on racquet, draws the spectator into a unique mood. You would normally expect the contrasting moods of relaxation and excitement to cancel each other out, but at the tennis tournament they fuse. The careless self who lingers at the champagne bar unites with the self caught up in the ritualized rhythm of the match, living two moods at once, simultaneously leisurely and intense.

Every few years, I've returned in June to Baron's Court, near where I once lived, for the annual men's tennis tournament at Queen's Club. A warm-up event for Wimbledon, it attracts many top players. British celebrities are among those often seen in the members' enclosure. The spectators drink Pimm's and bottles of rosé in the stands.

I noticed how my mood always lifted as soon as I entered the club grounds, but only when I started to research the history of the game did I think about why this might be, because it seemed to be more than just anticipation of a day given up to pleasure. I eventually worked out that to visit Queen's was to reprise the past, but it wasn't straightforward nostalgia.

I was a junior member of the club. My father paid the subscription from my thirteenth birthday until I went to university. My tennis hardly justified it. I was a less-than-average player – passable ground strokes, especially my (one-handed, of course) backhand, almost no serve – but I loved everything about playing tennis, in the slightly melancholy way you love things you're not very good at, or people who like you less than you like them. I loved the rubbery smell of the balls, I loved the feel of the racquet handle and the twong of the strings. I loved the climax of hitting a really good stroke to create a winning point. Years later, a lover compared successful sex to hitting a perfect forehand. That might sound a bit unhinged, but I did know

Figure 17.1 *Tennis tournament at Queen's Club, 2018. Author's photograph.*

what she meant. There was something orgasmic about the force that drove the ball to its destination.

My stepmother had been a Wimbledon player in her youth, and she and my father introduced me to the All-England Club, when, on a chilly spring day, we attended the Wightman Cup contest between American and British women's teams. I was transfixed by the tennis and particularly by the towering, sinewy American amazons, Louise Brough, Margaret du Pont, Doris Hart and Pat Todd, who destroyed their lady-like British opponents. They flashed around the court and leapt at the net, leaving the British 'girls' in ruins. A well-dressed crowd seated sedately in the stands, men in blazers, some women wearing hats and even gloves, applauded the most startling shots with clipped reserve. There was a garden party atmosphere as spectators strolled through the grounds in the intervals between play.

I loved the green and white aesthetic of the game and lost my heart to its glamour. Years before, Fred Perry, Britain's only male Wimbledon champion until Andy Murray came along, had immediately recognized its allure. He was a working-class boy, but the moment he arrived for his first big tournament at Devonshire Park in Eastbourne and saw the expensive cars parked outside, he fell for it and promised himself to overcome the barriers into that privileged world.

The year I was taken to the Wightman Cup, I also discovered 'Wimbledon'; in other words, 'The Championships'. From my school in Hammersmith, my friends and I rushed to catch the Piccadilly line to Southfields and then a shuttle bus to the club. With immediate entry for 5 shillings (50p), you could either make for the standing room on Centre Court or hang about by the court's exits, for, as they left, spectators handed the hopeful schoolgirls their tickets and in next to no time you were in a prime seat to watch play that went on well into the evening.

I recalled this in my history of tennis.

The rush to Wimbledon during that magic fortnight was the essence of schoolgirl innocence and enthusiasm. It was to give yourself up to pure play. For a short space of time, you lived in a carefree world of mown grass and Horrockses cottons. For the duration of a match you lived utterly in the present, all other worry, hurt and doubt screened out, so that *nothing mattered* except the next point, the next game, the *outcome*.

After university, I played very little tennis, but, in the 1970s, I became a dedicated tennis spectator. This was partly because the women's movement coincided with Billie Jean King's triumphs and her campaign for equal pay for women players. It was spectatorship rather than participation that drove me eventually to write a book about the sport.

Combat is at the centre of all sports. Indeed, until well on into the nineteenth century, 'sport' was largely about hunting animals. With urbanization and a more humane attitude, sport developed into mass-spectacle organized contests between individuals or teams. These were social, entertainment events, and as I researched the history of tennis and its evolution, I saw the similarities between sport, tennis in particular, and performance art.

Seeing *Anthony and Cleopatra* at the National Theatre reinforced this conviction for me. I knew the play well, so there was no suspense or revelation, yet as I watched Ralph Fiennes's very physical performance and the long, noisy production, with its raucous brutality and simulated battle, the sensations I experienced were not so different from being at a tennis or football match. The mere fact of watching a live performance and of experiencing vicariously the risks the actors took was unnerving. I was excited. There was violence. I was tense as the larger-than-lifesize emotions boiled over. This was in 2017, three years after I'd published my tennis book, but the experience in retrospect vindicated, I felt, my intuition of what all spectacles have in common. Sport, theatre and dance are not entirely separate spheres.

Sport does differ by being war by other means, that is symbolic war, for, as Boris Becker once said after losing his Wimbledon crown, 'no one died out there'. But *Anthony and Cleopatra*, Verdi's *Don Carlos* or even *Game of Thrones* speak to the same emotions in the audience. All are symbolic life-and-death struggles of passion, despair and triumph.

Rivalries and competition are what most interest sports enthusiasts and sports writers, but there is another dimension, one that tennis illustrates especially well. Tennis long had the reputation of being more refined than other sports and was for many years dismissed as a 'cissy' sport, not worthy of real men. (e.g. It wasn't taught in most English private boys' schools) Its origins are uncertain, but it may have had its roots partly in medieval jousts and tournaments and is therefore associated with the spectacular and theatrical side of combat. It was played by monks and there may have been street versions of it, but it was thought to have been first and foremost an aristocratic game. For Castiglione, author of the early-sixteenth-century *The Book of the Courtier*, it was part of the education of a civilized man about town.

It fell out of fashion in the eighteenth century, but in mid-Victorian Britain was reinvented in a new form: lawn tennis. This was played out of doors on grass instead of on an indoor court and was an upper-middle-class pastime associated with the vicarage lawn and suburban social life. Tournaments, at Wimbledon, in Paris and soon all over the world, became fashionable dates in the social calendar. This distanced and still distances tennis from sports such as football that originated in working-class culture. It immediately lends tennis some of the sheen of celebrity. Indeed, since the 1960s, its top players have become some of the most recognizable celebrities on the planet, in spite of the relatively niche status of the game. This is partly because its unusual rules and scoring system make possible the spectacle of two individuals squaring off against each other, possibly for several hours, an emotional drama seldom seen in quite that way in other sports, and today relayed all over the world on television.

Tennis, in other words, is a soap opera and has as much in common with *The Ring Cycle* or *Dallas* as with, say, hockey or football. In writing about tennis, I developed this theme. Operatic passions, on court and in the stands; players whose movements are like ballet in their elegant creativeness; fashion on and off court; and personal rivalries – all these make of it something unique and bring it closer to theatre and closer also to art. Its aesthetic dimension has attracted painters and photographers, ballet choreographers and film directors. My take on tennis was that it was fascinating precisely because it wasn't like other sports, because, although it was, of course, a sport, it was also an art form of a kind.

As I read and wrote about tennis, about past rivalries and scandals, cruel defeats and glorious triumphs, I relived the years I spent at Queen's with my friend, Ruth. We played tennis for hours, in summer on grass, in winter on hard courts or, best of all indoors, where the wood surface was blisteringly fast. After the game or a coaching session, we often hung out there almost all day. Queen's was (and is) one of the few centres in England to support 'real tennis' and we could watch this, the original and ancient game, which would have been familiar to Henry the Eighth. It was played on a gloomy indoor court with a cloister running down one side (memories here, perhaps, of the monks who played the game in their monasteries). To start proceedings, the server sent a leather ball underhand up onto the cloister roof, from whence it trickled down to be put into play. The game was incomprehensibly elaborate and the contestants, or a friend seated in the cloister, shouted out an arcane scoring system, which might as well have been in Middle English, or, more likely, Old French, and probably was.

When not actually out on court ourselves, or absorbed in real tennis, Ruth and I lolled about the members' room, eating crisps, drinking orange squash or ginger beer and reading old copies of *Punch*. The most special thing of all was that every summer we had free seats at the annual tournament, where, for a thrilling week, the club was stuffed with famous players and tennis 'characters' such as Teddy Tinling, then at the peak of his fame as the man who had designed the frilly knickers worn, to the scandalized horror of the All-England Club, by the American player, 'Gorgeous' Gussie Moran. So, all in all, Queen's was a carefree, charmed existence, and the hours whiled away there were untroubled in a way that my adolescence mostly wasn't, but only now, so many years later, do I understand why I always feel good when returning to Queen's Club. It is the echo of my teenage mood when, in the school holidays especially, the club was a refuge from the tensions at home and Ruth almost the only person with whom I felt truly relaxed.

After O-levels, Ruth left school and I attached myself to tennis fans Cynthia and Jennifer. We formed one of those triangular friendships in which the third wheel is more than a hanger-on, yet less than an equal partner and I was that third wheel. Even in A-level year – the exams that would set us on the way to Oxbridge – we still planned to carry on with the after-school dash to Wimbledon. Cynthia and Jennifer were devoted fans of the American player, Doris Hart. I didn't share their passion and I didn't think anything of it when they talked about the warm-up tournaments in Nottingham and Eastbourne, where Doris Hart would be playing. But one Monday, they were not at their desks when the register was called. There was no explanation. At first, no one knew what had happened to them, but gradually word seeped out. They had run away. They'd chucked up their A-levels and were following Doris Hart around England.

I was stunned. What they'd done was incomprehensible. In our innocent Enid Blyton *Malory Towers* world, their behaviour shattered every norm (and yet at the same time was like something out of Enid Blyton or Angela Brazil). They were immediately expelled from school for having committed this fearful crime. And, as criminals, their names, like Oscar Wilde's, could never be mentioned again. Silence stifled discussion. They had been erased from history. The scandal (Cynthia's father was a prominent public figure) was smothered. Today, sixth-formers revise for exams at home and could possibly be away at a friend's house overnight, but in the uptight world of the

1950s, adherence to the rules was strictly enforced and disobedience was fatal.

I was shocked and deeply hurt that Cynthia and Jennifer hadn't told me about their plans, but at the same time I was hugely relieved, in a cowardly way, not to have been involved. No one, it seemed, suspected me of having known about it. Alternatively, I may have been credited with refusing to join them, when actually I hadn't been invited to. Either way, strange as it seems now, no one, neither students nor teachers, nor even my mother, questioned me about the escapade. More strangely still, I never once lifted the telephone receiver to try to contact Cynthia or Jennifer, nor did they telephone me. I had no idea what happened to them. They were ruthlessly airbrushed from my life and the life of the school, and I never saw either of them ever again (although I did later hear a rumour that Cynthia had got into more trouble). It now stands as another dramatic example of how nothing was ever talked about, how my feelings were shut into the echo chamber of my solitary self, how things were always suppressed.

Wimbledon fortnight came as usual, but that year I didn't rush over after school. I did queue with Ruth and her older brother for tickets to the final, but the match was a disappointment. My favourite, the magnificent Louise Brough, was defeated by a bustling, head-bobbing teenage baseliner, Maureen Connolly, 'Little Mo'. And after that, the end of Wimbledon was always dismal anyway. There was a vast empty crater in my life where Wimbledon had been and now the silent absence of Cynthia and Jennifer made it worse. It was then, in the vacancy of post-finals Sunday afternoon, that I understood what I'd managed not to recognize until then: that I hadn't been in love just with Wimbledon, and I certainly hadn't been in love with Doris Hart. I'd been in love with Cynthia.

In the new millennium, immersed in tennis history, I recalled this schoolgirl episode, for decades entirely forgotten. It seemed so absurdly outdated as to be even more incomprehensible than it had been when it happened. I now also understood how naively unaware I'd been of the prestige of Queen's Club and how I'd taken my father's generosity entirely for granted. I never wondered then why my father encouraged my tennis, yet it was so obvious. He surely must have hoped tennis would bring my stepmother Gladys, the pre-war Wimbledon player, and me closer together and melt the icy distance between us. In this, it utterly failed.

I wasn't unusual in being a war child who hardly knew her father, but, after the war was over and he retired at the age of fifty-five, there would be no closer relationship. The divorce overshadowed my mother's life and mine too, and I accepted the image of my father constructed by her and my grandmother, as a selfish cad who'd never wanted children in the first place and had only married my mother for money. This was delusional, as my grandparents had no money and my mother inherited nothing, but in my grandmother's view my father was motivated solely by greed and selfishness. My stepmother was quite rich, and this was taken as conclusive proof that my father was a gold digger. He was even presented as a threatening figure, who whether from stinginess or malevolence, might try to remove me from my 'good school' or prevent me from going to university.

This was simply not true. He painstakingly observed his duties as a father. He saw me regularly. We sometimes went to the cinema, sitting through films by Renoir and Ingmar Bergman that obviously puzzled him. We went to the Messiah at the Albert Hall and to concerts given by the pianist Eileen Joyce, a glamorous figure who swept across the podium to the piano, her rippling red hair offset by magnificent amethyst or emerald-green gowns. We even stayed with Gladys's friend Mabel in Sussex, but that was a disaster, since I more-or-less refused to speak to anyone and sat buried in a book all day. When I was at Oxford, he visited me once a term. We'd have an

Figure 17.2 *My father in Sierra Leone. On the back he has written: 'Picture of an African administrator, having his first cigarette of the day and just beginning to thaw towards everyone and to become reasonably approachable.' Author's photograph.*

awkward lunch at the Mitre, and he'd ask me about my boyfriends and whether I was having a good time, and at the end of the three years, when I 'came down' after finals, he drove me home from Oxford with all my belongings, although he was already suffering from cancer. I never unbent to Gladys, completely at one with my mother and grandmother in thinking her 'common'. I despised her because she didn't read books and didn't have the right accent. She was older than my mother and I couldn't understand why my father had married her. In fact, I was just like my grandmother: stiff-necked, self-righteous and a terrible snob.

Even without the war, I doubt my parents' marriage would have survived. The British Empire was unkind to family life. In India, wives and children could move to the hills to escape the heat of the summer, but in West Africa the climate was so bad that children stayed in England. Many of them spent long months, including the holidays, at boarding schools or staying with relations. Quite apart from that, my parents weren't well suited. My father forbade my mother from travelling to Africa in wartime as the journey was too dangerous, but the marriage had already broken down. When he came home on leave in 1942, the situation was uncomfortable. I was only six years old, but perhaps because I was an only child and spent a lot of time either alone or with the three adults who paid such close attention to me, my radar system picked up every twitch of unspoken tension.

By the time I reached Oxford, my family's colonial past was one of my secrets, one of the things I never talked about. I'd internalized my mother's sense of shame about Africa, which was mixed up with her shame at being divorced. I didn't realize that there were sons and daughters of empire scattered all over Oxford who felt no shame at all. The last remaining descendant of my grandmother's ancestor, the Nabob, visited us during my first vacation. She was about the same age as my grandmother, in her early seventies, but very differently dressed. My grandmother had gone permanently into black after my grandfather died, but her kinswoman wore a fashionable, coloured flowered frock. Her hair was permed, and she wore bright red lipstick. She'd never married but had spent her life on extended trips abroad with her widowed father. 'She's had a wonderful life', said my mother wistfully – who would have loved to have travelled the world with my grandfather.

The silver teapot and the Rockingham tea set was brought out and over tea the Nabob's descendant blithely dismissed the East India Company and the whole imperial past. 'Oh, young people aren't interested in all that now, are they', she said and looked to me for confirmation. I supported her. My grandmother looked disapprovingly down her long nose.

It was actually worse than that. It wasn't just that the British simply lost interest after the Second World War when bits of the British Empire started to fall away. It was that the whole thing was swept under the carpet. The British Empire was a huge event, which altered or shaped the course of global history, but Britain never truthfully confronted what it had really meant. It was simply largely effaced, suffocated in pious generalities.

When, some time in my twenties, I read Graham Greene's *The Heart of the Matter*, my reaction to the novel was not what I should have expected. As someone who was 'against' the empire, I expected to fully agree with Greene's wholesale contempt for the society he described. The novel is set in Sierra Leone during the Second World War, where Greene spent time, possibly on a secret service mission. I was surprised to find that his attitude to the country's colonial community upset me as much as it did, in spite of my anti-imperialist views. He dismissed the civil servants as second-raters, who went to minor public schools. The empire may well have provided a career for cohorts of not very distinguished individuals, but Greene's sweeping disdain from his assumed moral high ground struck me as being motivated largely by snobbery. His novel displays loathing for Sierra Leone itself and for the benighted creatures that inhabit it, Africans as well as imperialists. In an essay on the novel, Elizabeth Hardwicke acknowledges an 'element of snobbishness in serious Catholic writers' but thinks Greene's book brilliant. I, on the other hand, cannot respond to what to me are contrived moral problems in Greene's novels, which give them a spurious or distorted solemnity. Hardwicke feels Greene expresses immense pity for the unhappy women he describes; I found it closer to horrified distaste. Greene has retained his place in the pantheon of British literature, but I have never quite understood why he has been so highly regarded. Perhaps it is because he, or rather his protagonists, take the position of sinners who know they are sinners, which does somehow give them a twisted kind of moral superiority. Perhaps the intensity of their moral agonies is compelling. Certainly, I remember a book group discussion of *The Power and the Glory* in which we (all unbelievers) almost seemed to end up arguing about whether the anti-hero, the priest, would or would not go to hell.

It is possible that my father and Greene met in Sierra Leone, but I feel sure Scobie, the central character of *The Heart of the Matter*, could not have been based on my father, for my father was a middle-of-the-road, moderate sort of man and not prone to the agonies of self-hatred from which Scobie suffers. But he died when I was twenty-four and I never knew him well. He didn't talk about his years in West Africa, nor about the history of Sierra Leone. He never told me, for instance, that the colony had begun as a country for freed slaves from many parts of the world. It was not until many years later when I visited Oxford with my cousin and his daughter, who was interested in family history, that I discovered that my father had loved Sierra Leone.

We looked at my father's papers, placed by my stepmother in Cecil Rhodes house, and now in the Weston Library. These consisted simply of notes towards an encyclopaedia of Sierra Leone, never completed, and letters soliciting contributions to the enterprise from fellow administrators. My father seemed only to have realized that he needed to include material from actual West Africans when he was well embarked on the project, yet his attitude, paternalistic as it was, must have been typical of so many British administrators throughout the empire.

Human beings like to believe in what they are doing, and it is difficult to admit you were wrong, still less that the whole basis on which you built your life was flawed. So, administrators managed to persuade themselves, however misguidedly, that they were doing the right thing, that colonial administration was benign and worthwhile, even as they restricted indigenous populations to inferior status and belittled or simply failed to recognize their capabilities. My father would certainly have been appalled had he lived to contemplate Sierra Leone's descent into corruption and authoritarian rule and then the terrible civil strife of the 1990s, but I expect would have found it difficult to acknowledge that the problems encountered not only in Sierra Leone but in so many parts of Africa, had their roots in the injuries of imperialism. Which is not to defend him or the empire, but simply to state what was the case.

Not long before he died, my father said one day: 'I could never compete with your grandfather.' By that time, I was in my early twenties and studying psychoanalysis, so I knew what he was talking about, but our relationship was too inhibited for me to respond, as he attempted to explain, to himself and me, the failure of his marriage to my mother. The way he suddenly, starkly volunteered this piece of information was similar, in an odd way, to the revelation my mother would make years later about the stillborn twins.

I'd always known my mother adored my grandfather. He was asthmatic and his bedroom smelled of the herbal cigarettes he smoked and of other medicinal substances. In a group photograph of Edwardian University College Hospital medical students, he stares cheekily at the camera, dashing in a bow tie and bowler hat tipped slightly sideways. When I knew him, he'd lost his élan, but still always looked distinguished. Tall, spare and bullet-headed, he was a dandy, who never wore a sweater or seldom even a blazer and grey flannels, but more often dressed in an old-fashioned three-piece suit as if for some formal invitation that never came. He was courtly to my grandmother, often declaring his devotion to her. I never saw her kiss or make an affectionate gesture towards him.

So, all those years later, my book on tennis, or rather the writing of it, revealed my father in a different light. He hadn't given up on me. Now I could see how in his undemonstrative way he'd tried to be a good father, to do his best. To understand the past so differently was a shock, yet, as I recalled the vanished summers at Queen's Club, it was also a kind of reconciliation.

18

Hedonism

In 2020, a pandemic interrupted the 'way of life' we took for granted. Throughout a century of conflict, this had developed into a global system. Now it was paused. The hiatus gave me an opportunity to think about my work (I had nothing else to do). I was surprised to recognize how much of it explored – hedonism. I'd never conceived of it in that way until now, but perhaps that was the theme that held all those different subjects together.

The common phrase 'way of life' suggests a culture chosen and coherent, but in retrospect it feels more as if it developed insidiously. We 'bought into it' – literally – without ever looking at it as a whole. There was never a pivotal moment of choice. There was just an accumulation of little choices: a washing machine, a TV set, a foreign holiday. Each was separate and we hardly noticed how they grew into a whole network, a system with implications we never fully thought through. The way we behaved changed without our ever having decided that that was how things were going to be. True, we invented theories after the event to explain the permanent revolution in manners and morals, but that wasn't quite the same. Life moved into the fast lane, and we could hardly keep up with ourselves. This was the twenty-first century.

The idea that there is one 'way of life' is an oversimplification. There are many life worlds and cultures within cultures. There are groups that have consciously rejected the way of life I describe and there are societies that barely aspire to it. There are immense differences between life as experienced in London and that found in, say, the Republic of Congo or Saudi Arabia; indeed, there are immense differences even within London, yet as a whole, Europe, the United States and large parts of Asia have made consumer culture the lifestyle of choice and aspiration, and there is no part of the globe that remains wholly untouched by consumerism. It is a way of life, at one and the same time both normal and aspirational. It is what we are told we want, and it is what we tell ourselves we want.

In the 1890s, a change of mood swept Europe. Oscar Wilde was imprisoned for loving men and music hall songs celebrated imperialism, but artists had been preaching a cult of beauty for twenty years and Joris-Karl Huysmans had recently published his ode to sensation, *Against Nature*. The *Yellow Book* periodical published Aubrey Beardsley's exquisitely lewd drawings and a developing counterculture expressed dissent in art, literature and performance. These years came to be known as the Decadence, but, far from being a period of decay, the *fin de siècle* was one of anticipation. Virginia Woolf was later to write that 'on or around 1910 human character changed'. She was alluding as much to modernist movements in art and to a changed sensibility as to changes in human relations, but if writers were producing books and artists paintings that differed fundamentally from those of earlier decades, this must mean that people were experiencing their world differently. Economic development might be at the root of it, but it was expressed in cultural terms. Art was intimately connected to human psychology and bore witness to changed subjective experience.

A century later, the zeitgeist was very different. After the collapse of the Soviet Union, the Japanese-American political scientist Francis Fukuyama declared history to have come to an end. He celebrated the triumph of 'the West' in *The End of History and the Last Man* and hailed the permanent dominance of liberal capitalism and market forces. Henceforth, human nature would not change. His book was a manifesto for the shallow 1990s, when the political rebellions of previous decades fizzled out, suffocated in the close embrace of consumer choice in a world of spectacle.

In progressive circles, there was hope that the end of the bankrupt Soviet system would liberate radical thought. Socialism, no longer associated with tyranny, could return to its roots. Radicals would build a different, fairer and more democratic future. It didn't work out like that. Every attempt at a progressive politics was tainted by the Stalinist legacy. Immersion in the pleasures of consumerism seemed a more alluring option. Mass culture swallowed up radical subcultures and remade them in its image. Punk was no longer a howl of rage, now it was merely a style. The decadence of the nineteenth-century *fin de siècle* had questioned the dominant culture, and had been oppositional; that of the end of the twentieth century emphatically was not.

Dissidence was to be found if you knew where to look for it. The runway shows created by Alexander McQueen used the unlikely medium of fashion to express extreme rejection of the status quo. Child abuse, the rape of the Highlands, the oppression of women and the slave trade themed successive collections. McQueen's radical art created extraordinary garments of ferocious power summed up as 'savage beauty'. Fashion was transformed. No longer the oppressor of women, it became the last stand from which to mount a radical critique of actually existing society. If it seems paradoxical that the gossamer wings of fashion should have hefted such weighty political statements, this was because, as Caroline Evans observed in *Fashion at the Edge*, radicalism lacked a foothold elsewhere in a time when opposition to the status quo seemed out of fashion. McQueen turned hedonism back on itself to expose the wounds beneath the mask. Yet, it is fair to ask whether such protest escaped the pages of *Vogue* or could ever be more than merely gestural.

Twenty years later, governments were still clinging to the model endorsed by Fukuyama. They continued to seek economic expansion and greater productivity, partly by promoting technological advance and increasing consumption through competition, but above all by driving down costs at the expense of workers. Damage to the environment, attacks on wages, declining living standards and mounting inequality might perhaps be mitigated but were essentially the regrettable but necessary by-products of deregulation and the relentless search for profit, as were rewards for shareholders and million-pound bonuses for CEOs.

The consent of the majority was secured by the lavish choices offered them. Spending money and having fun was reclassified as subversive. A cornucopia of goods in superabundance encouraged us to accumulate possessions and thereby assist the economy to grow, making our every purchase beneficial. The economy had to expand and our acquisitive behaviour made this possible, so that we as consumers were virtuous. To spend was ethical. And there were enough consumers to make this model work, on its own terms.

Globalization benefitted the populations of Asia and India as it had previously lifted those of Europe and the United States out of poverty, but this was just as the neo-liberal model began to falter in the West. There, having destroyed the organized storm troopers of the trade unions and hollowed out the working class, neo-liberalism was now coming for the bourgeoisie. It caused growing inequalities, fostered a newly insecure workforce, accelerated the climate emergency and nurtured right-wing populism. There was widespread discussion of the ways in which it didn't work, yet no alternative model gained traction, partly because of its uneven effects across the globe – for some, many, the benefits outweighed any downside.

Consumers meanwhile coped with the mismatch between their 'way of life' and environmental reality by a process of disavowal. Disavowal worked to reconcile the collective guilty conscience. We knew about the damage unfettered consumerism inflicted, but we genuinely needed a new dress – or three; Primark is so cheap! Work could be all-consuming and wearisome, so we needed easy-come pleasures to offset the tension it generated. Actually, it was better not to think about any of this. It was unfortunate that an impoverished class was having a hard time, but – hey! there are always winners and losers!

In any case, the current system was the only game in town. There was no alternative. It was just the way things are, just as 'human nature' never changed. It was natural to crave material well-being and material goods. It was common sense that the current model of consumer society was rational – and for some it did continue to work. It was rational that providers sought to fulfil our every desire, or indeed to anticipate each one before it even surfaced in our own consciousness, and it went without question that we should see success in life in terms of acquisition. The provision of goods – health care, education and public utilities – once provided within the family or socially, now used the discourse of choice; indeed, sexual orientation (positively) and suicide and crime (negatively) were routinely simplified as 'lifestyle choices' or sometimes 'mistakes'. Language was altered to smooth-over the glaring inconsistencies in our 'way of life', as we all became customers instead of passengers, patients and paupers.

Acquisition was presented as the fulfilment of desire, but unending desire surpassed material goods. It extended to the thirst for experiences, excitement and intensity. Mass global culture catered to this thirst for emotional stimulation. Film and television thrillers, adventure narratives, science fiction, reality shows, war movies and exotic travel, but above all sport, maintained populations in a continual state of expectation and, since the millennium, social media had provided yet further opportunities for heated emotions.

As these desires for acquisition expanded, so they evolved. At the beginning of 2020, Lucia van der Post of the *Financial Times* described how the idea of luxury had changed. At the turn of the century, it was still all about champagne and designer labels, cashmere sweaters and holidays at seven-star hotels. Twenty years later, when cashmere was on sale at Uniqlo and champagne at Aldi, luxury had become intangible. Now, consumers wanted experiences more than stuff. A holiday was no longer just a visit to tropical islands with sandy shores; it had to include, say, instruction in weaving from local artisans or lessons from a well-known tennis star. It was no longer about indulgence of the body; it was about expansion of the mind, about learning, about spirituality. Above all, claimed the late editor of *Vogue Italia*, Franca Sozzani, consumers desired ethical purity: purity through consumption. Financial and political crises temporarily undermined the complacency of earlier decades. The 2008 banking crisis led to talk of a Marxist revival, but that didn't materialize. In the post-crash world of austerity, governments continued to cling as determinedly as ever to the philosophy that had brought the world to its knees.

The system was already faltering before the pandemic, casting doubt on the promise of limitless opportunity, and was already resulting, in a number of countries, in threats to social order as tensions and protests mounted. Then, in 2020, came the Covid-19 pandemic. This forced whole populations to desist from the pursuits they loved. The sacrosanct laws of neo-liberal economics were suspended; a way of life ceased – for the time being – to exist in anything like its accustomed form, while offering the temporary alternative of a more leisurely world. To what extent the old system will resume after the pandemic is unknown at the time of writing, but it is worth considering what its philosophy is and how deeply it has become rooted in our collective consciousness. This philosophy is seldom named or acknowledged, but it does have a name. Its name is hedonism.

Far from being a modern concept, hedonism originated in ancient Greece around the fourth century BCE. The Cyrenaics, who came from what is modern-day Libya, were the first to develop a philosophy of hedonism. Their views were similar to, but also distinct from those of Epicurus, who is usually credited as the founder of hedonism, a 100 years or so later. Almost no works of Epicurus have survived, but they circulated widely in the ancient world and were developed and given literary form in the long poem, *De Rerum Natura*, by the Roman writer Lucretius.

'Hedonism' derives from the Greek word for pleasure. The Cyrenaics, Epicurus and their followers believed that life itself had no moral purpose and human beings should seek pleasure, rather than virtue, yet their definition of pleasure might come as a surprise to a twenty-first century hedonist, for theirs was a philosophy of tranquillity, prudence and the avoidance of pain, worry and agitation. Calm, they believed, increased sensitivity to pleasure. Pleasure was decoupled from accumulation, novelty and the search for continual change. To an Epicurean, the continual craving for excitement was self-defeating. It was simply a way of running away from yourself. It was a form of distraction. The lust for worldly advancement was equally worthless. Status should be a matter of indifference; a slave and a king each experiences happiness and unhappiness in the same way. It was particularly foolish to involve yourself in politics, as Epicurus explicitly stated. The prison of political involvement did not promote happiness but led rather to agitation and displeasure and was therefore to be avoided. Nor was religion the answer. The hedonists did not believe in nature as teleological, that is, as having an end purpose, and they were sceptical about religion. The gods might exist, but they were far away and did not influence human life on Earth.

Plato and Aristotle opposed these views. In their philosophy, nature was viewed as an ordered, cosmic whole; all things in nature were directed towards their own proper end and the proper end of humankind was moral virtue, justice and magnanimity. The hedonists also advocated magnanimity, but Plato placed hedonism in opposition to his own philosophical beliefs regarding morality and virtue. The Aristotelian view of natural law came to be embedded in Christianity and it was not until the rise of the modern era that a generation of innovative thinkers – Francis Bacon, Thomas Hobbes and Machiavelli – returned to the work of the pre-Socratic philosophers. They viewed nature differently from the scholastics of the Middle Ages. To the new men of what would become the Enlightenment, nature was not inherently orderly. It was imperfectly understood, and the role of the new empirical scientific philosophy was to unveil its secrets. Man was to conquer nature in order to increase human comfort and the flourishing of human life. The emphasis moved away from preparation for life after death to the improvement of life here on Earth. The power of religion gradually weakened as scientific advances favoured scepticism. By the late eighteenth century, as Richard Holmes described in *The Age of Wonder*, developments in astronomy and the possibility of the existence of thousands of suns and worlds made the certainties of Christianity seem inadequate in the face of the universe, which was so vast by comparison with an Earth so small and insignificant. The Creator became a shadowy and distant figure.

The new science arose alongside the development of a form of pre-industrial capitalism based on trade, on radical developments in farming, and a new financial system. Thomas Hobbes and later John Locke realized that this new world demanded a new politics that could accommodate and promote a way of life in keeping both with scientific enquiry and with wealth creation and accumulation. These philosophers essentially expressed the 'bourgeois vision'. John Locke stated that the restless pursuit of pleasure, or 'uneasiness' is 'the chief, if not the only, spur to human industry and action'. It is therefore good. He defined happiness/pleasure as the unrestricted acquisition of goods. Hedonism, even if he did not call it that, promoted progress, productivity and mastery over nature in order to make life more comfortable and enjoyable. He was a moral relativist, believing that 'virtue is everywhere that which is thought praiseworthy'. Virtue was what any given society deemed good. It was not ordained by nature, as it was for Aristotle.

Essentially, capitalism was amoral. It was simply a means of increasing wealth. For it to flourish, social order was necessary. Locke (although not Hobbes) believed that social order involved consent, to be achieved, as time went on, through liberalism and liberal democracy. It also required a moral system, based largely on religion, to support its claim to benevolence, especially once socialists began to argue that it was inherently unjust.

At first, it was supported by a Protestant ethic of work and piety, but, as consumer society expanded and flourished, new templates of pleasure developed. An expanding middle class desired more comfort in and beautification of their homes. Books and publishing flourished. There was a 'reading revolution' as the Bible ceased to hold a unique sway over people's lives. Literacy expanded and this gave rise to new literary forms, such as the novel (a genre in which women writers excelled) and made reading an enjoyable pastime instead of an aspect of scholarship or worship. The aesthetic dimension of life widened for growing sections of the population. Fashion played an important role in this.

The bachelor Parson Woodforde, living in Norfolk with his spinster niece, Nancy, as housekeeper and companion, recorded the late-eighteenth-century lifestyle of the gentry in his diaries. In spite of destitute parishioners, unwanted pregnancies, gruesome dentistry, ailing animals and even riots in other parts of the country, the easy-going parson led a sociable life filled with hare coursing, continuous visits to and from neighbours, concerts in Norwich, trips to Bath and excursions to London for shopping and socializing. The household consumed vast meals based around digestion-busting quantities of meat (e.g. rabbit, chicken and mutton all at one sitting), with the result that the parson and his niece suffered from frequent stomach upsets, usually treated with ginger and rhubarb. Nancy went to 'the best friseur in Norwich', received a £10 note (in today's money worth roughly close to £150) one New Year's day from her uncle, wore silk damask gowns and pearls and bought herself a black hat with a purple cockade, yet as a single, unmarried gentlewoman, she lacked agency; on 1 January 1791, the parson recorded that 'my niece hath been almost daily making me uneasy by continually complaining of the dismal life she leads at Weston Parsonage for want of being more out in company and having more at home'. Already, 200 years ago, the enemy of modern hedonism was boredom.

The squalor and ugliness of the new industrial towns and the misery of a new class of urban workers made nature and the charms of rural life seem increasingly desirable by contrast, yet the products of industry culturally enriched daily life and there was a new emphasis on aesthetic values. A growing section of the public, especially the urban public, came to expect exciting visual experiences and luxurious objects in their lives. By the 1870s, an 'aesthetic movement' had emerged, advocating beauty and appropriate design in all the objects the expanding middle classes surrounded themselves with. For the aesthetes, art and beauty justified human existence.

The British writer Walter Pater, friend and mentor to Oscar Wilde, was an ardent propagandist for this aesthetic philosophy. Epicureanism for him was far different from quietism. The philosophical hedonism he celebrated in his two best-known books, *Marius the Epicurean* and *The Renaissance*, proclaimed his ideal of intensity of feeling. Art for him was the greatest good because it was ecstatic, Dionysian. 'To burn always with this hard, gem-like flame', he wrote, 'to maintain this ecstasy, is success in life.' This was the very opposite of the ancient Epicurean view, which had equated pleasure with tranquillity.

During the course of the twentieth century, hedonistic consumerism became ever more concentrated on aesthetic enrichment through the spread of mass entertainment, until today our world is saturated with music and visual images, with objects to enrich our interiors and clothes for our adornment. Cultural events of all kinds are referred to as 'entertainment', spectacles to provide pleasure and excitement rather than moral uplift – although it is still claimed, rather optimistically, that morality resides in sport. Yet, when culture becomes a consumer item, developed for profit, it dwindles into an optional extra, a modern form of bread and circuses. Once radical and challenging subcultures have been relentlessly monetized, celebrity culture goes even further, because it is the commoditization of individual lives. Human life has become a spectacle. Hedonism is for sale.

It is rather contradictory that the seventeenth-century scientists looked to ancient philosophers, some of whose views were compatible with those of the classical hedonists yet created a world that differs so greatly from the Cyrenaic ideal of a fulfilling existence. Modern hedonism has rejected quietism and has embraced instead the intensity that enthralled Walter Pater. Intensity has become the touchstone of our valued experiences, yet paradoxically, the roller coaster of leaps from joy to despair and back, of continually heightened expectation and the ratcheting up of sensation, lead eventually to desensitization. A continuously heightened spiral of intensity is needed to keep us going. This is more like an addiction. We are addicted to excitement.

I experienced this as a tennis fan when I met someone who followed the game as I did. His favourite, like mine, was Roger Federer. We travelled to Paris and then Basle to see the Swiss star play. On later expeditions, our partners joined us, and the trips became cultural weekends, combining tournaments with visits to museums and art galleries, meals in restaurants and explorations of unfamiliar cities. But at the tennis, we were bonded with the community of Federer fans. The partisanship went beyond nationalism; 'Roger's' fan community transcended borders. There was a sense of belonging and camaraderie. When 'your' star lost, you could take comfort in sharing the disappointment and grief, but most of all there was an enormous emotional wave when he won. But where did all this emotion come from? It seemed to be based on an inherent human desire for sociability, but the reactions of the audience seemed also to come from some well of surplus feeling, as when a tragic film or an operatic aria made you cry. Consumerism is not just about material objects but includes emotional stimulation. It is easy to criticize the folly of football crowds or the insanity of parents, seduced by a PR event, who allow their children to queue at midnight for the latest *Harry Potter*, but these, however unhinged, are social celebrations that act to confirm the loyalty and passion of fans.

To enjoy material culture is not in itself to capitulate to some kind of false consciousness. Contemporary hedonism fulfils the human desire and need, for sociability. All those spectacles, those parades of fashion, those dinners, those shopping excursions and those holiday adventures cater to the human need for the social, for social contact and social stimulation. Hedonism as social spectacle is the clothing, so to speak, of part of what makes humans human. The greatest deprivation during the pandemic may have been the loss of human contact and sociability. There is a further dimension to the thirst for cultural events. Through these objects, stories, performances, consumers express their aspirations for beauty and fulfilment. They invest their personalities in objects that become symbolic embodiments of our needs and aspirations. There is a philosophical dimension to objects and, after all, those we leave behind us may represent the only immortality we have.

Yet critics have been right to question the way in which commoditization has encroached into more and more areas of culture and of personal life. As Guy Debord predicted in 1967, in *The Society of the Spectacle*, capital has colonized areas that used to be outside the reach of commoditization, such as social care, education and even romance. 'The individual's own gestures are no longer their own, but rather those of someone else who represents them to him', he wrote, anticipating social media and the power of influencers. Pleasure is commercially determined and defined. The sports organizers, the publishers and the film studios search at all costs for customers; their produce must be tailored accordingly. Was it really necessary, after all, to publish a new volume of *Harry Potter* at midnight, in the effort to create a slightly transgressive, exciting cultural event?

All this was what I'd studied and written about, fascinated by the way in which human beings invested their identities in objects, experiences and pastimes. North London windows in council estates and elegant terraces alike were transformed into shrines dedicated to the Arsenal football team. Federer fans brought flags to matches with messages – 'Genius at work', 'Greatest of all time' – to underscore their devotion. These events, I came to understand, were as much about friendship as they were about fandom. In public discourse, friendship is largely eclipsed by family, which seems to be so much more important. As a result, friendship has been less studied and researched than it should be (unless I've missed a whole sociology of friendship). It may be that lesbians, gays, trans and queers are more sensitive to and more apt to develop friendship, since, historically at least, they were not infrequently rejected by their kin and so were forced to create alternative sources of support. Informal communities of fans, also, however tenuously, operate in that way. The most important thing of all, though, remains the emotion of the living spectacle and the intense desire for Walter Pater's gem-like flame of transcendence.

The emotional world of consumption, then, fascinated me, but you could not ignore its darker side: the destruction of the planet. For hedonism in the modern world has now run up against forces that inexorably work against it. The continually expanding economy is pitted against a finite environment. Too much tourism, for example, destroys the spectacle the tourists have travelled to enjoy. The success of Airbnb has overwhelmed the centres of cities such as Amsterdam and Edinburgh, so that attempts have had to be made to halt the flow of visitors, since these are destroying the lives of those who actually live in these 'popular tourist destinations'. Meanwhile, more and more urgent are the voices of those who warn that the exploitation of natural resources will sooner rather than later lead to their exhaustion and even to human extinction. When the world population increasingly consists of two opposing tribes (tourists and migrants), escaping their countries of origin for diametrically opposed reasons, it is clear that the 'restlessness' of which John Locke spoke with approval cannot continue indefinitely, yet there is no sign so far that twenty-first century fans are ready to renounce Pater's gem-like flame of intensity.

The climate emergency is real. It demands that we change our habits, but those habits are ingrained and emotional. We have invested the material trappings of our lives with psychic significance. Therefore, to stall global warming involves more than turning down the heating; it demands a change in mentality. Human nature will have to change again. On the other hand, contemporary pleasure has been so heavily monetized and so often in forms that threaten the environment, that other forms of pleasure have been lost and forgotten. Just as after the 2008 crash, there was what turned out to be a superficial or at any rate short-lived demand for a different way of doing things, so during the pandemic it has been possible to read many newspaper columns expanding on the delight of hearing birdsong again or of seeing a bluer sky, undulled by pollution. There was rejoicing at the rumour that fish were once more seen swimming in the Venice canals. As in 2008, there are hopes for different ways of doing things, but there is more than a risk that once the pandemic has passed, the familiar imperatives will predominate in the effort to bring about economic recovery along the familiar, destructive lines. The economic system we know is as sticky as a spider's web. It is hard to know how to escape its entanglements, or if there is even the will to do so.

The question remains whether modern excitement or Lucretian tranquillity are the only alternatives. I spent years of my life seeking mythical political 'third ways' and more often than not ended up falling between opposing views. I was neither a Eurocommunist nor a Stalinist, neither a Blairite nor a member of Momentum. The result was I was always in danger of finding myself distrusted by both sides without having found the different path that could have worked. It may be that the choice between contemporary hedonism and the green emergency is stark, yet hedonism is not about brute materiality; it is about imagination. It surely can't be impossible to imagine a better way of doing things.

The pandemic has exposed the fault lines and structural vulnerabilities of consumer culture as a way of life. Commentators write uncertainly of a 'return to normal' or predict a 'new normal' of deprivation, without familiar pleasures and with new ways of living impossible to predict. In 2008, the opportunity to set a new course after the crash was not taken. The pandemic provides a second chance for a reset, at least for reflection on how we live our lives. Who knows whether that path will be followed?

19

Down there on a visit

*Even if you were in hell, you'd send a postcard, saying
'Down here on a visit'.*

Misquote from Christopher Isherwood, Down There on a Visit

It must be more than twenty years since I visited a prison. The last time
was on a dank February day, or perhaps it was November. We drove
through a landscape of ploughed fields, cross-hatched hedgerows
and skeletal trees inked in against the pale sky. I can't remember the
name of the prison, but it seemed to have been set down, for no good
reason, in a field somewhere in Essex or Suffolk. High wire fencing
surrounded what at first glance looked like dilapidated warehouses or
outbuildings, less bleak than merely neglected.

Once inside the perimeter, visitors waited in a kind of enclosed
bus stop. We carefully didn't look one another in the eye, speaking
in undertones, if at all, yet united in mutual disavowal. We were not
the guilty ones, yet guilt by association clung to us, like a faint but
embarrassing smell.

Eventually, we trailed in, were relieved of handbags and any gifts
we'd brought and waited again, subdued, but now at least warm. In
fact, prisons, like hospitals, were always too hot, a nudge to remind
us it would be hotter in hell. When the prison officer appeared and

called us, we were led away, were rattled and clanked through locked gates and along endless corridors to the visiting room.

On the drive home, the pearly sky was tinged with tangerine as the sun briefly appeared, only to sink behind the fields. My companion, Mary, my ex, and I, pondered for a while on the prisoner, depressed by the sense of failure that had pervaded our visit. We turned to other subjects and in fact, for most of the journey home, I was trying to persuade Mary to adopt my brown Burmese cat, Coco. We had had Coco for about six years when my partner suddenly developed an allergy to her and all cats. Coco relocated to my partner's mother for a time, but she, now nearly ninety, had vascular dementia and was moving into a care home.

I'd been confident that Mary and her partner would welcome Coco, because their own cat had just died. Now I discovered to my dismay that the last thing they wanted was an ageing replacement. Astonished and mortified, I continued to plead in vain. After we parted, I felt not only disappointed, but even betrayed; yet Mary and I hadn't lived together for more than thirty years, so I was hardly justified in expecting her to privilege my wishes over those of the woman who was now her other half. In the end, a mutual friend intervened and persuaded them to accept Coco, but the incident depressed me, because it made me feel, however unreasonably, that the special nature of my relationship with Mary, something I had depended on without consciously formulating it, had hollowed out. As usual, I doubted myself. Perhaps I was being sentimental as well as over-entitled in expecting more of it.

In 1970, Mary and I had barely separated before we were swept up into Gay Liberation and then the women's movement. The politics of the early 1970s somehow kept us close as we embarked on new relationships, but the feelings that endured were never discussed or articulated. I am now really not sure what Mary felt

Figure 19.1 *Mary McIntosh. Author's photograph.*

for me in later years and my attachment to her was something I never questioned. It was as though she was someone I had always known. She came to represent permanence and possibly the kind of family I never had.

I got to know her in my last term at Oxford or just before that, when a group of us stayed on in college through the vacation to revise for our finals exams (something that would be out of the question today, since, now that universities have become businesses, students are decanted from their rooms during holiday periods to make way for conference delegates who pay more).

Mary's family was of a type unknown to me until then. Her grandfather had been a grocer in Jedburgh and her grandmother had worked in the Dundee jute mills. Her father, always known as Mac, was a successful businessman, but not all grocers' offspring are Tories and he had been a communist in the 1930s, as had Mary's mother, Jenny. Mac was the only member of the London District Committee of the Communist Party to resign when the party endorsed and supported the 1939 Nazi–Soviet Non-aggression Pact (although Harry Pollitt, one-time general secretary of the party and John Ross Campbell, editor of the *Daily Worker*, also opposed the pact), but he remained a socialist throughout his life and, after his retirement, advised the Labour governments of the 1960s.

I was amazed to learn that a businessman could be left wing. This was a world I hadn't known, in which successful middle-class individuals supported the Labour Party and believed in equality. In my mother's more lurid view, being what she called a 'labourite' was confined to rabid leftists who wanted to nationalize everything yesterday and probably send the middle classes to a gulag. Mary and her family helped me in a positive sense to move further away from the political constriction of my own family. Jennie and Mac were principled. For them, socialism was normal: moral and rational. If they were disappointed their daughter chose to live with another woman, they never showed it, but on the contrary warmly welcomed me.

Mary also was a principled person, one of the few truly good people I have known, a goodness developed out of that upright, solid family from the Scottish borders. I'm not even sure how I would define her goodness; perhaps she was admirable because she stood by her principles. Or it may have simply been that she was patient and kind to difficult, scratchy me.

Perhaps I idealized her, at the same time only half-aware of my dependence on her, on her good sense, but anyway, I continued unreflectively to assume her affection long after we no longer lived together. Our feminist activism and our socialism kept us on the same track, so we did remain close for many years. One result was that we visited women in prison.

In 1971, I began a relationship with a woman who was soon afterwards arrested, one of eight activists accused of 'conspiracy to cause explosions' as alleged members of the Angry Brigade, an anarchist groupuscule that had, in 1971, placed small bombs, not intended to threaten life, outside the Miss World contest of 1970, at the house of the then-Conservative home secretary, Robert Carr, and at the fashion boutique, Biba, in Kensington. I often wore a signature short-sleeved Biba cardigan, fashion garment du jour in the women's movement, when, very much to my surprise, I found myself visiting Holloway prison and got involved with a women's group that was trying to improve the situation of women prisoners and their families.

Until released on bail, my new girlfriend shared a cell with Joan, an American who had no friends in Britain. She'd entered the country, accompanied by her two small children, on a crazy scheme with her boyfriend to make a killing with the enormous quantities of grass they'd managed to smuggle in. They purchased a pantechnicon, hid the marijuana in it and had various plans for selling it, but these came to nothing, because they were stopped by the police when they tried to run a roadblock set up to catch someone else. Now Joan was marooned in Holloway, while her two small daughters had been returned to the United States.

My friend suggested I might visit Joan, totally alone as she was. By the time I started going to see her in Holloway, she had been sentenced to five years in prison. I asked Mary to join me on the visits. I'm not sure how or why this came about. Perhaps it was typical of the way I sought her moral support or approval in many situations, but she was a radical criminologist, so a professional interest may also have partly motivated her.

It certainly felt better going in with a friend, rather than braving the gaping prison jaws alone. The old Holloway prison, a Victorian castellated fortress, was a grim and intimidating place with its medieval portcullis and enclosed courtyard. Even to enter its portals was to make you feel, if not actually guilty, at least vaguely at risk. Its separate world of incarceration kept normal life out. To get inside felt dangerous – as if the bolts might rattle into place behind you and you'd be imprisoned too.

At the same time, to enter the prison was to go backstage, to get 'behind the scenes'. You became privy to secrets hidden from the normal world of streets and public transport, parks and shops. You felt it was full of unmentionable secrets of which everyone was ashamed.

Far fewer women than men went to – or still end up in – prison. In the ferment of the 1970s, with campaigns concerning equal pay, abortion, childcare and sexual stereotyping, the situation of female prisoners, a minor afterthought in the judicial system, might have seemed relatively unimportant, but female prisoners symbolized the situation of all women in a particularly stark way. Women who committed crimes were more harshly treated than men in similar situations. Many were merely caught up in their partners' misdeeds. They were banged up for minor offences that, if committed by a man, would never have attracted a custodial sentence. If they were mothers, they were further punished by being separated from their children. The few women who killed their violent partners were given much longer sentences than the many men guilty of similar crimes, who often got off with as little as a couple of years, or were even acquitted because the murdered victim had 'nagged him'.

A therapist later commented that prison appeared to have some special significance for me. If it had, this may have been to do with the idea of prison as a forbidden place, containing shameful secrets and therefore mixed up with the silences and shames of my childhood. Or perhaps it was that my mother had seemed imprisoned in her circumstances. It also felt as if my grandmother had locked herself in an emotional prison and I think that, as I grew up, I was always afraid of being locked in myself – locked into myself – and perhaps I did have my own invisible prison. I was afraid to reveal myself, in case I too turned out to be unacceptable in the way my mother had seemed to feel she was.

To actually enter a prison was, although alarming, paradoxically demystifying. The bureaucratic routines normalized what was really a peculiar and irrational situation. I didn't encounter the minotaur at the heart of the labyrinth. I was not a prisoner. I was free to leave. W. H. Auden thought that the appeal of reading crime fiction is that, at the end, when the murderer has been unmasked, the reader experiences a sense of absolution: 'I am not the guilty one.' It was a bit like that as one left the prison.

Joan, of course, could not leave. In New York, she had been a hairdresser, a bit into drugs, her life rather chaotic. I remember her describing a visit to a cinema when she sat through the whole film wearing sunglasses. That seemed rather to describe her life until then – and even mine, up to a point, my young womanhood anyway. The women's movement changed everything for her. After her return to the United States, where she was eventually reunited with her daughters, she renamed herself Sage Mountain Fire, moved to California, worked as a teacher at an alternative school, bought 'women's land' in the northern part of the state and lived with another woman.

Visits to Joan took place in a lofty hall in the old Holloway. There were two long rows of small tables, and, at each table, a prisoner sat opposite her visitors. I remember there having been tea and biscuits, but that may have been at a different prison. Young men visiting their girlfriends made hopeless attempts at some sort of sexual activity under cover of the tables. Everyone brought in cigarettes. Dust and smoke hung in the air.

On one particular afternoon, a pale sun shone through the high windows. On entering, I saw that Anna Mendelssohn was at another table. Anna was one of the four now-convicted members of the

Angry Brigade and was near the beginning of a ten-year sentence. I strolled over to say hello, but this turned out to be against the rules and caused a flurry of agitation.

I knew her only slightly, as a result of the Angry Brigade trial. She was at least a decade younger than I was and a student – or ex-student – at the time of her arrest. Striking, with her mass of black curls, her dark eyes and generous, curling mouth, Anna was considered beautiful, but it was her vitality that was so arresting. She demanded attention. At the concrete modernist megalith which was Essex University, set down in the middle of a field (and rather like the Suffolk prison in that respect, although architecturally more interesting), she had flung herself into the student protests, transforming the campus into a crucible of the revolution. Jean Luc Godard came to film the scene and wanted Anna to become his next leading lady. She could have been his muse and a famous film star, but she despised the idea as bourgeois and would have nothing to do with it. The breaker she wanted to ride wasn't French New Wave film, but the total transformation of everyday life.

Her sexual allure was magnetic and drew men irresistibly into her orbit. Enviable as that might have seemed, it did not work in her favour. The zone of desire encircled her but didn't necessarily fit with her desires. The men who wanted to possess her offered her only a distorted image of herself, perhaps a falsely powerful one.

Knowing her so briefly and superficially, I responded to her vivacity and enthusiasm, but did not notice the vulnerability beneath. Prison damaged her. Her unruliness was twisted and bent by the stupidity of the system.

In 1980, I was researching women's political activities in the 1950s and, while reading through the old pamphlets and magazines of the Women's League of Peace and Freedom, held in the Fawcett Library, I found a description of a fund-raising event in Stockport.

The star of the concert was Anna Mendelssohn, aged seventeen. She accompanied herself on the guitar as she performed a repertoire of socialist and peace songs. She got a rave review. The reporter was sure she was destined for stardom.

By 1980 Anna was out of prison; she'd been paroled in 1976, to predictable outrage from the tabloids. I encountered her once more, unexpectedly, at an exhibition of modern art. As memories often do, this one lacks context. I don't remember where it was held or much about the exhibits, save one, a large section of the floor, paved with mirror glass. If you stepped out onto it, you looked down giddily into infinite regress. Terrifying.

And there was Anna. A great hug. A huge smile. Larger than life. She, of course, leapt out onto the floor of mirrors with no fear. She was bold. I envied that fearlessness. Yet there was uncertainty. It was as if we were still under the shadow of prison and didn't know if we were allowed to speak to each other. We found a café and had a rather stilted conversation.

She moved to Cambridge. She had children. There were difficulties. She had problems doing things the way the authorities always want you to.

My friend, Tony, met her on a visit to the north of England. Her unannounced visit, to someone they both knew, put Tony's nose out of joint. It sounded as though, once Anna appeared, the friend they shared took no further notice of Tony. Anna was still beautiful, Tony said, though rather haggard, but she was fearfully demanding and talked about nothing but herself.

Years later, the political dramatist, James Graham, wrote a play about the Angry Brigade and, in 2014, Angela and I went with Tony to see it in Watford. It was non-judgemental and sympathetically captured the cracked romanticism and exaggerated rhetoric of amateur revolutionaries as well as the incomprehension of the

Special Branch detectives, who couldn't make head nor tail of the utopian politics. In one scene, Anna produced a pretty little tea pot she'd bought. This served as a symbol of her wish for a different kind of life, a life of beauty and love. Her boyfriend ranted on in the

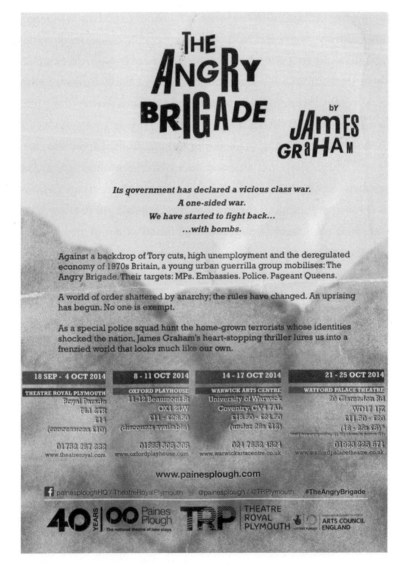

Figure 19.2 *Angry Brigade play flyer. Courtesy Paines Plough.*

revolutionary rhetoric of anger and destruction, but she wanted to get away from all that.

When I re-read this paragraph, I realized I'd made a strange mistake. It was not Tony, but another friend who had noticed the play was running and thoughtfully organized the excursion. We could not have seen it with Tony, because he had committed suicide seven years previously, yet we ought to have seen it with him, for he'd been such an important part of that period of our life, long ago. Surely he must have been our invisible companion, with us in spirit at that matinee.

After her release from prison, Anna renamed herself Grace Lake and became a poet, rejecting politics and embracing art – as if the two spheres of activity were opposites and incompatible. In 2009, she died. We discovered somehow that the Birkbeck College Poetry Society was to host an evening in her memory, to celebrate her work. We found the event, in the Gordon Square house, an outpost of the college, once lived in by John Maynard Keynes, but I don't remember whether or not the event took place in the library, its most imposing room. When we arrived, members of the poetry society, none of them known to us, were preparing refreshments and arranging the chairs. There was a slight atmosphere of tension and, when the programme got underway I understood why. This was to be very much a celebration of the poet. The spokeswoman who opened the event emphasized Anna's self-distancing from her political past. She had re-fashioned herself and become a different person.

It was hardly surprising that Anna should have tried to rid herself of the albatross of the Angry Brigade and should have refused the identity forced upon her by that brief period of her life. But there we were, a half dozen of her politico-anarchist friends from the old days, like vampires refusing to die, or rather, haunting the scene as unwelcome reminders of a past that lingered and which came, with passing time, to be almost romanticized with a sentimental gloss as unreal as the way the press had demonized the group in 1972.

The writer Pauline Melville was the only one from our group to speak. She had taught in Holloway and had got to know Anna then. She spoke about Anna in prison rather than Anna's politics. Even so, I could tell her words were vaguely unwelcome, the poetry society bristled a little, but I was glad she'd spoken, for Anna was, after all, a political prisoner of a kind. Nor in the end, can art be set against politics, they are not polar opposites. Even Proust, so often seen as the greatest aesthete of all time, knew that and placed the huge political scandal of the Dreyfus Affair and its anti-Semitism at the centre of his novel.

Someone read one of Grace Lake's poems. Its undisciplined anger seemed barely distanced from the revolutionary rhetoric of the past. I felt it expressed the uncontrolled and violently oppositional aspect of Anna's personality, but the poetry society loved its authenticity. Peter Riley, in an obituary in the *Guardian*, described her writing as 'outrageously ludic and surrealist', but I was dismayed that such anger had stayed so raw, so unreconstructed and unreconciled. And she remained isolated. She had, Riley wrote, been at odds with society. She had never managed to establish a bohemian circle around herself and had developed 'an increasingly hermetic way of life'.

After the poetry reading, a friend who'd known her in Cambridge, where she'd lived since the mid-1980s, talked of her eccentric character in later years, when she became a familiar figure walking the university streets, and described her tiny house, which grew increasingly filled with books, papers and furniture from her parents' home, so that eventually the interior was little more than a corridor between the ever-encroaching objects; and she told us that Anna did not rage during her final illness, that she did go peacefully in the dying of the light.

The final speakers at the celebration were Anna's three beautiful children, now young adults making their way in life. She could not have had a more fitting accolade than the warmth with which they spoke of their mother.

Before the women's movement, I had few, if any, close friends. I did not talk about my feelings or my childhood, but, in the women's movement, individual feeling was transformed into intellectual ideas and political projects and, in this new situation, I found communication easier. There was a culture of self-exposure and self-revelation, of 'letting it all hang out', but there was also activism, organization and polemical writing. So, the friendships I formed were not confessional, but formed around a common purpose. The women's movement of the 1970s, largely white and middle class as it was, expanded the horizons of those who engaged with it. I'd always feared that, behind my dark glasses, I was a tourist of radical ideas and equally of the subjects I researched. I saw life through shades. I wasn't in prison; I visited prisons. I wasn't truly bohemian; I wrote about them. I wasn't a *flâneuse*, or only in my imagination. Maybe I could never be more than a tourist, always 'down there on a visit', never for the duration. In the women's movement, everything was more direct and urgent and I was no longer a bystander.

Mary, Joan/Sage and Anna were just three of the women associated for me with the women's movement and the politics of that past time. They were neither representative nor unusual and my sketches of their lives hardly do them justice. Different as they were from one another, all three were courageous in taking things to their conclusions, that is, in living out the reality implied by their belief.

An individual life can never be finally defined or adequately pinned down. In *Proust's Overcoat*, Lorenza Foschini described how she managed, after much effort and frustration, to see and even handle Proust's fur-lined coat, which is preserved in the Musée Carnavalet in Paris. She described the sensation of unfolding the tissue paper and the smell of camphor and mothballs as she actually looked at and then stroked the worn garment, as if she were almost in the presence of the writer himself. This uncanny moment condenses into a single image, a relation between self, object and the force of imagination and symbol. It is a special kind of communication, that brings together the inner self and the outside world. The coat spoke simultaneously of privilege and suffering, representing both Proust's wealth and his chronic illness and neuroses. As a concrete object, it demonstrated the way in which things mean so much more and are more than utilitarian appendages. The coat was a metaphor of Proust's life; in a way, it was Proust. At the same time, it suggested the impossibility of pinning down and defining any life; Proust was much more than his coat, just as he was much more than the myth that has come to define him – and that myth in turn makes it hard to read his novel 'innocently'.

Djuna Barnes likened a person's life to a damaged classical statue that, over the course of time, has been damaged or chipped. A life, even when ended, was, she felt, incomplete, the story is always unfinished, there are loose ends, there can always be a different interpretation. My work has been largely concerned with interpretation, sometimes dignified as hermeneutics, the study of meaning. Susan Sontag argued against interpretation because, she felt, it fatally divided 'content' from 'style'. This division led to moralism and disrespected the work of art or literature. 'Interpreted' in this way, an artwork was only justified insofar as its attitudes were in tune with the interpreter's views and the views of the contemporary world. In Sontag's terms, an interpretation is always in danger of seizing upon a 'truer', permanent meaning behind the manifest one instead of, with more humility, seeking to understand the intentions of the artist.

Yet we cannot avoid interpretation. Facts, like objects, artworks, lives, are inevitably subject to different understandings. To state that does not imply that there are no truths and I'm not endorsing the sort of revisionism that ends up arguing that any and every 'truth' is as good as any other.

Nevertheless, when it comes to culture, perhaps what is most illuminating is when different interpretations are layered together, so that they achieve a richer understanding one, rather than cancelling one another out in conflict.

Djuna Barnes used the broken statue as a metaphor for the life that, even when complete, is in some way unfinished; loose ends left untied, untold stories concealed by those revealed. The wear and tear to the statue during its existence through time is an addition to its story, just as, in Japanese *kintsugi*, the repair to a broken object becomes part of its distinction; and just as Japanese *wabi-sabi* values objects that are damaged or incomplete, for they are reminders of impermanence and yet of what persists.

References

One

p 8 George Devereux, *Ethnopsychoanalysis: Psychoalanysis and Anthropology as Complementary Frames of Reference*, Berkeley: University of Berkeley Press, 1978.

Two

p 13 Alan Johnson, *This Boy*, London: Corgi Books, 2013.

p 18 Lucy Mangan, *Bookworm*, London: Vintage Books, 2018.

p 20 Walter Mehring, *The Lost Library: The Autobiography of a Culture*, Yardley, PA: Westholme Publishing, LLC, 2010, trans. Richard and Clara Winston, pp. 18–19.

p 26 Peter Quennell, *Byron, The Years of Fame & Byron in Italy*, London: Collins, 1974.

p 28 Alison Light, *Forever England: Femininity, Literature and Conservatism between the Wars*, London: Routledge, 1991, Chapter 2.

p 29 Nicola Beauman, *A Very Great Profession: The Woman's Novel, 1914 to 1939*, London: Persephone Press, 1983.

p 30 Ernest Jones, *Free Associations: Memories of a Psychoanalyst*, London: Hogarth Press, 1959.

Three

p 45 In *Taking it Like a Woman*, Ann Oakley does discuss her mother's conflicted life as a housewife and mother, 'dedicated if irascible' and describes her ironing sheets with a cigarette in her mouth, but otherwise this is misremembering on my part. Ann Oakley *Taking It Like a Woman*, London: Cape, 1984, pp. 30–31.

p 45 Anna Gavron, *The Captive Wife*, Harmondsworth: Penguin, 1965.

p 48 Jeff Nuttall *Bomb Culture*, London: Paladin, 1970, p. 129.

p 50 Michel Foucault, *The History of Sexuality: Volume One: An Introduction*, Harmondsworth: Penguin Books, 1978.

Four

p 57 Alberto Manguel, *A History of Reading*, London: Flamingo, 1997.

p 60 Siegfried Kracauer, *Der Detectiv Roman: Ein Philosophischer Traktat*, Frankfurt-am-Main: Suhrkamp, 1979.

Five

p 66 François Maspero, *Roissy Express: A Journey Through the Paris Suburbs*, London: Verso, 1994.

p 68 Simone de Beauvoir, *Force of Circumstance*, Harmondsworth: Penguin, trans. Richard Howard, 1965, p. 43.

p 71 Shusha Guppy, *A Girl in Paris*, London: Heinemann, 1991.

p 71 Gilllian Tindall, *No Name in the Street*, London: Cassell, 1959.

p 71 Françoise Sagan, *Bonjour Tristesse*, Paris: Juillard, 1954.

p 72 Nancy Mitford, *The Blessing*, London: Hamish Hamilton, 1956.

Six

p 77 Erich Mühsam, *Unpolitische Erinnerungen*, Berlin: Verlag und Welt, 1958 (published posthumously).

p 80 David Brooks, *Bobos in Paradise: The New Upper Class and How They Got There*, New York: Simon and Schuster, 2000.

Seven

p 88 Terry Castle, *The Apparitional Lesbian: Female Homosexuality and Modern Culture*, New York: Columbia University Press, 1993.

p 93 Elizabeth Mavor, *The Ladies of Llangollen: A Study in Romantic Friendship*, Harmondsworth: Penguin, 1971.

p 99 Katrina Rolley, 'Cutting a Dash: The Dress of Radclyffe Hall and Una, Lady Troubridge', *Feminist Review*, Vol. 35, Issue 1, July 1990, pp. 54–66.

p 105 Lisa Cohen, *All We Know: Three Lives*, New York: Farrar, Straus and Giroux, 2012.

p 108 Lisa Cohen, *All We Know: Three Lives*, New York: Farrar, Straus and Giroux, 2012.

p 108 Rachel Cooke, 'The Show Must Go On: Three Trouser-Wearing Characters – Nancy Spain, Writer and Personality; Joan Werner Laurie, Magazine Editor; Sheila van Damm, Rally-Car Driver and Theatre Manager', in Rachel Cooke, *Her Brilliant Career: Ten Extraordinary Women of the Fifties*, London: Virago, 2013.

p 109 Jack Babuscio, 'Camp and the Gay Sensibility', in Richard Dyer, *Gays and Film*, London: British Film Institute, 1977, pp. 40–57.

Eight

p 122 Charles Nicholl, *Somebody Else: Rimbaud in Africa,* London: Jonathan Cape, 1997, p. 63.

Eleven

p 153 William Pietz, 'The Problem of the Fetish 1', *Res*, Vol. 9, 1985, pp. 5–17; 'The Problem of the Fetish 2: The Origin of the Fetish', *Res*, Vol. 13, 1987, pp. 23–45; 'The Problem of the Fetish 3a: Bosman's Guinea and the Enlightenment Theory of Fetishism', *Res*, Vol. 16, 1988, pp. 105–123.

p 160 Caroline Evans, 'Elsa Schiaparelli and the Decentered Subject', *Fashion Theory*, Vol. 3, Issue 1, 1999, pp. 3–31.

p 167 Walter Benjamin, 'Manorially Furnished Ten-Room Apartment', in *One Way Street*, London: Verso, pp. 48–49, trans. Edmund Jephcott & Kingsley Shorter.

Fourteen

p 188 Janet Wolff, 'The Invisible Flâneuse: Women and the Literature of Modernity', *Theory Culture and Society*, Vol. 2, Issue 3, November 1985, pp. 37–46.

Fifteen

p 206 Siegfried Kracauer, 'Strasse ohne Erinnerung', in *Strassen in Berlin und Anderswo*, Berlin: Suhrkamp, 2009, p. 20.

Sixteen

p 213 Kennedy Fraser, 'Retro: A Reprise', in *The Fashionable Mind: Reflections on Fashion 1970–1982*, Boston: David R Godine, 1985, p. 237.

p 217 Elke Gaugele, 'The New Obscurity in Style: Alt-Right Faction, Populist Normalization and the Cultural War on Fashion from the Far Right', *Fashion Theory: Special Issue: Fashion as Politics: Dressing Dissent*, Vol. 23, Issue 6, 2019, pp. 711–732.

p 217 Charlene K. Lau, 'Taste and Transgression: Gender and Sexuality in the Contemporary Avant Garde Fashion of Bernhard Willhelm', *Fashion Theory*, Vol. 24, Issue 1, pp. 5–31.

p 219 Janet Malcolm, 'A Girl of the Zeitgeist', in Janet Malcolm, *Forty One False Starts: Essays on Artists and Writers*, London: Granta, 2013, pp. 199–273.

Eighteen

p 240 Virginia Woolf, 'Mr Bennett and Mr Brown', in *Collected Essays, Vol. 3*, London: Hogarth Press, 1966, p. 423. (Originally published in 1923.)

p 244 Lucia van der Post, 'How We Spent It: The Changing Face of Luxury', *Financial Times*, 13 December 2019.

p 245 This condensed and simplified account of Hedonism has relied heavily on: Kurt Lampe, *The Birth of Hedonism: The Cyrenaic Philosophers and Pleasure as a Way of Life*; and: Frederick Vaughan, *The Tradition of Political Hedonism: From Hobbes to J S Mill*.

p 246 Richard Holmes, *The Age of Wonder: How the Romantic Generation Discovered the Beauty and Terror of Science*, London: Harper Collins, 2009.

p 267 Lorenza Foschini, *Proust's Overcoat: The True Story of One Man's Passion for All Things Proust*, London: Portobello, 2010.

Index

Acknowledgements

Different versions of the following chapters previously appeared in:

Dressing the Post-war Young Woman, in *The Catalogue: The Chloé Exhibition*, Palais de Tokyo, Paris, 2012.

What Does a Lesbian Look Like, in Valerie Steele, ed., *A Queer History of Fashion: From the Closet to the Catwalk*, London: Yale University Press Newhaven and London in association with the Fashion Institute of Technology, New York, 2013.

Bad Decade, in *The New Humanist*, Autumn 2018.

The Vulgar, in *Fashion Theory* Volume 23, Issue 1, 2019.

Haunted Houses, in *AA Files No 68*, Autumn 2013.

Cracks in the Pavement, as 'The Invisible Flaneur' in *New Left Review* Number 191, January/February, 1992.

In Search of Lost Streets, in Georgia Giannakopoulou and Graeme Gilloch, ed., *The Detective of Modernity: Essays on the Work of David Frisby*, Abingdon: Routledge, 2021.

All have been considerably revised for publication here.